Alfred Rimmer

The Early Homes of Prince Albert

Alfred Rimmer

The Early Homes of Prince Albert

ISBN/EAN: 9783337164768

Printed in Europe, USA, Canada, Australia, Japan

Cover: Foto ©ninafisch / pixelio.de

More available books at **www.hansebooks.com**

THE

EARLY HOMES

OF

PRINCE ALBERT

BY

ALFRED RIMMER

AUTHOR OF 'OUR OLD COUNTRY TOWNS,' 'RAMBLES ROUND ETON
AND HARROW,' 'PLEASANT SPOTS ROUND OXFORD,' ETC.
AND JOINT-AUTHOR WITH DEAN HOWSON
OF 'CHESTER AS IT WAS'

With Illustrations

WILLIAM BLACKWOOD AND SONS
EDINBURGH AND LONDON
MDCCCLXXXIII

PREFACE.

In this Volume it is not so much proposed to give a narrative of Prince Albert's early life, as to show by pen and pencil the scenes which were familiar to him, and among which he spent a youth of singular happiness. The excellent work entitled the 'Early Years of the Prince Consort,' and Sir Theodore Martin's admirable 'Life of the Prince Consort,' leave nothing to add to the biographical part of the subject; but it lay out of their province to describe the quiet, quaint old Thuringian towns and fortresses, with the many legends that cluster round them. This Volume, while serving as a pictorial companion to these works, also contains some account of the game in the Thuringian forests, and the hunting and shooting which have been invested with so much interest in the pages of German literature. An account is also given of the visit which the Queen and Prince Albert paid to Germany in 1845; and some of the places they stopped at are illustrated. Drawings will be found in it of some of the curious old German buildings, which have for long been growing in estimation in England, and which are admirably adapted as models for the architecture of our own country towns : and there are views and descriptions of Rosenau and Reinhardtsbrun (the latter the favourite residence of Prince Albert's father); Callenburg, near Coburg; and the old Festung, the original palace of the Coburg family. The life of a student in a German university, when Prince Albert was at Bonn, is also delineated, as well as some of the surroundings of Bonn, which are among the most beautiful scenes on the Rhine. A sketch of the history of Luther from original sources is included in these pages, with drawings of Wartburg, where he was for so long held in friendly captivity by an ancestor of Prince Albert's; while it is shown that the history of the great Reformer had much to do with the fortunes of the house of Saxony. Rural life in Thuringia, which affords the best opportunities for studying in its purity the surroundings of the ancient Saxon people, also receives especial notice.

In addition to its special biographical interest, the volume will be found adapted to serve as an interesting pictorial souvenir of the localities described.

The numerous illustrations which give the book its peculiar character have been reproduced from sketches specially made by the Author.

December 1882.

CONTENTS.

LIST OF WOOD ENGRAVINGS.

LIST OF TINTED PLATES.

EARLY HOMES OF PRINCE ALBERT.

CHAPTER I.

INTRODUCTION—SCOPE OF WORK.

EVERYTHING which concerns the early life and surroundings of Prince Albert must have an interest for Englishmen. He was the father of their future kings, and the circumstances of his early years will be eagerly read. These have been well recorded by General Grey and Sir Theodore Martin, and they have been a delight to many an English fireside. But they have been much more than that. They have tended greatly to raise the tone of what is called the upper classes of England. These saw in Prince Albert a man unsparing of himself, and always resolved to act up to the high principles which he had laid down as his guide in the early dawn of life. How often life begins with great aspirations, and an honest contempt of all that is unworthy or mean, let our own recollections tell,—and let them

tell, too, how often these high aims have been ship-
wrecked! But to the last, Prince Albert to the best
of his powers did his duty, and he has left his reward
behind him in an unsullied name.

The Duke sadly said to Lucio in 'Measure for
Measure'—

> " No might nor greatness in mortality
> Can censure 'scape ; back-wounding calumny
> The whitest virtue strikes : what king so strong
> Can tie the gall up in the slanderous tongue ? "

Yet it may fairly be claimed for Prince Albert that even
calumny did not touch him; and he went to his grave
amidst the sorrows of more than a hundred million of
British subjects. Often during the progress of this
work the reflection has occurred to me what England
might have been if Prince Albert had proved, as many
before him were, neglectful and self-indulgent. The
times in which he came to England were very eventful,
and even threatening in many respects. If it cannot be
said that any foreign foes menaced us, it may occur to
those who have kept account of events, that there were
other foes, and those of our own household. The change
of tone in the higher ranks of English life in the last
forty years is something wonderful: the upper classes
have altered so much, and so much for the better, that
we should hardly know they lived in the same century
as our own. A roisterer of even forty years ago, who
caused no reproach, might say, as Henry V. to his
father in the Jerusalem Chamber at Westminster, that
he would "live to show the incredulous world the noble
change he purposed." How much of this is owing to

the example of Prince Albert! His life was not one of display, but of influence; and, as we can see in its records, it was the influence of doing daily duty, of redeeming the misspent moments past, and of living each day as if it were the last. There is no use disguising the fact, that when Prince Albert came to England, excesses in living, whatever form such irregularity might take, were not looked upon with any special horror; and this brings us to an important consideration which may be overlooked because it is not at first apparent. In the politics of England, Prince Albert from his position could not take a very active part; and yet he could not ignore them. His position was one of the utmost difficulty, and the highest praise that can be offered is that he filled it well. But his influence for good was above the range of politics. During his comparatively short stay among us, it is not too much to say that temperance and virtue—or, in other words, the righteousness that exalts a nation— were greatly advanced. The fashions, and habits, and tastes of the upper classes, are always copied by those who are not socially so well placed, so that in the course of time leaven in the highest, penetrates the whole mass. What would have been tolerated and condoned, I had almost said admired, in 1840, would not be suffered for a moment now. Let a single instance suffice, which will appear in a fuller form in its place in the book, and that in intimate connection with the "early homes" of the Prince. Few people would be prepared to believe at the present day that, when Prince Albert came to England, such a preposterous practice as duelling was countenanced; yet even four years after, we find him engaged in putting it down, and even meeting with some difficulty where it might have been least expected. The last chapter in the book will best illustrate how he made his appearance before an English public, and that a captious and fault-finding one—and it will show how he left the scenes of his usefulness.

I was living in Canada when the news of his early decease arrived in that province, and I am sure the feeling of grief was as deep as any that was experienced at home. The day of his burial was publicly observed as a holiday, and this was kept with every demonstration of sorrow. There was nobody who did not feel that a friend had departed, and one who would have been always willing to lend a helping hand to every good and worthy object.

The publication of the records of his early life has been of great advantage to England; and how grandly they compare with those of the scion of any other Court whose history we have access to ! The exacting tasks he laid out for himself at the age of fourteen, when living at Rosenau, would appal many a student, and yet they were the result of his own free wish ; and indeed, though surrounded with splendour, the life he led, even to his latest day, would have had few charms for a man of pleasure. I can say advisedly that this life has had good influences where he never could have expected that any detail of it would reach.

Legh Richmond wrote a memorable book on the ' Annals of the Poor;' but had he lived now, he might have written another on the annals of the great—almost as short, and quite as simple. The records of Prince

Albert's life have been read by millions; and the love of truth they display, the simplicity of character, and the endeavours after the right, have been a beacon for many a tempted wayfarer in his pilgrimage through life.

> "Duncan
> Hath borne his faculties so meek, hath been
> So clear in his great office, that his virtues
> Will plead like angels."

The present work lies, however, more with what may be called the picturesque side of the subject. 'The Life of the Prince Consort' and the 'Early Years of the Prince Consort' will be continually referred to, and illustrations will appear that may throw further light on these works; and some narratives that could not have been included in them will also be offered. The influence of the old German Fatherland was present with Prince Albert all his life; and the realisation of the scenes amid which he was reared aids greatly towards a better understanding of his nature. Some few remarks on the quaint cities of Thuringia will appear in their proper place, and also a few pages on the legendary lore of this interesting country. The Prince's family were always regarded as great sportsmen; and some account of the game of the Thuringian forests, and the sporting of his youth, will be included. But it is more with the picturesque aspect of the early life which surrounded his homes, that it is proposed to deal, though other subjects may of course, and indeed must, present themselves. The fine legend of Albert the Landgrave of Thuringia, who rode round the outer walls of Kynast Castle, is not often quoted, but it is one of the most romantic in history. The stealing away of Albert and Ernest from Altenburg Castle will be narrated as far as

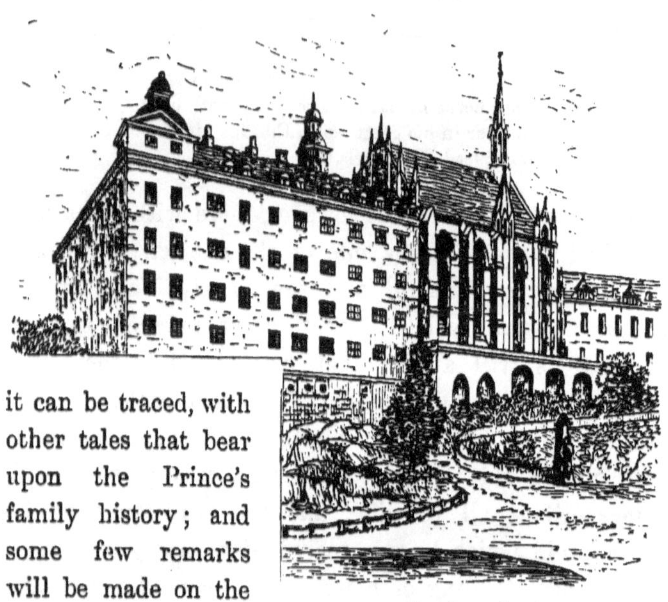

Altenburg Castle.

it can be traced, with other tales that bear upon the Prince's family history; and some few remarks will be made on the German customs and habits amid which his Royal Highness grew up to manhood.

A chapter will also be added on the agriculture of Thuringia, which now is a subject of great interest in England. Thuringia consists principally of peasant proprietors; and as the change in the tenure of land is comparatively recent, we may regard the issue with interest. The Prince's efforts to advance agricultural knowledge in our own country are too well known to need any remarks in the present volume.

CHAPTER II.

ORIGIN OF THE DUCAL HOUSES OF GERMANY—FREDERIC, ELECTOR
OF SAXONY — MARTIN LUTHER — ERNEST THE ASTRONOMER —
HILDBURGHAUSEN, OLD PALACE—ROAD TO RAILWAY STATION.

THE origin not only of the Coburg house, but of other
great German houses, is often involved in confusion, owing to the continual wars that swept over Rhineland. During the middle ages, in fact, Germany would
seem to have been in almost a normal condition of
war. Territories changed hands continually, sometimes
with, but quite as often without, reference to the wishes
of those who were most interested in the transaction.

In the time of Charlemagne, the Saxons in their
Thuringian fastnesses fought long and gallantly against
the conqueror; but at last his legions proved too
many for them, and they were obliged to accept his
yoke. When at its height of power, Charlemagne's
empire extended from the Baltic to the Ebro, from
the Atlantic to the Vistula, and from the North Sea
to Central Italy — or, in other words, it embraced
France, Germany, part of Spain, and more than half of
Italy. When, after his death, his empire was dismem-
bered and divided, the central part retained the titular

supremacy.   On the west lay France—which did not differ very materially from France of the present day in its boundaries,—on the east was Germany; and between these two lay what was called the Roman Empire. The connection of Germany with the Empire was productive of much good in one sense.   Up to Otto's time, in the tenth century, there had been little national feeling among the Germans.   They called themselves Franks, Saxons, or Swabians, and they did not consider themselves a very united people, nor was their country one in which they took any particular pride.   But when their kings were crowned at Rome, a different feeling came over them, and they all felt a common pride in the German name.   Their country, as we shall see further on, had dark periods in its history, to one of which King Leopold touchingly alludes in his letter to the Queen, as it related to matters within his own personal recollection. But even in the darkest hours, and when it was trodden under foot by the conqueror, the feeling of German nationality that was aroused saved the country.   Before Saxon rule in England was crushed, this patriotism had taken root in Fatherland; and it went on rising in tone and in spirit, till in recent years Germany has taken her place among the foremost of nations.   But through being emperors the German kings were frequently involved in quarrels that they had nothing to do with, and these quarrels led to interminable troubles and complications, even within the limits of their own territory, shadowy though these limits may have been.   " It would be difficult," says a very able reviewer, " to trace the frontiers of a dominion in so great a degree imaginary."   The central or imperial part became divided, and the endless disputes that subsequently arose as to the possession of its provinces occasioned great complications. Indeed, what might be called the territorial history of imperial Germany at this period is much too confused to be followed with accuracy in the present day. The various German provinces dissipated and divided the national strength and unity. Each one was virtually independent, and in its narrow confines forgot too often what was due to its neighbour.

Not long before the birth of Prince Albert, as we shall see, a great change had come over the land. Germany awoke from her long sleep, at the presence of a common foe, and resumed her place among the nations of the earth. The difficulties in tracing a connected history between great German families and the territories with which their name is generally associated, seems to be almost universal in the history of the country; and Prince Albert's family is not an exception.

Frederic the Elector of Saxony was on the throne at the same time as our own Henry VIII., and his sheltering care of Luther is well known, and will be remembered for ever in Protestant countries. The Emperor Charles V. determined to stamp out heresy; for though he was no friend to the secular power of the Pope, he felt bound to be a good Catholic. There were many foes with which he had to contend. The peasantry all over south Germany had a desire to cast off their rulers. They had been harshly treated, it is true; and when Luther spoke of freedom, and preached it in the market-places, they did not comprehend that the freedom he spoke of was not of this world.   Indeed, when they appealed to Luther for help, he told them to render to Cæsar the things that were Cæsar's, and gave them no encouragement beyond.   Yet, in the face of this, Charles V. waged a fierce war against the Lutherans, and in 1547 he defeated the Saxon army at the battle of Mühlberg, and took John Frederic prisoner.   Then the Saxon Electors paid for their devotion to the Reformed faith, and lost their inheritance.   This was conferred on the Albertine branch of the family, who still continue to hold it.   Perhaps it would be impossible now, even with any records before us, to trace the history of this time clearly.   But one thing is certain—after losing the Electorate, now the kingdom of Saxony, the Thuringian duchies were conveyed to the Ernestine branch of the great Saxon family, and they remain with them to the present day.   If anything were required to thoroughly confuse the subject, it would be that the Saxon dukes used to divide and subdivide their inheritance among their sons.   Sometimes these, either by death or intermarriage, changed hands again, or they reverted to the original branch.   Thus, as General Grey has pointed out, "the dukedoms of Saxe-Gotha-Altenburg, of Saxe-Meiningen, of Saxe-Hildburghausen, and of Saxe-Coburg-Saalfeld, were, on the death in 1679 of Ernest the Pious, Duke of Saxe-Gotha-Coburg, and great-grandson of the last Elector of the Ernestine branch, John Frederic the Magnanimous, divided severally among his sons.   Of these the eldest, Frederic, inherited the duchies of Saxe-Gotha-Altenburg, while Saxe-Coburg-Saalfeld fell to the share of the youngest, John Ernest, the immediate ancestor of our Prince."

If field-sports held high place among these princes, as indeed they did, it must not be forgotten that the arts and sciences always found in them kindly and fostering patrons ; and that the more especially, as the remoteness of the Thuringian land was in itself a protection : often indeed the tides of war have swept over the duchies ; but their way of life was a quiet one, if compared with that of their neighbours. Among the men of science who graced the Gotha family we may well instance Ernest, who was a liberal supporter of astronomers during the last century.

Ernest, who was born in 1741, was remarkable for his zeal in the promotion and encouragement of astronomical science, and his knowledge was very abundant. He built an observatory near Gotha at Seeberg, and assisted any attempt that was made to extend the advancement of his favourite study. He defrayed the expenses of works on the subject, when the authors were not exactly able to conduct their own researches ; and the mensuration of a degree by Zach found in him a warm and liberal patron. In many things his love of science, and his desire for the progress of knowledge, resembled Prince Albert's, as did also his dislike of display. He directed in his will that no monument should be raised to him ; but at the same time, he left an abundant provision for the preservation and the due working of his observatory. I doubt, indeed, whether Herschel ever had a more worthy countryman.

To quote General Grey again, Ernest, the father of Prince Albert, "succeeded his father as Duke of Saxe-Coburg-Saalfeld, under the title of Ernest I. To this inheritance, by an arrangement made in 1825, on the death of Frederick IV., the last male descendant of Frederick, Duke of Saxe-Gotha-Altenburg, eldest son of Ernest the Pious, and which was confirmed in November 1826, he added the duchy of Gotha. But in accordance with this arrangement he had to surrender the duchy of Saalfeld to the Duke of Meiningen." Meiningen is a charming old town, and it is referred to often in the Memoirs, having been visited by the Royal party in 1845, when the memorable trip to Germany, and to the early homes of Prince Albert, was made, under circumstances, in nearly every sense of the word, of unclouded sunshine. Saxe-Altenburg was separated from the duchy of Gotha at the same time, and given to the Duke of Hildburghausen.

Hildburghausen, which also appears in the account of the Royal visit, has become a town of the past, and Englishmen rarely set their foot in it. The Court has departed, and the prestige of the Court has departed too. But we can see traces yet of its old importance, and these traces are not far to seek. The streets are broad and well constructed, and there is still the old palace at the end of the town, which was a ducal residence even during the lifetime of Prince Albert. But if we explore some of the side streets or lanes, we shall soon discover traces of ancient Germany. I was somewhat struck with a very quaint old brewery and brewer's house, which is shown here. The black and white construction more nearly resembles the English style of building than many others in Germany; and the shady lane it terminates is very like one of those off the principal streets of Warwick or Stratford. The courtyard of a very curious inn is also shown here, which lies not far off. This is a very admirable example of one of the most picturesque host- elries that I ever remember to have seen. There is not a beam or a win- dow or door that is not ready for Prout or Nash to copy, and that without any alter- ation. The hollow red tiles that cover the roof are East- ern in character, and are found in

Brewery, Hildburghausen.

many parts of Europe, though they are not very common in England. A fanciful resemblance might be discov- ered between this inn - yard and the Eastern courts, which may have been copied by the Crusaders that fol- lowed Conrad, as our own inns that are built in a hollow quadrangle, and have nearly disappeared, are said to have been the importation of the followers of Richard. But even in the more remote parts of Germany these hospit- able abodes are less common than they were, and the railway hotels have pushed their older neighbours away.

I found this one a very hospitable resting-place on a hot August day.   There was a large kitchen sitting-room with an open roof, and several rustics had come in from their labours in the Thuringian hills.   They were all very polite and companionable, and at the end of a long table a small cloth was laid for me.   I remember that an excellent lunch of sausage and bread, and a pint of good light wine, cost what, in English money, would be equal to about ninepence.   But there is a much more touching record of departed greatness in Hildburghausen than the quaint country inn, and that is the enormous ducal palace.

The few English visitors that explore Hildburghausen are struck, among other relics of the past, with the dismantled palace that lies at one end of the quaint town. It stood in all probability on the site of some older residence, but the present palace was commenced in the same year as James II. came to the throne, 1685; and as its date is so clearly defined, it may be interesting to compare its architecture with that which was common with us.   Then we had what is called Jacobian architecture.   The " Queen Anne " style, which has made so much progress of late, was not thought of; but even that came and went before the Hanoverian style, as it is called, was introduced into England.   This palace is purely Hanoverian in its character, and resembles the façade of a West-end square in modern London.   When the duchies underwent such sweeping changes as they did in 1826, Hildburghausen palace was in its pride and glory; but how it has changed!   Soldiers, with their wives and families, occupy its chambers; and its gilded saloons only afford a roomy space for tennis or boisterous play—and many exciting games seemed to be

Inn, Hildburghausen.

in progress when I visited it. Still it was hardly possible to forget what these rooms had seen. A thousand times they had been filled with the nobles of the land; often

the walls had echoed the plaintive music of the last
century; and what tales of joy and of sorrow they have
looked down on!   How often has all revelry stopped in
its *salons* at the sound of the drum !

> "Ah ! then and there were hurrying to and fro,
> And gathering tears, and tremblings of distress,
> And cheeks all pale which but an hour ago
> Blushed at the praise of their own loveliness."

We cannot help thinking how eagerly the news which
travelled so slowly in those days has been discussed.
Blenheim, which rolled back the tide of war from Germany; the first and the second Silesian wars, and all
the calamities of the Seven Years' War.   There was the
departure of its Duke to fight the battles of Maria
Theresa against the Great Frederick, and his discomfited
return after the loss of Rossbach.   There is always
something melancholy in departed glories : an ancient
farmhouse that has been at one time a baronial residence,
or a Roman mosaic unearthed along the line of Watling
Street, are intensely interesting, but they suggest many
thoughts of sadness.   The grounds in front of the palace
are grown over with rank grass and wild flowers, and the
pool is coated with weeds and fringed with rushes and
flag.   There is still some little life in the old town; and
a trade in toys, sausages, and condensed milk affords
occupation for the inhabitants, who number about 5000.
At Hildburghausen there is a monument to Queen
Louise of Prussia.

One drawing more is given of this interesting old
place—the turn of the road on the way from the railway
station.   The tall, steep roofs, which are covered with

red tiles, are backed by the deep green of the uncleared
woods of the Thüringerwald ; and the pale buff-coloured
houses form a wonderful break to the dusty foreground

Wing of deserted Palace, Hildburghausen.

of the road.   The combination of colours seems almost
perfect, and is a peculiarity of this part of the world.
The Queen says : " What is so beautiful is, that between
the noble and solemn forest of silver and spruce firs, you
come to the greenest and most beautiful little valleys,
overshadowed by those deep-green firs, with here and
there some beeches and oaks among them.   These re-

minded us of Windsor—only the latter seems tame and stiff after this.   And then the peeps you get down such heights, and the bursts of sunshine between the trees, were so beautiful."   This is a description we can all appreciate; but how many scenes that would have delighted as much are hid from the eyes of a Royal visitor! We perhaps could hardly say now with Henry V.—

> " O majesty ! thou dost sit
> Like a rich armour worn in heat of day,
> That scalds with safety."

But even if there were fewer restraints, the time which could be spared in a Royal visit to see the country in its simplicity would afford only a meagre opportunity.   In passing through the turn of the lane here shown, the view would be lost; it only lasts for a few score of steps.   And there would be crowds of eager eyes, and many demonstrations of welcome and joy that had perforce to be acknowledged; and as there is no lingering or turning back, the view is lost.   This scene may be described in a few words.   First of all, it may be remarked that the house to the left of the fountain is the inn with the old-fashioned courtyard that has been illustrated.   When I saw it, the sky was a beautiful blue, of that clear ultramarine colour that speaks of days of sunshine to come.   The thick belt of wood was clear and sharp against it, and of a dense olive-green ; and the little clearing which is shown was golden after the ingathering of the harvest, and not a few crops of grass-land were ripening again for the sickle.   The red roofs formed a rich warm resting-place for the eye ; and the houses were of that pleasing tone which is obtained by mixing a little ochre with the whitewash. The road was the colour of other dry roads, and not obtrusive; while the house on the left was of old greystone. The most unskilful artist could not fail to make a picture out of such a scene.

Since Hildburghausen ceased to be a ducal residence, it has the air of a sleepy old country town; and the change might not inaptly be described as resembling that which was seen in England when railways diverted the traffic from some busy market, and the coaches that used to gallop up the main street with four horses were consigned as relics of the past to the stable-yard of the principal hotel. One almost wonders what the feelings of the last Duke of Hildburghausen must have been when he left his palace, and the town that bears his name, to take up his residence at Meiningen. The distance between the two places is about fourteen English miles, and the palace at Meiningen is just the counterpart of the one he had left, though the town bears the traces of greater activity, owing doubtless to the removal of the Court.

CHAPTER III.

IN the year 1862 the Queen applied to the King of
the Belgians for some record of the early years of
the Prince and his family, and this request was responded
to in reminiscences of much more than ordinary interest.
He writes: "Your uncle Ernest and myself, only fifteen
years old, left Coburg to join the Russian army in Moravia;
but Austerlitz put an end to it. We went to Berlin,
where we met the Grand-Duke Constantine, and returned
afterwards to Coburg. In 1806, the war with Prussia became evident. There was still a great notion that the
Prussians, who spoke with great contempt of the Austrians,
would do wonders. Towards the end of September my
brother joined the King of Prussia. My parents, aunt
Sophia Mensdorff, little Hugo, and myself, went to Saalfeld, hoping that, owing perhaps to the Thüringerwald,
we should remain perfectly quiet. Poor Prince Louis
Ferdinand of Prussia, however, took an absurd position
near Saalfeld, which clearly, once the fact known that

the French were in great force, could only lead to his destruction. So we who went to Saalfeld to be out of the way, got into the very midst of a battle—Coburg having only had the passage of the French, but no other inconvenience.

"We returned *tant bien que mal* to Coburg. Towards the end of November and the first days of December our beloved father sank very fast, and died on the 9th of December 1806. The situation was a sad one. The French had occupied, but not yet seized Coburg, as our father was present. But after his death the question was immediately put, 'Where is the new Duke?' Hearing that he was with the King of Prussia, Coburg was taken possession of, and a military *intendant* took everything in hand. He was not an agreeable person— a M. Vilain, bearing well that name." More complete details of this terribly dark night will appear in this chapter, but even the slight reminiscence of King Leopold is startling enough in itself: " Nearly all the men of good families who did not live in the army were *utilisés* as *auditeurs du Conseil d'Etat.* Molé, Duc de Broglie, &c., were all in this position, and generally employed in the administration of conquered countries. At the same time, Colonel Parigot was named military commandant," —and here follows a sentence that is startling enough, as coming from the late King Leopold, who subsequently held so prominent a position among the rulers of Europe. " My good mother and all of us had no means of existence but what was clandestinely given by our *employés,* and a little tolerated by the *intendant.*" This is emphatic enough ; and those who remember King

Leopold and his dignified career, will now have some difficulty in believing that such things could be, and that in the present century. Yet we have King Leopold's own word for the truth of it. But he goes on further to say: " Our mother, in the hope of obtaining the means of getting your uncle back, and also to make Coburg enter into the Rheinbund which the other Saxon houses were going to obtain, went to Berlin, and was ready to go to Warsaw to see the great man. She got, however, not beyond Berlin, Napoleon not being very fond of those visits. General Clerke, Duc de Feltre, the Governor of Berlin, was very kind to her. I am sorry to say that our cousins behaved very badly, particularly the Duchesse de Meiningen, whose plenipotentiary was the famous Baron Erfa." The touching account of the Napoleonic occupation is brief, and it may be well supplemented by the accounts of contemporaries, that will always rank among the most pathetic and eloquent narratives in history.

It will be seen from these what the condition of Germany was before the birth of Prince Albert, and I have been tempted to attribute much of his character for self-devotion and self - restraint to the marvellous change that had come over the life of his country when the wars were ended. Not only those of high degree were changed, and that so very much for the better, but even the artisans and rustics had become heroes in their struggles with Napoleon, and women brought their jewels, and even their wedding-rings, to melt down, to raise funds to free the country from the oppressor. The straits to which King Leopold describes the household at Coburg as being reduced, were paralleled in all other States of Germany, excepting any that might have joined the common enemy through fear; but it was, as some of the wisest said, the real beginning of German unity.

How sadly the disintegration produced on the small States by the French invasion told against German power, we learn from the touching but eloquent narratives of Steffens and Arndt. But the description of the army and its officers, as told by Count Henkel, is appalling. "We were always wishing for war," he says; "with whom, was a matter of perfect indifference. It never occurred to any one to reflect what the Government was or ought to be. We stood far more in awe of the inspector than the King. The annual visit of the former furnished the subject of all the thoughts, conversations, hopes, and fears, of our little world for the whole year. We hardly knew where Berlin was. Königsberg was the ' residency; ' and if any of us went thither on leave he brought us back all the news, and was regarded as a travelled man. There was a dragoon regiment near us quartered at Tilsit we never met; but that did not prevent us from entertaining a mortal hatred to each other." At the close of the last century, Henkel thus describes the staff officers of the army at a general review: " Lieutenant General von Marwitz had the gout very badly, loved his ease, and abhorred exercise : he was seventy. Another had gout in both hands; another was obliged to be lifted on his horse; another was a corpulent *bon vivant*, sorely incommoded by a brisk pace; " and so follows the dismal list of commanders that were soon to meet

Napoleon. "The reign of Frederic William had left the finances of the country in a state it would have required all the order and frugality of his successor to retrieve even in times of peace." But though himself virtuous and temperate, he could not stem the tide of licentiousness that had infected the country, and feared to offend old friends and servants if he attempted to make a change. But even at times the King seemed to fear for the worst. Before the terrible slaughter of Jena, he said to Count Henkel, " This cannot end well; the confusion is indescribable. The gentlemen will not believe this : they say I am too young, and don't understand these matters. I wish I may be wrong." How right he proved to be, the battle of Jena, with all its horrors, showed. Steffens, who was an amiable and an excellent man, and a profound scholar, had been appointed to a professor's chair at Halle. Before Jena, Steffens had made the acquaintance of some officers of rank, and he was far from being impressed in their favour. The following, which is a translation of his remarks, will show : " They were among those," he said, " who afterwards, panic-stricken by the war, betrayed the most disgraceful and disastrous spirit ; but even, I must confess, their language alarmed me. There was none of that healthy enthusiasm which springs from the fresh and copious fountain of the heart. It was narrow arrogance, and a kind of superstition which attaches superstitious powers to obsolete and rusty military forms. A courage like that of the English before Agincourt, as described by Shakespeare, would not have been blind to the impending dangers. But not one of these men seemed to have a suspicion of the tremendous strength of the brave army which, having overturned all the existing theory and practice of war, flushed with victory, and sharing in the vehement excitement of a whole people, now threatened us with annihilation. The ghost of the Seven Years' War, they fancied, would strike terror into the enemy. The Prussian soldier, a slavish hireling, enjoyed no consideration among his own people, had no national interest, and was only kept to his duty by fear of punishment." Steffens then describes, in language of deep interest, the shock which was received when the first news of Napoleon's successes reached them —how helpless they felt when the French were at their gates. At first, as is usual, the news of the rout was preceded by reports of a signal victory, and the joy was great. Every one believed in the invincibility of the German army, and a solitary French prisoner that was brought into the town was an object of great curiosity, until at last the terrible news was forced upon them, and the army they trusted in was a wreck!

Perhaps Immermann's account of the German army as it passed the house where he was then but a boy, has few equals for graphic power: " The city [Magdeburg] was soon the scene of a continued passage of troops: regiments of horse and foot, ammunition and baggage waggons, and pontoons, which peculiarly struck us boys, marched for weeks in at the Bruck and out at the Sudenburger Thor. An army in movement then had very different appendages from what it has now. These imprinted themselves on our childish imaginations. The pack-horses carrying the tents, with their intricate mass of linen and cordage, above which balanced the long poles, were obliged to pass in single and interminable file. Then, still more strange, the red-striped kitchen-waggons of the generals and colonels, with great hen-coops hanging on both sides, from which were heard the cackling, and screaming, and gobbling of all sorts of live poultry, destined to secure these heroes the pleasures of the table. This precaution astounded us children, and one of us naively asked whether there were no chickens in the villages on the way ? " But the Magdeburgers were soon awakened from their dreams of security. Jena was fought, and the actual rout of the Germans is best told in the language of Immermann : " As the confused rout came in by the same gate through which they had marched forth, the people gathered in knots, looking on with alarmed but still incredulous wonder. ' These are the first fugitives,' I heard people say ; ' they are never in order : have patience, the regular regiments will soon come.' But noon came—afternoon came—evening drew on, and the pell-mell had not ceased. The disorderly mob which had been an army still filled the streets. At length came some troops in marching order, as exceptions to the miserable rule. Covered were now the banners which had floated so proudly in the breeze. Most of them marched in in silence. Once only the music sounded, loud and clear, like the laughter of despair. It was the trumpeters of a cuirassier's regiment. Their regiment was not behind them,—they were quite alone, and blew the Dessauer march just as if all was in the best possible order. They looked well too, and were mounted on high-fed horses. Indeed, generally speaking, the men did not look jaded, nor hungry, nor worn; and the contrast between their personal good condition and the general destruction, exhibited in the strongest light the depth of the calamity. In the evening everybody knew that a Prussian army no longer existed. A helpless grief sat on men's faces. But even then, the indescribable spirit which characterised that period was not extinguished. I heard a man say to his neighbour: 'That may be as it will; things have gone badly, no doubt; but we have lost with honour, for I heard just now that the Prussians didn't once lose their step through the whole battle!'"

But to return to Steffens. The description he gives of the battle of Auerstadt is very graphic and touching, and it was as usual heralded by the news of victory:—

"The troops assembled in the neighbourhood marched out; rumours of the approach of the enemy grew stronger, and it became certain that the field of battle would be in our neighbourhood. An anxious silence reigned through the city; the Duke of Würtemberg marched into Halle, and from that moment the inhabitants felt that they were involved in the fearful struggle. It is a singular and awful feeling to be obliged to surrender one's self, passive and without an effort, into the hands of a foreign power. We were still protected, indeed, by our army; but we ourselves, inactive, had only to wait the destiny in which that might involve us. Tranquillity and order were destroyed. Men and women wandered about the streets in a state of anxious excitement; for it was evident from the position of the hostile troops that a great battle was at hand. At length a vague rumour, and then the certainty, of the unfortunate battle[1] of Saalfeld, and the death of Prince Louis, arrived. His rashness seemed like the effect of despair, and this despair infected us all. The unfortunate 14th October drew near. An unquiet crowd filled the streets. The news of a great defeat came heralded by the report of a great victory. The people exulted; the general joy even infected my friends. This lasted for a whole day, during which one French prisoner was brought into the city. He was the first enemy we had seen, and his appearance excited an immense ferment among the people, who were with difficulty restrained from falling upon him. It seemed as if we had gained a great advantage! On the evening of the 15th, I ascertained that the battle of Auerstadt was lost, and concluded that the Halle reserve would be attacked." How well Steffens judged, the following narrative shows :—

" Very early in the morning," says he, " came Schleiermacher and his sister, to be witnesses of the fearful sight. They were joined by several professors and others. To unskilled eyes, all appeared undecided; and so wonderfully blinded by the good news, so firmly trusting in the invincible character of a Prussian army, were most of them, that they saw in this attack of the French a victory. 'Poor French!' said one of my colleagues, 'I could find in my heart to pity them; they will soon be cut to pieces before our eyes.'" But the terrible truth was not long in coming. The attack of the French was successful, and soon the town was filled with scattered

---

[1] This is the circumstance alluded to in King Leopold's letter to the Queen.

troops. "My dwelling," says Steffens, "in a distant, unfrequented part of the town, was exposed to danger. We determined to take our infant and seek refuge in Schleiermacher's house. Schleiermacher, and his sister, and my wife, went first. I followed by the side of the maid that carried the child; but the danger was pressing. Shots were fired in the streets, otherwise utterly deserted. The houses were all closed; only here and there was seen a workman tearing down some tempting sign. The nurse was herself a mother: she wished to go to her child, but trembled, and could hardly walk. I threw her cloak over my shoulders, took the child from her, and hurried on. On arriving at the market-place we saw our danger: the retreat of the reserve corps lay through the city, and we had to cross the whole tumultuous body at right angles. How we got through I know not. In such moments consciousness is turned into a blind but powerful instinct of self-preservation. The enemy was pouring into the streets; a volley was poured in the direction of my flight; the bullets whistled about my ears. We were but a few steps from the place of shelter, but our retreat might any moment be cut off. At length we reached the house. The street was silent and empty. The closed door was hastily opened and re-locked: for the moment we were saved." But soon after, some French soldiers came to rob the little party, and it was evident that the Prussian power was annihilated. Finally, Napoleon himself came; and though Bernadotte promised that the funds of the university should be untouched, and that all the professors and students should remain unmolested, Napoleon cared nothing for this, but simply closed the university, and ordered the students to go home to their parents.

"The council of the university met, and we found the funds had been seized. A letter from Berthier had arrived from Dessau, in which he informed me of the Emperor's displeasure. Men of letters, he said, should not trouble themselves about politics, their only office being to cultivate and diffuse science. The professors of Halle had mistaken their vocation, and therefore the Emperor had closed the university. The whole corps of teachers were therefore left without occupation, and the greater part of them condemned to poverty and want (!) "—and then, to the dismay and disgust of Steffens, it was proposed by some of the professors that they should endeavour to free themselves from any charge of disloyalty to their conqueror; and even abject apologies and submissions were made, and made, of course, in vain. Still in some form the distinguished scholars whose names remain as a bright light in the gloom that overspread the country, continued to live as best they might, and even to continue their abundantly useful work. "We determined to throw the little sum at our disposal into a common fund, and to form one household. Schleiermacher removed into my small confined dwelling. My wife, with her child and Schleiermacher's sister, slept in one very small room, which opened into a larger; while I and my friend slept in a similar room, and each pursued his studies in a common apartment. In a corner of this room it was that Schleiermacher wrote his essay on the Epistle of Paul to Timothy. We lived in great indigence, saw few people, scarcely ever left the house; and when money fell short, I sold my little stock of plate. But though we lived so poorly, our minds were not subdued. It was our fixed persuasion that from this time the fate of our country lay in the firm and constant spirit of every one of her sons. *That* strengthened and elevated us ; and in spite of our poverty, we assembled the friends and young men who had the courage not to leave the town, around our humble tea-table. Luckily we had just laid in a stock of tea and sugar when the storm broke on us. These evenings we shall never forget. At first our minds were occupied with the fearful and wretched events of the day, especially the prompt and unintelligible surrender of Magdeburg." Nearly all that was great and noble in Germany at that time had been smothered by pedantry and frivolity. It was little understood except by the great minds who never lost hope that the country was passing through a fiery ordeal, from which it emerged so gloriously. The spirit of Arndt, and Schleiermacher, and Steffens has indeed lived till later days, and was still exercising a strong influence upon the country while the mind of the future Consort of the Queen of Britain was being moulded. What would they have given to see the deliverance they had wrought in our own time for their country !

CHAPTER IV.

IT is a singular and unpleasant reflection that when
the news of the battle of Jena was first announced,
many civilians even took comfort from the fact that
the soldiery had received so severe a check; and the
thoughtful saw that there would be no salvation till
the whole army was remodelled.

When Napoleon entered Berlin, a very acute observer
says that the French were more than usually inflated,
and full of vainglory, and that they attributed their victory to their own valour, and even considered that they
had conquered the troops of Frederick the Great.　Very
few officers admitted that it was the antiquated organisation of the Prussian army that gave them so easy a victory.　The easy careless air of the French soldiers proved
a strong contrast to the stiff pedantry of the Prussians.
"Napoleon made his entry into Berlin in a lovely day
of October, to the sound of the same bells that had so
often heralded the wonderful and daring victories of
Frederick the Great—so often awakened the national

pride of Prussia. He entered with unequalled military pomp; but this did not make the impression he expected." The writer remembers an elderly gentleman very well who used to describe this entry; and he said Napoleon and his staff resembled circus-riders. Every one was disappointed with his appearance, which, according to the same authority, was so very far from military or imposing. But great humiliations were yet in store for Prussia. The remnant of the Prussian army, under Lestocq and Kalkreuth, joined the Russians on the Prussian frontier, and at first some advantage seemed to rest with the allies; but at Friedland the French gained a complete victory, and Buonaparte had an interview with the Russian Emperor on a raft in the middle of the Niemen, and the peace of Tilsit, which was signed on July 9, 1807, was the result. The hardest of terms were exacted : all the territory between the Rhine and the Elbe was taken away, and, together with Brunswick, Hesse-Cassel, and part of Hanover, an independent kingdom called Westphalia was created, on the throne of which Buonaparte placed his brother Jerome—so that the Prussian King lost 5,000,000 of his subjects, and had to pay an idemnity of 140,000,000 francs ; and it seemed almost impossible that a country which had fallen so low could ever rise again. "The truth," says Arndt the patriot, " is beyond all power of description. We look back as upon a black dream, and are amazed at what we have seen and suffered, and can hardly believe it. Years must elapse before it can be described, nor will our grandchildren believe what was the state of Germany in 1808, '9, '10, and '11. The base and bad openly triumphed and domineered; the indolent and the cowardly served with hopeless and thoughtless obsequiousness; many of the good despaired; only a few noble spirits still hoped." The hopes of these great men were founded on their own keen insight into the workings of human affairs, and the certainty that the cruelty and oppression of the aggressors must in the end go the way of all acts of tyrants.

They had sown the wind, but ultimately the whirlwind must follow. All this is admirably told by Steffens: "The more all prospect of external help vanished, the more threatening the aspect of things around us, the stronger became our firm conviction that the holy and the good, the germs of which were springing up in Germany, could not be annihilated by the rude trampling of a conquering soldiery. In this view, I often ventured to express what was the guiding principle of all my thoughts so long as the French occupied the land, even in those days of despair. I maintained that the battle of Jena was the first victory over Napoleon, for that it had destroyed the weaknesses which were his best allies, and had awakened a spirit which in the end must rise and conquer. The certainty that I should witness his fall never left me." This is noble language; and how Steffens's hopes for his country were realised, history is at hand to tell. If the digression appears somewhat long, it must be excused from the following considerations. There were, as both Arndt and Steffens say, some lofty spirits that never despaired of final deliverance and success—who seemed, indeed, to rise in greatness with their country's wrongs; and among these were several of the professors at Bonn who were Prince Albert's instructors. For these men he always entertained a warm friendship and respect; and from them he learned much that was to fit him hereafter for his high position in England. Again, I should wish to reply to those who used to say that the German invasion of France in the war of 1870 was harsh and cruel:—Take it even on any showing, the rights and private property of the French were respected as far as that was possible by the invaders; and it is certainly true that the Germans who were left behind in France behaved with great consideration. Yet let us remember that the appalling pictures which Arndt, and Steffens, and Immermann have given us were almost fresh in the minds of some of the German invaders. A cry went up indeed from many Englishmen that we ought to help our "old ally." But that was merely the kind of generous impulse that feels a sympathy for the losing side, and would have called quite as loudly, and, so far as we were concerned, more justly, for aid, if the fortunes of war had been different. It must not be forgotten that when the tyranny and oppression of the first Napoleon were doing their worst, and when not a ray of light appeared through the cloud that hung over Germany, King William was in his fifteenth year. He was just at the age when the most lasting impressions would be made on his mind. The German army of occupation, however, when the war was over, acted with great dignity, and, in cases within the writer's knowledge, with much forbearance.

The last time I left Gotha I was sailing down the Rhine—it was in the August of 1880—and as I had noticed a large panorama of the country in a gentleman's hands, I asked him if he would kindly let me look at it. It was in his valise then, but he immediately went forward to get it, and pointed out to me where we were. He was comparatively young, hardly more than forty years old, but one of the most attractive and capable-looking men I ever saw—tall, very straight, and singularly handsome, and I had hardly a doubt that I recognised a field-officer that I had seen at Coblenz inspecting the Landwehr.   He saw me shortly after looking over the map to find out a place, and he asked me with great politeness in English (I had spoken French to him) if he could assist me, for, he said, with half a smile, " I think I know every part of Germany ;" and indeed he pointed out almost at once the place I was looking for.   When I returned the map, with cordial thanks, he said, " I am always glad to speak to an Englishman in his own language, for I have a great desire to know it well."   We travelled about sixty-five miles together, and he seemed to have an exhaustive knowledge of many things I wished to know.   He had shot repeatedly in the Thuringian forests, and knew them well.   Some of his remarks about the game will appear in another place ; and he was well acquainted with the early homes of Prince Albert, such as Gotha, Reinhardsbrunn, and Coburg.   Unfortunately, I had begun to speak in the first instance about the Franco-Prussian war, in which he had served, and consequently much time was lost—for it is not easy to find any one who has any great variety of information relating to a district so little traversed as Coburg and Gotha. One remark, though, he made, in speaking of the war, struck me much, and that was the complete dislocation of all our finer feelings during a battle. Brothers or nearest and dearest friends may be struck down, but they are unheeded; and men who could not see a limb taken off in a hospital—and these are many—pass by with total unconcern scenes a thousand times more frightful.

For himself, he said he not only as a youth had almost a dread of seeing a corpse, but even now would feel disposed to cross over the way to avoid one; still, as he remarked, on a battle-field you think no more of them than of the pine-stems that you see lying down in a Thuringian forest. This gentleman had been in the army of occupation in Paris, and he confirmed what had been stated about the desire of the Germans to treat their conquered foes with courtesy. I felt almost inclined to say that for himself and the men under his command no such assurance was needed; and I parted from him with great regret when he had to leave the steamer at Cologne.

The King of the Belgians also writes the following significant description of Germany to the Queen. This is the Germany as it existed seven years before the birth of Prince Albert. He says: " Germany was, at the beginning of 1812, in the lowest and most humiliating position; Austria and Prussia sank to be auxiliaries; everybody frightened and humiliated, except Spain, supported by England.

" The two elder brothers were chiefly at Coburg. The Mensdorfs came also; as well as Victorie, the Princess of Leiningen.

" All the news that reached Germany were favourable

to the Emperor Napoleon. In November only there came vague reports of non-success in Russia. In December there appeared the famous bulletin which told the end of the disastrous campaign in Russia. The Duke of Coburg went to Berlin to act upon the mind of King Frederick William III., who was known, though dreadfully maltreated, to come with great reluctance to any decision, and who took, in general, gloomy views of everything. The enthusiasm of Germany cannot be described. After seven years of slavery, a ray of hope animated again the people.

"The 1st of January 1813 saw Germany happier than it had been for a long time." But Germany had begun even before this to wake up to new life, and indeed had begun to be a nation of heroes. In that year the battle of Leipzig was fought, and Napoleon's downfall commenced. King Leopold says in the same letter, "Prince Leopold was the only general who knew the country, which proved of great importance;" and General Moltke has almost gone so far as to say that the knowledge of a country is the surest key to victory. "After some delay the allied army went into Saxony in October; and on the 16th, 17th, and 18th October, battles took place at Leipzig, finally liberating Germany."

The enthusiasm for Fatherland that had been aroused, and sent shop-boys, and mechanics, and farm-labourers to the front, met its reward here; and there is a simple tale told of a meeting in some church on the anniversary of Leipzig, when the clergyman used to read the names, and sometimes the deeds, of those who had fought there.

When the list was completed, a youth who had only just entered the stage of manhood called out, " Oh that it would come again !"—he was too young to join the army during the war. The self-denial and self-sacrifice we read of were universal; it extended from the highest to the lowest, and it was in such an atmosphere that Prince Albert was born.

CHAPTER V.

ROSENAU, THE BIRTHPLACE OF PRINCE ALBERT — DESCRIPTION OF ITS SCENERY—WATER-MILL, THE FAVOURITE HAUNT OF PRINCE ALBERT—RESTAURANTS IN GERMANY—ABELE POPLAR.

ROSENAU, the birthplace of Prince Albert, is situated about four miles from Coburg market-place. Even to the last the Prince was passionately fond of the place where he had spent so many happy hours in his early days. There is a very excellent account of it and its beautiful situation in General Grey's work, from which I shall borrow a few extracts. The day when I first saw it was a lovely one in August, and the sky was so fair and bright that it seemed almost impossible for a storm and frosts ever to come over the scenes again. The walk to Rosenau may be varied in several ways, but perhaps the most pleasant course is to take the bridle-path to the right, which goes by the beautiful little river Itz, a river which is very like some of the Scottish brooks, and is not inferior in beauty even to these. To any one whose love for the beautiful in nature was as strong and sensitive as Prince Albert's, it is not wonderful that he always fondly remembered the spot, which, during his sojourn in England, he rarely revisited. " It is charmingly situated on a knoll that rises abruptly from, and terminates to the south,—a ridge running out, their last offshoot,—a range of wooded hills which divide the lovely valley of the Itz from the broad and undulating plain through which

Rosenau from Plateau.

passes the main road from Coburg to Hildburghausen, Meiningen, &c. This ridge is cut a quarter of a mile above the house, and again half a mile higher up, at the little villages of Unter and Ober Wolfsbach, prettily situated on the right or western bank of the Itz, by openings through which country roads ascend to the open country to the west; while from the latter village it runs back to a steep ascent, first to the picturesque ruins of Lauterbourg, and thence to the summits of the Herrn Berg, the last of the range of wooded hills above mentioned.

"The eastern side of the ridge falls steeply, covered with wood, to the narrow valley through which flows in serpentine form the pretty little stream of the Itz, sometimes, as at the villages above mentioned, drawing close in below the ridge—at others, diverging in wide sweeps to the further side of the valley. To the west, the ridge slopes gently, just above the house, to a meadow shut in by thriving plantations, and with a large piece of artificial water in the centre."

In the part that has been so excellently described here, where the bridge passes over the Itz, is a beautiful water-mill, which the old country people say that Prince Albert, in his younger days, used to delight in. It had a romantic charm for him, and any of the mill-hands might be sure to engage him in conversation. Often, they say, he used to lean over the railing and watch the fish (trout, I think), that looked like shadows in the little pool below. The mill itself is a perfect marvel of picturesque beauty, and one such as we do not often see now in England, though formerly we might, before science had improved mills out of the range of the artist's pencil. This mill is covered with red tiles, and a frail gallery extends from the miller's house to the mill and store-room. The ruins above spoken of are perfectly visible, and the foliage on the hills is very dense indeed.   The Itz, which is shown

Mill at Rosenau.

here, is fed by ten or twelve rills that issue from springs in the mountains, and is never dry. The fish in it are all of the best quality, owing to the limpid streams they inhabit ; and at the "Grün Baum" hotel, which stands at the corner of the market-place in

Coburg, the landlord is sure to recommend his table more highly if Itz trout are included in the bill of fare. " The knoll on which the house stands, rises abruptly to the southern extremity of this ridge. It falls precipitously on the east side of the Itz, which again draws close in here beneath the house, and by a very steep descent on the other three sides, to the plain on the west and south." There are many beautiful walks through the woods ; and the resemblance of the scenery to Balmoral and the country that surrounds it, may have been the cause of Prince Albert's untiring love for the latter. There is another road which, leading to the Rosenau under the walls of the great fortress that overhangs Coburg, and leaving the little village of Waldsachsen to the right, is not inferior in beauty to any of the others. Indeed, I counted as many as seven different routes by which Rosenau could be reached; and it goes without telling, that such a goal at the end of a pleasant walk is highly prized indeed. About a furlong from the house is a restaurant, which is the favourite resort of citizens on holidays, and it was not at all uncommon for members of the Royal family to mix with them and cause no surprise whatever. In this respect the Germans are certainly superior to the English, and higher in tone. Nothing can exceed the excellent management of this restaurant. It is in reality within the grounds of the Rosenau, but no let or hindrance is placed on any one who wishes to enjoy open air, and shady trees, and the hospitality of the Wirthshaus. There is an excellent plan here, which is common in Germany, for a card to hang up on a conspicuous place, with the prices of everything indicated

clearly; and so the wayfarer can just suit his requirements and his purse. I went there one Sunday afternoon and joined the company who had come from Coburg,
and perhaps Neustadt, or the villages that lie between
Rosenau and Shalkau or Rodach. They had come from
different parts, for a German has a great desire always
to see his own country, and the tables and restaurant
were very well filled. The company were certainly not
total abstainers, if one might judge from the tall wine-
bottles, and the flagons of lager beer; but I must confess
that I felt pained and humiliated at the contrast, when I
remembered what I would have seen in my own country
if similar hospitalities had been afforded in any park
within four miles of a country town. There was plenty
of cheerfulness and gaiety, and there was nothing beyond;
yet this was at an hour on Sunday when the laws have
decided that it would be against the public good if even
a glass of the lightest German or French wine were re-
tailed to the consumer—and indeed, as far as England is
concerned, they have decided well. But in the shady
groves of the Rosenau, where there is no restraint except
any one's own ideas of right and wrong, all was order.
Musical as the Germans are, there was no singing; and
though, as recent years have shown, they can hold their
own against any aggressors, there certainly was nothing
even approaching a combat; whereas in England, with
such opportunities near a large town, Sunday afternoon
would hardly have struck any foreigner as being a day
of rest! "The top of the knoll, as is said in the ' Early
Years,' forms a small plateau, on the southern edge of
which stands the house—a solid building of no archi-

tectural pretensions, with high gable-ends to the north and south." It might also be said that simply, as far as the architecture is concerned, it belongs to a style that has been sometimes copied in England, but has never become popular. It resembles in many respects some of the older Scotch castles, with the large round tower or keep, and what is technically called the " crow-step " gables.

The situation, as will be easily understood from the illustration, is very grand. It may not be exactly as inaccessible as the old fort at Coburg, or the castle at Wartburg where Luther spent so many useful and happy days under the sheltering care of Elector Frederick, but it is equally beautiful, and much more homely. As far as I could trace its history, it belonged to a German family of the highest standing. This family became extinct about the time of the accession of Charles II. to the English throne. The last of the race was one Adam Alexander von Rosenau ; he was childless, and sold his residence to the then Duke of Coburg. In the year 1805, however, it came into possession of the house of Saxe-Coburg-Gotha. When the property was conveyed to that house, the building was, as may be easily supposed, in evil case : indeed, it was little more than a gloomy shell. It was restored, however, by Prince Albert's father, and the wilderness of a park was brought back to its present beauty. The ancient walls were preserved, and the old style of German architecture, to which he was particularly attached, was adopted. The entrance, as will be seen from the illustration, is in the round tower, which is approached through a grove of pines. A broad wind-

A Rimmer

ing staircase in the tower leads upwards to the principal rooms on the first floor, and downwards on the other side to the marble hall or dining-room, which stands on a lower level than the rest of the house owing to a sudden fall in the land. The thing that strikes an English visitor most is the modest size of the mansion. It would, so to say, not be considered cumbrous or excessive if it were the adjunct to an English estate of fifteen or sixteen hundred acres, and yet it seems better adapted to its beautiful situation than an imposing residence. General Grey, in his description of the surroundings of the Rosenau, says: "A small terrace-garden commands a lovely view of the valley of the Itz, beyond which the country is broken up into a succession of wooded hills and picturesque valleys, with occasional clearings, and smiling tidy villages standing in the middle of rich meadows and orchards, the hills gradually rising in height up to the highest points of the Thuringer Wald."

This charming terrace-garden is shown here, and excepting the celebrated view from the terrace at Wynnestay called Nant-y-belen, which it much resembles, I hardly know any scene to equal it in England. The balustrade is formed of pierced quatrefoils with vases on the pedestal for flowers. The parterres are laid out with simple native flowers—such as violets, and roses, and campanulas—in great taste. This garden, they told me, was the favourite resort of Prince Albert. About a mile and a half or two miles from Rosenau is the Thiergarten, where the Dukes of Coburg have a preserve for rearing wild boars, which are much more formidable animals than English readers often suppose. Everything here looks like nature, and hence the charm it had for Prince Albert to his latest day.   His favourite tree was the *Abele* poplar, which flourishes here in great force and strength.   There are many magnificent specimens

Terrace at Rosenau.

of this tree along the road that leads from Coburg to Rosenau.

I have read that he planted it extensively at Windsor and Balmoral.   It is just the tree that might have captivated his youthful fancy, for when the sky is clear and no shower is threatening, this tree may still be seen quivering, even though no draught is felt. The leaves below are deep green, and above they are silver white. A somewhat similar tree grows in America, and is there called the Aspen. There are not a few along the Thames; and in the grounds of Rosenau are some very fine specimens, especially one near the house. This tree grows freely in even exposed situations, and recently the timber has been found very useful. It is better fitted for railway-brakes than any other wood that is known, and more especially for the heavier goods trains.

CHAPTER VI.

ROSENAU—EARLY EDUCATION OF PRINCE ALBERT—BREAKFASTING IN OPEN AIR — GREAT ADVANTAGES OF THE SYSTEM — RUSTIC BUILDINGS ROUND ROSENAU — GERMAN CHARACTERISTICS OF THURINGIA.

AT Rosenau the Prince and his brother received their earlier education. They were singularly happy in having so excellent a tutor as Councillor Florschütz, and their education was conducted on the most enlightened principles. When only fourteen years of age, the Prince laid down for himself at Rosenau, the programme of his studies for each day in the week. The programme on page 98 of 'Early Years,' should be reprinted and sent to every public school and private school in England. There are fifty hours allowed for each week by the Prince, which seems rather a full demand upon the time, according to modern ideas of a student's life. But then he undertook things of utility, and things that interested him. "The labour we delight in physics pain," and he became what in any class of scholars would be called an accomplished gentleman ; but yet the whole time allowed for the classics was six hours in the week, and those six hours were devoted to Latin. The rest of the fifty hours was employed in acquiring information that enabled him to fill so well the high position for which he was destined.

There is a very natural complaint of the tutor's that the system of breakfasting in the open air at ten o'clock interfered with their studies; but the kindly father of the Princes saw things in a different light. We all of us know how delightful the open-air *déjeuners* are on the Continent, though they are literally unknown in England, even when weather would almost invite such gatherings. But the excellent tutor was exercised at the loss of time, for, as he said, nearly the whole forenoon was wasted; and though I cannot think that his grievances were so great as he would have us believe—namely, that these open-air breakfasts "prevailed from early spring to late autumn," for the climate would hardly admit of this —yet the distances travelled were considerable. Thus, when the family was staying at Coburg, the breakfast was held at the Hof Gardens, at the Festung, or even Rosenau (four miles distant), or Callenburg. The Councillor Florschütz may possibly have thought that anything taken from study was wasted time; but as it happened, the beautiful scenes his pupils saw, and the opportunities which these open-air breakfasts gave them of observing nature, and all its wonders and changes, were not thrown away. Will the day ever come to England when lessons are to be regarded as things not to be dreaded? No one of even early middle life can forget their being called " tasks ! " It would have been a good day for England if Prince Albert, from his great influence and knowledge, had written a programme, in the same form as his own, for the education of the sons of the middle and upper classes.

But to return to the narrative. The sites chosen for the meeting were always very beautiful, though none could be more exquisitely charming than the one shown here. It was perhaps the favourite rendezvous near Coburg, and nothing can excel it in beauty. The sketch was made in a glorious August morning. The weather was warm, and the sun had not dissipated the dews that were rising in mist from the low lands. The great Festung of Coburg, that had withstood so many attacks, was clear in outline, and here and there a white farmhouse was just visible. The long avenue of Lombardy poplars was raised above the mist, though their stems were scarcely visible, and the waggon that lumbered between them with its load of wood was more known by sound than sight. But as the sun rose it was wonderful to see the mist pass away, and the smallest object become visible along the highway. This bower was shaded by clematis, and creepers, and honeysuckle, and it seemed to me as nearly a perfect arbour as could be invented by man. The flora and fauna that Prince Albert and his brother collected in after-years, and that form the nucleus of a museum at the great fortress they saw in the distance, received many additions during these happy gatherings. In the plaintive words, indeed, of Councillor Florschütz, " The greater part of the forenoon was inevitably wasted, to the interruption of useful studies and occupations. The Duke was indifferent to this, and we can only wonder that the Princes, notwithstanding, retained their love for study."

But it may occur to others that the Duke knew very

View from Arbour, Callenburg.

well what he was about, and would not have been so

indulgent unless he had been well assured of the character of the Princes.

> " Hath not old custom made this life more sweet
>   Than that of painted pomp ?   Are not these woods
>   More free from peril than the envious Court ?
>
>   .   .   .   .
>
>   And this our life, exempt from public haunt,
>   Finds tongues in trees, books in the running brooks,
>   Sermons in stones, and good in everything."

We are told, indeed, that, years afterwards, the sight of the old collections of natural history that had been formed by the two brothers brought back a flood of recollections such as can only be known to a student " to whom every object in his collection has an interest, not merely from local or personal association, but because it marks a step in ' the pleasant path that winds by stealth ' to knowledge."   Continually we find references to Prince Albert's love for Rosenau in his letters, and there is a touching allusion to it in one which he wrote to Baron Stockmar in May 1839.   He had just returned from his Italian tour, and was looking forward to a quiet time in his beloved Rosenau, the repose of which place, as he truly said, would be well suited for the study of English and history; and for this, he writes his friend, he had formed the finest plans.   But these plans were rudely crushed when he found that he had to accompany his father to Carlsbad,—" a place," he says, " that I hate mortally; " and the restraints of the most fashionable and exclusive watering-place in Europe were not likely to be to his taste.   But in order to understand more fully the strength of this sentence, we should consider what the life at Carlsbad was at the time it was

written. The " season " here is from June to September,
just when Rosenau and its lanes and streams and hills
were in their glory.

In addition to the many beauties of hill and dale, and
all that in nature can delight, some of the farmhouses
round Rosenau and the little villages are charming.
There are also buildings where the peasantry dwell
that are very picturesque ; one especially, that was no
very great distance from the Rosenau, I met with in a
ramble, and it seemed to enclose a kind of open courtyard—but unhappily I did not sketch it. There is a
farm, however, shown on the next page, which lies on
the road to Coburg, which is very pleasant, and much
resembles a homestead in Cheshire or Shropshire. In
the latter county I could enumerate more than one that
it resembles very closely.

There is one thing that strikes us in this class
of architecture, of which Germany affords so many examples—I mean the " post and petrel " style, as it is
termed, or " black and white," as it is also called—and
that is the lightness of the framing. In Cheshire or
Shropshire, when a tree was cut for a building, it was
only dressed with an adze, and then carted by teams
of oxen, and helped with rude levers into its place
—an operation that required many hands. I could
point out cottages in Cheshire that contain quite enough
timber to build a moderately-sized mansion. One reason
of this lightness in the framing of the houses is that the
Germans had more science, and perhaps they were also
compelled to economise their hardwood. This farm is,
speaking from recollection, about a mile from Rosenau.

The buildings follow each other in picturesque confusion, and the large enclosure before it is used for empty waggons or heaps, and for the cattle to roam about in. I could hardly help remarking the military air of some of the

Farm at Rosenau.

peasants on the property ; but this, as it at once appeared, was owing to the recent French war, when nearly every one had to qualify for service ; but everything about, from the ploughshares to the farmers, looked very contented and happy.

There was a trifling incident that was very suggestive of the simplicity of the German children; but certainly it was impossible not to be interested in it. Behind a thicket hedge that bounded a small garden I heard a plaintive German song sung by a very young girl, perhaps not more than six years of age; and this was kept on monotonously for as long at any rate as my sketch took. She was evidently walking backwards and forwards along a small garden-walk; and when I had finished and looked for a moment over the hedge, I saw a young damsel, with flaxen hair and clear round eyes, walking backwards and forwards by a little cradle that held a wooden doll, and she was playing at putting it to sleep. But there is a simplicity about all the inhabitants here which is very charming and attractive. Thuringia is said to be the most thoroughly German of all the States; and it is not a little curious to notice the resemblance to some of the old Saxon MSS. figures that the inhabitants bear. Some of the Cottonian and Harleian MSS. show us Saxons with long hair, and hands and arms in angular positions, which we may have fancied were the result of bad drawing—but in reality these ancient pictures are well drawn; and if we stop in a field to ask the peasants who are following a plough any direction, it is much if at least one of them does not forcibly remind us of some old document that we have seen in the British Museum.

CHAPTER VII.

VISIT OF PRINCES TO MECKLENBURG-SCHWERIN, AND OTHER PARTS
OF GERMANY — ARRIVAL AT VIENNA — MAJOR HÜBNER AND
EHRENBREITSTEIN—PERSEVERANCE OF GERMANS IN LEARNING
A FOREIGN LANGUAGE—RESIDENCE OF PRINCES AT BRUSSELS.

IN the year 1835, when the Prince was sixteen years
of age, he went with his brother to visit his great-
grandfather, who was the Grand Duke of Mecklenburg-
Schwerin, and to congratulate him on the fiftieth anniversary of his accession to the dukedom. He succeeded,
it may be remarked, in the same year that Frederick the
Great formed the celebrated League, which was joined by
the temporal princes of Germany, and by the Elector of
Mainz, and was in fact the first attempt of Prussia to
seriously contest with Austria the leading place in Germany.

This was indeed short-lived, but the general scheme
was renewed in 1867, and is now the foundation of the
great German Confederation. There does not seem to
be any journal of the Prince's travels on this occasion,
though doubtless he kept one. The road in those days
would occupy fully a week, unless great expedition were
used. The capital of the Grand Duchy of Mecklenburg-

Strelitz is the quiet town of Strelitz, which, at the time of the Prince's visit, was estimated to contain about 5500 inhabitants, and the area of the state was as nearly as possible half as large again as his native one. Mecklenburg-Schwerin adjoins it, and their public debt was so interwoven that it often complicated the balances.

After spending a few days here they joined their father at Berlin, and left this city almost immediately for the travels they had so often looked forward to make together. Nothing can indeed be more delightful than the prospect which was opened out before them. They went to Dresden, Prague, Vienna, Pest, and Ofen—places they had so often heard of, and now saw for the first time in their lives. Railways were unknown, and the diligence, or post-horses, were the only means of conveyance, excepting where there was a river. But what picturesque delights would be opened out where now a railway hurries a traveller by! With every advantage that high rank and opportunity can afford, with well-spent lives, short as they had been, to look back upon, and the prospect of an exalted future before them, the Princes set out on their journey. May is a charming time to visit the places they went to, perhaps the most pleasant period of the year; and they were received with all the hospitality the Courts they visited could show. Who cannot remember some journey in early life, when all nature was bright, and before a single cloud had come across the summer sky! On the 20th May the Duchess of Gotha speaks of the arrival of the Princes at Vienna; and as this must have occurred some few days before, they would reach that city about two months after the death of the Emperor Francis, who was succeeded by his son Ferdinand, and who would be the Emperor when the Princes arrived, though Prince Metternich was in reality the ruler of the state. It would be interesting to read the impressions which the town made on Prince Albert, and doubtless he wrote very fully what he saw.

In May 1836 we find the Princes writing their Rhine experiences, which must have been very delightful. They made the acquaintance of the Princes of Isenburg, and dined with them at the hotel. Major Hübner, who built Ehrenbreitstein, was one of the company. They went over after dinner to Ehrenbreitstein, for it is hardly necessary to add that the usual dinner-hour in Germany is soon after mid-day. Some of the views from the commandant's house, where the Princes were received, are among the most beautiful in Germany, or perhaps in Europe. The town, with its zigzag fortifications, lies below, with all its outworks, and the four bridges which span the Rhine and the Moselle are distinctly visible, while the hills of Maiengau and Maifeld slope away into fruitful plains. Singularly enough, when the Princes were looking at the scene, they saw the site of the old Roman city of Victoria. Major Hübner was directed by the general commanding to show the Princes everything; and they spent the afternoon in looking over the fortifications; and next morning they visited the forts Alexander and Franz. In the afternoon they went on board the Rhine steamer, where they met their father, and proceeded to Cologne on their first visit to England, where in after-years Prince Albert was destined to fill so conspicuous a place. One thing is noticeable in his letter which he writes home from Rotterdam. He says,—" We arrived here after two days more on board the steamer, during which I tried to practise my English in conversation with some Englishmen whom we met." This is precisely where the Germans can teach us a lesson. They lose no opportunity of practising and acquiring knowledge of a language, and it gives them an immense advantage in the markets of the world. If we will take the trouble to remember the names of the Champagne houses at Epernay and Rheims, we shall find that there is always a German name among the partners, if indeed the house is not entirely in German hands. The reason is that Champagne is more generally consumed than any other wine; and while the French are almost the worst linguists in Europe, the Germans are by far. the best. I remember, when staying at the Hotel du Géant in 1864, to have met with a slight incident of which the Prince's letter reminds me, and if I mistake not, in the same building where he stayed. I had finished dinner and was in the hall of the hotel, when a gentleman came up to me and shook hands, and I recognised at once a stranger I had met in the early part of the day. He had given me some interesting information about the locality, and especially recommended me to visit Mosselweiss, and Laach, and Elz, all of which he described to me more or less in intelligible English. But he came to me in the hall, and after a very courtly recognition, he asked me if he might venture to renew our acquaintance. I said that nothing could give me greater pleasure, and sat down, inviting him to do the same. But I must confess that I was a little puzzled, and the more so when he handed me a wine *carte*, and begged me to name any wine on it, that he might order for us. To English habits this seemed very curious, and even suggested some hesitation; but I said to him that I had just dined, and as I believed a pint of Rudesheim was coming up for me, I would ask him to join me, especially as he had favoured me by paying me a visit. I well remember how his eyes twinkled as he apprehended my meaning; and he signalled a waiter, who seemed to know him, and addressed him in German with great respect, and then he said to me in English that was perfectly intelligible, " I understood you so well this morning that I came to speak English again; 1 understand your accent, and I want to profit by speaking to you." This was of course an excellent opportunity for me to acquire some knowledge of the country; and he soon showed that he was a gentleman of culture. The incident seemed to an Englishman a little odd at the time, but had escaped my recollection till reading the extract quoted from the Prince's letter. I remember now he said that he recollected the Princes well at Bonn, and used to see them. The Duke of Mecklenburg-Strelitz, he said, was there at the same time, and he knew him personally, and he was, he said, within a few days of the same age as Prince Albert. He had been introduced to the latter, and had had several conversations with him; and though his acquaintance was of the most transitory, he had seen enough in a short time to convince him that he was one of the most exemplary young men he ever met with in his life; and yet, as he said, he himself was born in the first year of the present century. An accident prevented me learning the address of my friend, which he obligingly gave me; for just as I parted with him at the door of the hotel, an old friend whom I had left in America landed from the Rhine steamer, and in my hurry to greet him, I lost this gentleman's card without having even read the name.

The Prince's account of his visit to England will be read with interest, but it hardly belongs to the present subject. He was in his seventeenth year, and of course was well able to appreciate the scenes he saw for the first time in his life. He speaks, in a letter that he writes home, of the interest he felt in meeting the Duke of Wellington at a grand ball given in the Princes' honour. Here he also met with William, Duke of Brunswick, and the Prince of Orange and his two sons. The next day they went to visit the Duke of Northumberland at Sion House: and his biographer mentions a curious weakness he always had to struggle with, and that was a tendency to sleep; and he speaks of the "hard battles to fight against sleepiness at these late entertainments." Some of his descendants have been sorely tried in the same direction by their sojourn in Canada; because it is utterly impossible for any English person to spend an evening in a Canadian house any time during their winter at least, without a feeling of drowsiness overtaking them, owing to the way in which the houses are warmed. On returning from England they went to Brussels, where their father left them in the excellent charge of Baron Wiechmann, a retired officer of the English German legion. Both of the Princes profited much by their residence at Brussels;

and some years later, when there was an international statistical congress, Prince Albert was the president. Among the deputies was M. Quetelet, who represented Brussels, and whose works have long been standard ones in England; and the Prince gracefully reminded him that it was to himself he owed the information which he possessed on the subject of statistics. While the Princes were at Brussels they availed themselves of the opportunity of visiting Paris, and of course saw everything that could be seen, and were much struck with the beauty of the surroundings that met their gaze on all sides. They stayed at the Hotel des Princes, which no longer exists as a hotel. It was situated in the Rue de Richelieu, not far from the Palais Royal, and was, as Prince Albert described it, " a most horrible place—such a noise in the street that you could not hear your own voice." This is literally true. The Rue de Richelieu is so called from a garden that was planned by the great Cardinal in 1629; and we can well understand the Prince's description of it if we remember that it is the principal thoroughfare from the Rue de Rivoli, the Rue St Honoré, the Louvre and Tuileries, and the northern districts of Paris.

At length they are settled in Brussels, and they commenced again their studies with great ardour. They lived in a very pleasant little detached house, with a garden in front; and though in the middle of the city, it was free from noise and disturbance. The Prince's letters home at this time are full of interest. Sometimes they may excite a smile, as when he speaks of going out at Ostend with his brother shooting, and killing some sea-gulls; but the few records are so exceedingly artless, that they command our warmest sympathy the moment we read them. There is one letter that must be quoted, though to properly estimate it we should remember the circumstances under which it was written. Germany, we need hardly say, is the land where, beyond all others, Christmas is enjoyed; and our own Christmas festivities are copied from German models. We learn, of course, that Prince Albert had no taste for the sumptuous entertainments that it became his lot to attend in after-life, and said with Sir G. Cornewall Lewis that " life would be very pleasant but for its amusements." Yet, as it happens, it is just to such natures that Christmas enjoyments are most pleasant; and those who shrink from a stately assembly of any kind, look forward with the greatest anticipation to the family gathering at Christmas. The journey also from Brussels to Coburg, which would have been exciting and delightful in the company of the brother he loved so well, was in itself full of attraction; yet we find the following written on the 29th November 1836, to his father, who had asked the Princes to spend their Christmas at Coburg, with all its charming associations of Rosenau and Callenburg :—

" Dear Papa,—We should be so glad to accept your invitation to go to Coburg for a few days, and to spend Christmas there. But if we are to profit by our stay here, I am afraid we must deny ourselves that pleasure. Such an expedition would require five or six weeks, and our course of study would be quite disturbed by such an interruption. We told dear uncle the purport of your letter, and he said he would write to you on the subject."

It is not often that, with the authority of a parent for such a holiday, it would be disregarded on the grounds that it might interfere with the course of study. How many youths from Eton or Harrow would have returned such a reply to a paternal request to visit their home for a holiday? supposing always—which is perhaps supposing a great deal—that the masters of these schools had been perfectly agreeable to the arrangement.

CHAPTER VIII.

THE period at length arrived when the Princes were to commence their university career, and for a time at least bid farewell to the plains, mountains, and valleys of Thuringia, and the sylvan delights of Rosenau, though indeed their residence at Brussels had severed them from these for ten months. They went to Bonn in April 1837, and remained there for a year and a half. Their tutor, M. Florschütz, accompanied them, and they lived in a small detached house near the cathedral; and we have his testimony to the rigour and assiduity with which they pursued their studies. If, indeed, students more frequently resembled his scholars, and especially Prince Albert, the life of a tutor would be very different from what it often is. Writing of the Prince he says: "He maintained the early promise of his youth by the eagerness with which he applied himself to his work, and by the rapid progress which he made, especially in the natural sciences, in political economy, and in philosophy." But while study was so congenial to him, he did not forget the necessity of developing the body as well as the mind. The *mens sana* is not always of use unless it rests in *corpore sano*. He would seem to have been especially dexterous in the use of the rapier, and had indeed few equals in that weapon at Bonn.

He also practised what is so much neglected in England—the art of swimming,—and became such an adept that he swam on one occasion a distance (down the stream) of three miles. But walking with a friend was a great delight to him always; and we well know that in the neighbourhood of Bonn the walks are not surpassed in beauty by any walks in the world.

I met one or two elderly inhabitants who remembered him well on these excursions, and always speak of him with affectionate remembrance. He used to walk along the roads with his brother, or his friend Prince Löwenstein, who was at the university with him. Godesberg, with its ruins and its old chapel, was a resort of untiring delight to these friends; and often the Prince used to pore over the legends that surround it. The castle is a picturesque old pile; and it was built by Archbishop Dietrich out of money which the Jews whom he incarcerated paid him for their ransom. It is surrounded by many places of interest, such as the Abbey of Heisterbach and Königswinter. I was assured that there is hardly an inhabitant along the road who can count sixty summers that does not remember the Prince well; and often in those days they would leave the cottage garden, if they saw him coming in the distance, simply to touch their hats, being sure of a polite acknowledgment. A veteran officer, who had seen many wars, was always in the habit of returning salutes most punctiliously; and if he made any exception, it was to be more

Godesberg.

polite to his humbler wayfarers, because, as he said, he would not be outdone in politeness by them; and if we regard what the old people round Bonn and Godesberg, and indeed that part of Rhineland, said, we should think Prince Albert adopted his system. In a letter written by his friend, Prince William of Löwenstein, in 1864, which has recollections of Prince Albert, he says: " I recall with much pleasure our excursion to the neighbouring Siebengebirge, so rich in legend; to the valley of the Aar, where the celebrated Walportzheimer wine is produced; and up and down the Rhine." More than one of these legends would seem to belong to other mountain districts of Germany, and certainly are told of hills in Thuringia. Prince Albert was said to take a great interest in legendary lore; and the weird quaint stories of Germany that have delighted so many English firesides, as well as those of Fatherland, must have some separate notice. The story of the white doe of Rylstone that Wordsworth has made so celebrated, really is a Thuringian legend, and has been told, though in a different, and some might think better form, many a time round the firesides of the rich and poor. Prince Löwenstein further says: " As the Prince excelled most of his contemporaries in the use of intellectual weapons, in the art of convincing, in strictly logical argument, so he was distinguished also in all kinds of bodily exercise. In fencing, and in the practice of the broadsword, he was very skilful. In fencing especially he excelled so much, that once in a fencing-match he carried off the prize from all competitors." It was my fortune to meet an old keeper of his at a rather out-of-the-way place called Newport, on the borders of Shropshire and Staffordshire, and he gave me some interesting information regarding Prince Albert.

He said that he was an admirable shot, indeed one of the best he remembers to have seen, and what is called a steady shot. Sometimes, as we know, a man shoots very well for a day, and the next day he can only give a poor account of his empty cartridge-cases; but with Prince Albert he says it was quite different: his nerves were always well braced, and he was the most even shot that went over the covers of Windsor or Bagshot; but the information I had from this keeper will appear when considering the game of the Thuringian forests, and the sporting they afford. We learn from the same college companion that Prince Albert had a great talent for caricatures, and the eminent professors, Fichte and Löbell, were always ready subjects for his pencil. Rath Wolff, who was in attendance on the Count of Erbach, was near-sighted, and was constrained to wear concave spectacles, as so many Germans—and of recent years, indeed, so many Englishmen—have been obliged to do; and though, as we know, through life the Prince was always a sympathiser with misfortune, it was too much for him when he saw Rath Wolff stop in a race to find his spectacles which had fallen off. One word of explanation is due here, and that is, that the calamity of near sight is not thoroughly understood by those who are not afflicted by it, and indeed they cannot understand it. The keeper I met with in Shropshire said that Prince Albert's eyesight was remarkably keen, and he could see a woodcock in the thickets of Bagshot or Windsor much more readily than even an averagely quick keeper or beater. It has indeed been said, with reference to this extract, that near-sighted people are generally keenly sensitive to their defect; but on the other hand it is often not apparent at all to any companion; their eyes are frequently as bright and clear as their neighbours, and their hearing and other faculties enable them to join to the fullest extent in the surrounding society, though it is often not even suspected that objects round them appear as though they were seen through obscured glass.

Nothing could be more ridiculous than the incident which materially moved Prince Albert's humour, unless it were another that is said to have occurred on a Rhine steamer, during his residence at Bonn, and in which one of the college professors figured conspicuously. He was, if I remember rightly, a professor of chemistry, or some kindred subject, and he happened to sit next to an English manufacturer, who was a gentleman of much dignity. The British magnate happened to possess very large brown hands and long arms, and as he reclined back, one of these hands, closed, rested on the edge of the table, and indeed rather encroached upon the space that fairly belonged to the professor. The latter having surveyed it closely and curiously, though unhappily without his concave glasses, had no doubt that it was a French roll, and suddenly struck his fork into it (!).

Bonn is well known to every one who has sailed on the Rhine; it is beautifully situated on the left bank, about fifteen miles above Cologne. At Bonn the most charming part of the Rhine commences, and the gorge begins which extends nearly to Mayence. The university where Prince Albert was educated is one of the noblest in Europe. There are in it 80 professors, and 800 or 1000 students. Bonn is also the seat of many learned associations and societies. The Leopoldine Academy of Physical Science was founded at Vienna in 1632, and transferred to Bonn in 1818. It obtained a university in 1786, which was, however, suppressed during the sway of France of which Arndt has left us so touching and eloquent an account. The present university was founded in the year 1818, and received from Government the electoral buildings, which had formerly been the palace of the Electors of Cologne, with the other buildings attached to them ; and it also received Government aid to the extent of £15,000 per annum. There are two theological colleges, the one Protestant, and the other Roman Catholic. This splendid college has a library of 150,000 vols., some splendid museums, and collections of Roman antiquities. There is also what is so much needed in our older educational establishments in England—an agricultural[1] school, a botanic garden, and a riding-school. Indeed there is no more perfect educational establishment in Europe. While Prince Albert was at Bonn, August Willem von Schlegel was the professor of history: he was the brother of Friedrich Schlegel, and an equally celebrated man, though the works of the latter are more commonly read in England. He was born at Hanover in 1767, and studied at Göttingen, where he soon became conspicuous for his devotion to classical and philological studies, and he was also one of the first Sanscrit scholars in Europe. Schlegel translated Shakespeare into German, and was the author of many works in his own language which

[1] See chapter on the Prince's Windsor farm and Thuringian agriculture.

are text-books in Germany : he died in his seventy-eighth year.

Niebuhr was also a professor here when Prince Albert was a student. He was born at Copenhagen, and went at an early age to Göttingen to study law, and in his nineteenth year he removed to Edinburgh to devote himself to natural sciences. It is said that his precocity caused him to be regarded as a sort of infant prodigy ; but, unlike other infant prodigies, his powers for acquiring knowledge kept pace with advancing years. His feelings were so strongly anti-Napoleonic that he had to resign several appointments when Napoleon's sway was all-powerful in Europe. He was appointed ambassador to Prussia in the Papal Court in 1816, and retained his office until 1823, when he went to Bonn, and there, by his excellent lectures on classical and archæological learning, he greatly contributed to the advancement of the university. He was employed with his university work when the revolution of 1830 broke out, and this he fancied would be a repetition of the horrors of the French Revolution, which so shocked his sensitive nature that an attack of prostration was the result, and he died in 1831. Niebuhr's acquirements embraced a more extensive range of subjects than most men are capable of attaining. He was not only an able diplomatist, but a scholar and a man of original genius. He had mastered twenty languages before he was thirty years of age. He left his mark permanently in Bonn University, though it was not the lot of Prince Albert to be among his students ; but the year before he entered Bonn a very eminent scholar was appointed to the professorship of philosophy—Immanuel H. Fichté, a son of the illustrious Johann Gottlieb Fichté. The political principles of Fichté, we can easily see, were absorbed by Prince Albert, and they have been well summed up in the following words : "The principles of real Conservatism are those of constant well-planned reform ; and all revolution consists either in attempts to precipitate prematurely the future, or to go back to ideas that are effete—the last being only the chrysalis state of the first." Fichté suggested meetings of philosophers similar to those held by physicists ; and at the one held at Gotha in 1847, he delivered his address "On the philosophy of the future." Perthes also was the professor of law at Bonn during the time that Prince Albert was among the scholars. He was a second son of the able and patriotic Friedrich Christoph Perthes, who tried to rouse his countrymen to shake off the iron rule of France, and a nephew of Johann Justus Perthes who established a printing-house at Gotha from which the celebrated 'Almanach de Gotha' is now issued. Holburg, Kaufmann, and other great German scholars were among the professors ; and it is recorded that Prince Albert pursued his studies with the same eagerness under these masters as he had shown in former years for his earlier reading ; and happy it was for him, and indeed for England, that his efforts were aided by men of such ability and experience, and of such lofty aims. There is an interesting association connected with the University of Bonn. It was at one time the palace of the Electors of Cologne, having been removed there in consequence of the many feuds between them and the citizens of that place. In the chapel of that building was a tenor singer of some excellence, who had a son born in 1770, and whose genius for music was so great that it was carefully cultivated when he was only five years of age. In his eighth year he astonished every one by his performances on the violin, and when only twelve he published a work of great ability consisting of variations of a march, songs, and sonatas. This was Beethoven, who may indeed be said to have made a new development of some branches of music.

It is at Bonn that the beauties of the Rhine fairly commence, and for myself I must confess that each time I have sailed up that glorious river I have felt a greater love for its delights. It is partly the atmosphere, and partly the grand scenery along its shores, that leave it with hardly a rival, certainly without a superior, in the world. It is not a little significant, also, that the majority of the travellers we meet on the steamers are German—and Germans, too, who have opportunities of seeing other parts of Europe if they so desired, but Fatherland has sufficient attractions for them. When shall we see London merchants, or bankers, or Manchester manu-facturers, exploring the beauties of Lancashire, Cheshire, Shropshire, or Merionethshire? yet I could give a list of old towns, and shady lanes, and quiet rich valleys, which few of them ever saw (and which are by no means con-fined to the counties named), that would so fill them with astonishment that they would say, "Surely this cannot be England;" nor would the romance be quite dispelled if they heard the natives speak. For—leaving out Wales, where indeed he might hear a tongue spoken, compared with which even Russian *patois* sounds like easy and holiday work—he would be quite as much puzzled in Lancashire, and that in some of the most beautiful parts, if he asked a direction, as he would in any State on the Continent. Cheshire and Shropshire are not so obscure in their dialects; but there are some parts of Cheshire where a Londoner might feel very much at fault occasionally. The Germans, as before said, are among the principal excursionists that we meet with on the river, though of course there are others from all parts of Europe, and not a few from America. Every one seems happy on these steamboats. Each bend of the river gives us new delights. Sometimes a castle is the first object we see, and it is so singularly large and looming that we wonder why it was built; and as the number of these is so great, and the available land for their feudal support so comparatively small, this is always a mystery. Much of their revenue must have been drawn from rather doubtful sources. These ancient fortresses, it is sufficient to say, are a picturesque delight to us, and perhaps if we knew more of their history we should not be more impressed with their beauties. Even more beautiful than the castles are the old-fashioned villages that fringe the water's edge. The steamboat stops only for a few moments while a boat that has been waiting with peasant passengers unloads, and is refilled by others who are going ashore. Every stroke of the oar in the reflections of the turrets of the little town is picturesque; and as the steamboat hurries along, I have often looked back with almost a feeling of envy at the voyagers as they slowly approached the landing. Of course we can hardly avoid making some comparison between the scenery of the Rhine, to which Prince Albert was accustomed from his early days, and that of English rivers, and perhaps more especially the Thames, which at Windsor is developed in its beauty. But the Thames is of course not the only English river that can boast of charms, nor perhaps the most beautiful of all our rivers. We have the Severn, the Wye, the Trent, and the many streams of Yorkshire; but there are very general characteristics among them, whether they run through hilly or plain countries. They have all a peaceful appearance, and they look as if they belonged to a land that had never seen a foreign invader. All the wars their banks ever saw have been waged among the dwellers on their own shores; and whether the combatants were claimants for the crown under the red or the white rose, or whether they were fighting for the falling fortunes of the Stuarts, one thing was certain, they had no foreign armies to fear. Perhaps a military canal and some slight attempts at fortification may be excepted from the category, if we traverse the south coast of Kent from Folkestone to Rye or Hastings; but these are exotic, and they only give emphasis to what is said, and indeed they almost provoke a smile. The characteristic of English rivers is their homeliness. The banks are rarely high, and they flow through fresh meadows, and past alders and poplars, and quiet villages. Village churches, with their towers or spires, are sure to appear at intervals of greater or less distance. Sometimes they rise from a clump of elms or beeches, and sometimes they come down to the water's edge, flanked by a village. Then, in all the English rivers there are shoals and shallows which give a charm to them, and on these cattle cool themselves, or a ford is made from side to side. The Thames is of course

Mill on Rhine.

more of a typical English river than the rest, and its even quiet stream flowing past lawns and country-houses, with gudgeon and barbel fishers moored in square-ended boats to stakes, is all its own. The locks also are a specialty, and the barges and gigs and wherries, as they ascend and descend, have to learn their business, while the floods of water that one seems to think could be utilised in London are impounded, and place the fishers often in perilous positions. But, excepting a slight turmoil at the locks and weirs, the Thames flows quietly on; and other rivers, such as the Severn and the Trent, are even more remarkable for the even tenor of their way. Perhaps we should have to go to the Wye or the Conway to find, though on a small scale, a parallel to the Rhine, and even then the resemblance soon vanishes. They have some hills indeed, and some feudal recollections, and a few international wars to make them conspicuous in their history, but these are shadowy; and the castles, which were at any time but few, have disappeared, all except a few crumbling walls. The Rhine is, of course, in every way different in its characteristics from English rivers.

We do not see cattle sheltering themselves under overhanging boughs, and cooling themselves in quiet placid contentment from the rays of a midsummer sun. The circumstances and the landscapes are quite different. In place of the tranquil shallows and lazy current of an English river, we have a stream that runs rapidly through high banks, and carries a constant and exceedingly picturesque commerce along its clear waters.

Then we hardly dare to venture a descent into the cabin of a Rhine steamer for fear of missing some of the quiet quaint old towers that nestle on the banks. No modern science could reproduce them: we may have, indeed, many copies—and some of the London suburbs have tried with more or less success to imitate them. It is a good intention, and one for which the passer-by should be grateful; but after all, there seems to be

something about medieval architecture so real and so
unstudied, that the actual groups of gables and chimneys
nearly defy the attempts of modern architects to reproduce them. As we ascend the Rhine these quaint surroundings seem almost as if they partook of our joy,
the villages and hamlets are so very bright and happy.

Goarhausen.

To trim the vines, and gather the fruit in its season high
up on the hills, is not only a delightful but an easy task ;
and the eyes of the tillers are for ever refreshed when they
look away from their work by the glorious windings of
the river that flows below—

> " The river nobly foams and flows,
>   The charm of this enchanted ground,
>   And all its thousand turns disclose
>   Some fresher beauty varying round.

F

A blending of all beauties ; streams and dells,
Fruit, foliage, crag, wood, corn-field, mountain, vine,
And chiefless castles breathing stern farewells
From grey but leafy walls, where Ruin greenly dwells.

And there they stand, as stands a lofty mind,
Worn, but unstooping to the baser crowd ;
All tenantless, save to the crannying wind,
Or holding dark communion with the cloud.
There was a day when they were young and proud :
Banners on high, and battles passed below ;
But they who fought are in a bloody shroud,
And those which waved are shredless dust ere now,
And the bleak battlements shall bear no future blow.

But Thou, exulting and abounding river,
Making thy waves a blessing as they flow
Through banks whose beauty would endure for ever,
Could man but leave thy bright creation so.

A thousand battles have assailed thy banks,
But these and half their fame have passed away ;
And Slaughter heaped on high his weltering ranks ;
Their very graves are gone,—and what are they ?

Adieu to thee, fair Rhine ! How long, delighted,
The stranger fain would linger on his way !
Thine is a scene alike where souls united
Or lonely. Contemplation thus might stray.
And could the ceaseless vultures cease to prey
On self-condemning bosoms, it were here,
Where Nature, not too sombre nor too gay,
Wild but not rude, awful yet not austere,
Is to the mellow earth as Autumn to the year.

Adieu to thee again ! a vain adieu !
There can be no farewell to scene like thine :
The mind is coloured by thy every hue.
And if reluctantly the eyes resign
Their cherished gaze upon thee, lovely Rhine,
'Tis with the thankful heart of parting praise.
More mighty spots may rise, more glaring shine,
But none unite in one attaching maze
The brilliant, fair, and soft,—the glories of old days."

Bonn, which, as before said, opens out the glories of the Rhine, is at the mouth of the river Sieg, where in days of old the Sigambri lived. It is supposed that it was not far from Bonn that Cæsar constructed his celebrated bridge over the Rhine, and that it was not at Weissen-thurm, which tradition gives as the spot. Probably, if it had been there, some mention would have been made of such an invaluable help as the island that is opposite.

CHAPTER IX.

Picture of Bonn, drawn when Prince Albert was a student—Concert at Bonn, and demeanour of students—Musical surroundings—Schiller at Bonn—"Landsmannschaften"—Duelling, and the Prince's dislike for it—The Prince's skill as a swordsman and a sportsman—Fatal duel between Lieutenant Munroe and Colonel Fawcett—Prince's attempts to induce the Duke of Wellington to take the matter up, and his own influence in stopping the practice—University of Jena founded by the Coburg family.

THE following is a description of Bonn from a very intelligent observer, just before Prince Albert matriculated—a lady who wrote down what she saw as she saw it : " If Bonn had nothing but its university, this would be sufficient to detain the traveller delightfully for several days ; but there are many other circumstances to repay such a delay. It is full of interesting antiquities, and it happens to be the first point at which one's expectations of beautiful scenery begin to be realised. There are views in the environs of Bonn equal in extent and richness to almost anything on the Rhine." An account is given of how the Electoral palace became a university, and the writer proceeds : " Everything connected with the university is upon a noble scale. The schools, the library, and the academy walks ; the gardens are all handsome, and arranged in a grand and expensive style. To those who have their fancies over-full of the Gothic glories of Oxford, or imagine that on any other spot of the earth they shall meet the perfection of King's College Chapel, or the magnificence of Trinity College, Cambridge, Bonn may cause a sensation of disappointment; but to all who are sufficiently instructed to be aware that the academic magnificence of England stands alone, it will appear what it really is—a noble and beautiful seat of learning. The bronze statue of the Empress Helen, the sainted mother of Constantine, is the most interesting object in the cathedral, which has been too much defaced by repairs to claim any great share of admiration. The walk on the *entresol* should by no means be neglected, both from thence and from the gardens behind the *café.*" Speaking of a concert she says: "I was extremely pleased to find myself in a room well filled with German company, at a point sufficiently distant from any metropolis to enable me to judge of the national style, when divested of the conventional air and tone which have made almost all characteristic national varieties disappear in the great cities of Europe. This must inevitably be the case whenever people agree to submit themselves to the uniform laws of high breeding and cultivated taste. But at Bonn this livery of elegance was neither to be hoped nor feared; and I found as many points of difference in the assembly between Madame Milden's concert and all other assemblies of the same kind I had seen elsewhere, as I could possibly wish. Yet there was nothing in the slightest degree unpleasant or uncouth. The extreme simplicity of dress was the first thing that struck me, while reviewing the female part of the company; but a few moments of prolonged examination of the faces, around which the luxuriant tresses were so simply braided, sufficed to convince me that the fair girls were right to trust more to their blooming complexions and sweet countenances than to any elaborate toilet.   We remarked many lovely faces among them.

"After the room appeared to be perfectly full, a door opened to admit a party, some of whom had a very decided air of metropolitan *bon ton*.   They placed themselves on chairs on one side of the foremost bench, and the performance almost immediately began.   A fair neighbour, who appeared very willing to converse, announced their names and titles, but I forget both : I think she said they resided in the neighbourhood.   One of the party was as lovely and graceful a woman as I ever saw.   They were immediately surrounded by a party of officers ; and on the broad chest of one I counted seven decorations." A description of the concert is given, but it hardly has specific differences enough from other concerts to make it desirable to record at any length ; the appearance of the students in 1833, however, is extremely interesting. "Of course," the writer adds, "no public meeting can take place at Bonn in which the young students do not make a distinguished figure.   On this occasion they did not appear to mix much with the company, but stood almost entirely apart in groups of three or four, and formed pictures which made me fancy myself in a saloon with Vandyck and Rubens ; for, certainly, some like the students I was observing must have been their models.

" I suppose it is the nature of all young gentlemen, particularly when congregated together, to mix a little fancy, and perhaps *tant si peu* of affectation, in their outward seeming. Something of this may assuredly be seen both at Oxford and Cambridge, despite the gown and cap, which so greatly curb the display of individual whim : but at Bonn, where no academic dress is worn, the costume of the young men is sometimes marvellously imaginative. Whenever a set of European youths assemble to receive the last finish of their education, it is probable that some will always be found among them upon whom the stamp which marks the gentleman is too strongly impressed to admit any vagary of dress to conceal it—and of such, many are to be seen among the students at Bonn ; but the majority are much more picturesque. Hair long and exquisitely dishevelled ; throats bare, with collars turned back almost to the shoulders ; with here and there a miniature beard, curiously trimmed into a perfect triangle, or moustaches long, thin, and carefully curled,—might be seen repeated in one knot after another through the whole length of the room. Some present a fair young forehead, carefully curled *à la* Byron, and looked about them with a wild eye rollicking *à la* Juan. One had the pale cheek and deep-set eye of a premature philosopher ; while another looked with such a dashing reckless sauciness upon all around, that I felt inclined to watch him, half in fear and half in fun, to see what madcap frolic would deliver him from the load of merry mischief that lay laughing in his eyes.

" Not the slightest indecorum, however, to the amount of an audible whisper, disturbed the entertainment ; and notwithstanding the boisterous licence assumed by the students of Germany, I question if so large a party of young men could often be seen assembled, and remain so long together, so entirely without noise or disturbance of any kind."

This picture of Bonn was drawn the year before Prince Albert entered the university. And it may almost be doubted if at that time, or indeed even now, so large a concourse of young gentlemen, brought together promiscuously from different parts of England, would be quite as quiet and decorous. Bonn occupied very much the same place in Germany as, if we could make a comparison, Eton and Christchurch do in England. There were not, of course, the same number of students who entered in order to pass their early days without any intention of turning their studies to practical account afterwards, for such a class is hardly to be found except in England; but there was always at Bonn the same high tone that we find in those places, and a dislike and contempt for what was untruthful or mean. Bonn is extremely musical; and the organist of an English cathedral, who has written some anthems that would seem to have made their way in Germany, says that as he sat at dinner in his hotel, a band of street musicians—as it appeared to him—came to salute him at his inn, and they performed upon the harp, the violin, and the horn. They played several minuets and polonaises, which were extremely well executed, and then treated him to a selection from Bach. He remarks that often a high state of proficiency in music is acquired at school; but the pupils go afterwards to the plough, and other laborious employments, "so that their knowledge of music turns to no other account than to join the village choir, and sing in their parish church, or else as an innocent domestic re-creation." He further mentions—what travellers such as Nugent and others have frequently said—that the German nobility retain musicians in their houses; and adds, "but in keeping servants, how could it be otherwise, when all the children of the peasants and trades-people are taught music, excepting at Prague, where music forms no part of the school system?" "Some-times," the same authority says, "there appears in the common country schools a musical genius, as was the case with Stamitz, whose father was the cantor of the town;" and he gives other instances where "genius" may have been the result of culture continued and transmitted through generations.

It was at Bonn that Schiller wrote 'Wallenstein.' The students used very commonly to repair to a hill to watch his movements, and he is said to have followed a plan which publishers would hail with delight in the present day. He walked up and down the room and recited the verses he had written; sometimes he stopped at his table to scan over his manuscript, and commenced his walks again, reciting his verses once more, until they were in proper form, and he could send them to his publisher without an erasure. Schiller's private history adds to the interest that his name inspires. His disposition was gentle and very sensitive, and his life was almost one of patient agony; but, whatever it was, he endured it with great fortitude, even though at last it brought him to a premature grave. Those who knew Schiller well say that his domestic virtues were as conspicuous as his talents. Of course there is no reason why Shakespeare, or Spenser, or Milton should not have possessed in the highest degree all the domestic virtues that we are capable of—and, for the matter of that, we have no possible pretext for believing that they did not; but their private life happens to have been less before the public than Schiller's. We know that in Schiller's case his descendants followed him to the grave with bitter mourning; and his wife, who was a woman of great talent, wept over her loss so much that she became blind. The habits of Schiller were not only singular but injurious. He wrote at night, beginning at eleven, and continuing his labours till four or five in the morning—exactly reversing the order of a very well known English writer of romance, who rises at five o'clock, and writes until ten or eleven in the day, and then has the remainder of the twenty-four hours for rest, and study, and amusement. But as he is said to have succeeded beyond the average lot of men who take up the pen for their profession, he is able to adopt the last way of spending his time—with every accessory of luxury. Schiller was a great man, and the historical plays he wrote will live; but even his own countrymen repudiate anything in the shape of a comparison between Schiller and Shakespeare. They have indeed been compared, but Schiller would never have been content to allow such a comparison. There is no doubt that the brilliant staff of professors, and the recollections of Schiller, Arndt, and Schlegel, did much, and even yet do much, for the renown and efficiency of Bonn University.

When Prince Albert went first to college, a system of quiet opposition to any law, which was not agreeable to students, seems to have been almost universal. At Leipzig and Jena it was most formidable, and it was called " Landsmannschaften." The name quite describes them— a *countrymenship*. This does not arise from the constitution of the university, nor does it form, indeed, any part of it. On the contrary, the association was proscribed, and that not only by the statutes of the university, but even by the laws of the country. It was supposed, though not perhaps correctly, that these associations, which prevailed over the land, had some concealed political object, some kind of advanced republicanism, in view, and were intended to propagate wild theories and reveries ; but it is more probable that they really were the result of egotism and mischief. This huge association was regularly organised, and each lodge had its president, and clerk, and councillors, who formed what is called a "Convent of Landsmannschaft." It arranged everything about duels, and all their senseless codes, and causes ; and totally illegal, and hateful, and oppressive as these secret societies were, it was dangerous not to belong to one of them. They met in secret, in spite of the utmost vigilance of the police. They cost many a learned professor a sleepless night. The Governments of the State used to censure the senator for not at once suppressing these brotherhoods, and the senator retorted upon the Government that they did all they could, but were in despair. Since open war was declared upon them, they took extra pains to secure secrecy, and even trampled the first principles of honour and honesty under foot. If a student was arrested as belonging to one, it was enacted by the "council" that he was at once relieved from all ties by his arrest, and he might declare that he was not a member. In some universities it was enacted that any inquiry dissolved the body, and whoever belonging to it was taken might say that no such institution existed at all. In others, a vow was required from the student that he would do all in his power to convey the idea that no such society existed. Some of the professors hit upon the expedient of taking from each student a solemn promise that he would belong to no secret society; but in such an atmosphere of deception, such promises were not very binding always. Some of course regarded them as sacred, and as a rule the more reasonable convents left it to the honour of the party himself to decide whether he considered his promise binding; but the Leipzig fraternities showed no such compunctions, and boldly published rules saying that any such promise given under such circumstances was null and void. It is said that whenever societies are formed their object is generally for preservation or protection, but the Landsmannschaften existed simply for mischief. When a sufficient number of these fraternities came into contact, each tried to be uppermost, and if not the most respected, at least what was more prized, the most feared. If their ambition had been to excel in rowing or cricket, like our English schools, all might have been well; but the stupid Landsmannschaften only cared for what was vulgar. They desired, as they termed it, to *renown*, or, in other words, to do something at which sensible people would wonder. The wrenching off knockers, or in any way annoying the police, was a mild form in which such vagaries were reflected in England; but in Germany more serious mischiefs were practised. As quarrelling was the soul of the system, the most careful rules were laid down, which were called a "code of honour."(!) Thus the exact words were prescribed which were deemed offensive, and with pedantic solicitude the scale is finely graduated. The penalties also are exactly laid down that attach to each opprobrious epithet. There was one expression, however, which conveyed a deeper affront than any other, and this could only be wiped out with blood. That expression was *dummer Junge* (stupid youth). One thinks it might well have applied to many of the prime movers of these secret societies; but when the word was once passed, there could only be the one result,—and a meeting was arranged with swords, that were duly regulated as to length and shape by the ruling powers, and according to a code.

When any of the words or expressions were used that appeared in the index, the youth to whom it was applied was declared to be affronted; and though it was not necessary at once to challenge the offender, he was expected to "put himself in advantage," as it was termed —or, in other words, to select some higher epithet, until the terrible expression *dummer Junge* was reached, and then the challenge followed. To have this reproach applied, would seem—and I am not sure that we ought to wonder — to hit the presidents of all the secret councils very hard. In some way it appears to have touched them in a sensitive part more keenly than any term in the criminal code. If the outraged youth allows any of the tabulated expressions to be used without either giving a challenge or capping his neighbour by one more honourable, he is punished with the lesser excommunication, and his life is a burden to him till he has recovered his rights by fighting a certain number of duels; but if he fail to do this within a given time, the sentence is declared irrevocable, and his life becomes a torment to him. This has been dwelt upon at some length, because it will make the ninth chapter of the 'Life of the Prince Consort' more readily understood. Bonn was not more free than the other German universities from the contemptible and tyrannical system. The Queen, in her journal, in writing about Bonn, says: "Several of the students were there in the fine dress worn at the Beethoven festival, with the rapier in their hands; many fine young men with loose hair and beards and moustaches, and most with sword-cuts across their faces." Many of these young men would be the students at Bonn University when Prince Albert was there. He himself would not have been likely to have taken any part in such broils, as the sword-cuts seem to indicate; the position he held in social life placed him principally in the society of those that had no fear of the so-called "courts of honour." But he would have been able to give an account of any student that attempted to interfere with him, as the narration of his extraordinary skill in fencing, elsewhere spoken of, would show. And his exceedingly even way of life would insure that his nerves were braced up to the finest point.

Allusion is made in another page to a gamekeeper who was in his employ, and whose father was the head keeper at Windsor for a number of years. He says that on one occasion at Bagshot, the Prince had been in some way challenged to show his skill. The origin of the feat the keeper would hardly be likely to know, though it would be interesting to learn, but he supposed that it arose from some conversation about cold water being the best beverage for the nerves,—and a sum of money was to be given to a certain charity by the loser of what we should call the wager. The rabbits, of course, followed the money for the same charity, or were to be divided among other kindred institutions. Rabbit-holes were stopped; and it must be remembered that this was before the days of breech-loaders, though there were keepers behind to load. The result was that the Prince left his friends the losers, and had ten or fifteen minutes in the two hours to spare. He killed 180 head in that time. Now, to any one acquainted with field-sports, it is unnecessary to say that the difficulty in shooting like this is to keep up to the mark. Even at the rate of a shot per minute it would require an excellent man not to give way after a dozen shots, and require a little breathing-time after making one or two misses. Yet this shooting was nearly at the rate of nine head in five minutes ! The bombast of the duellers was indifferent to him; but it is interesting to find, in the ninth chapter of the ' Life of the Prince Consort,' that his detestation of the custom was as stern as ever. Public attention had been called to the practice by the notable duel (the last in England) between Colonel Fawcett and his brother-in-law Lieutenant Munroe. The latter had been greatly provoked, and the code of honour which then prevailed in the army required him to go out, though he did so literally under protest, and in every way against his will.   Lieutenant Munroe was therefore under the ban of this law.   All the world would have said he was in the right in the quarrel; and he went out all the more unwillingly, because the majority of English people had already set their faces against the absurd custom, and it only lingered on in some sections of the service.   Prince Albert saw that the first thing to be done was to stop duels in the army; and the Duke of Wellington told him that public opinion, which it was so very necessary to enlist, would be the best and perhaps the only means of stopping the scandal.   This chapter in the 'Life of the Prince Consort' is deserving of all interest, as it shows how the Prince had set himself from the first against the practice in Germany; and the students of Bonn, as the Queen says, had for the most part indications of their weakness in succumbing to the rule, printed on their faces.   It really once was thought to be rather derogatory in a German college to be without a healed cut; and tales are not wanting that students who wished as it were to live to fight another day, would use the same devices with their features that Falstaff did with his sword, and " would make believe it was done in fight."   It is impossible to conclude this brief episode in German college duelling without saying that when the fatal duel alluded to had taken place, the part Prince Albert took in the matter caused it to be the last that ever was perpetrated in England.   In 'Nicholas Nickleby,' Dickens, who was writing almost a contemporaneous account of English life, spoke of the duel between Sir Mulberry Hawk and Lord Verisopht as an ordinary occurrence; and this was written so recently as 1839! There can be no doubt that if any prince in his position had loved the universal system in German colleges as much as Prince Albert detested it, and had let his partiality be known, a hundred duels would have been fought since the one alluded to came to an untoward end.

The family of the Prince has been instrumental in establishing another university in Germany; and though it perhaps could hardly boast of such an illustrious line of professors as Bonn, it had a powerful, and yet has a weighty, influence in the education of the country. Jena is connected by many ties with Halle and Bonn, and was founded more than two hundred years ago by the ancestry of the Prince—that is, by the sovereigns of the Ernestine line of the houses of Saxony, Weimar, Gotha, Coburg, and Meiningen,—and the crowned heads who established it shared in turn the patronage, and named the professors.

The road from Weimar to this quaint old town is very romantic and beautiful. It lies through lofty ridges in the Thuringian Mountains, which terminate abruptly at the Saale. This river flows quietly through a rich fertile valley in which are meadow - lands, and hamlets, and orchards, and cottages, that are sometimes hidden by elms and beeches, and literally abound in all that we are accustomed to consider beautiful. Before descending into the town we pass the battle-field of Jena, and are tempted to wonder by what possible means the Prussians contrived to lose the day when we see before our eyes the defiles the French army had to pass, and the steep ascents it had to climb, and the batteries, all in position, it had to face. Yet they not only lost it, but lost it so thoroughly that it decided the fate of the empire! However, when we arrive at Jena, we find an old-fashioned town with high-pitched roofs, which contain many storeys and quaint gables. The old city gates and the market-place are all, and more than all, an artist could desire; and the great church has a lofty tower. But it is with the university we are most concerned; and when Prince Albert was at Bonn, which had a higher social standing, the professors of the two universities kept up the most cordial relations. The cost of instruction at Jena was very moderate, but the professors' fees were at the same time proportionably low. Of course we must not compare old sums with modern ones, even in a country where the cost of everything was on a primitive scale; but the sum of 500 rix-dollars paid to a learned professor, which represents not more than £80 sterling, is, under any circumstances, to say the least, rather moderate. The usual fee for a session was five rix-dollars, or 15s. 6d., for an ordinary professor; but men of eminence could command a guinea for a term. It was calculated that a student could enjoy the same privileges at a German college which the Scottish students possessed, for half the sum! though indeed the Aberdonians were always regarded by the members of English universities as being singularly happy in the liabilities that faced them at the expiration of each term. Michaelis of Göttingen did much to improve the status of the professors, and altered the system of remuneration very much for the better.

The orderly conduct of the Jena students was always conspicuous when they were in college. Every man, when the professor appeared, put his bonnet in his pocket, unfolded his small folio, produced an inkhorn armed with a spike, which he stuck into his desk, and then listened to the lecture—which was not read, but repeated, or spoken *vivâ voce*.

Heidelberg.

CHAPTER X.

PRINCE ALBERT IN ITALY.

THE PRINCE'S VISIT TO ITALY — FLORENCE AS IT WAS WHEN THE PRINCE SAW IT—NOW MUCH ALTERED—HIS ADMIRATION FOR ALL HE SAW—SKILL AS A MUSICIAN—ITALIAN JOURNEY—REPORTS OF ROYAL MARRIAGE IN GERMANY—HOW RECEIVED.

PRINCE Albert's visit to Italy was destined to sever the two brothers who had been such close companions for years; and indeed it was perfectly clear, from the destinies which were before them, that in all human probability their future intercourse must of necessity be limited. Prince Ernest was to go to Dresden and commence his military studies; and at that time, the high position which Prince Albert was to occupy was something like an open secret among those who were most nearly connected with him, even if it were not known by the multitudes who in after-years reaped so much good from it.

On the 24th December 1838 the Prince and Baron Stockmar reached Florence, and took up their quarters in the Casa Cerini, where they remained for three months. Of course Florence was full of delights of every kind to any one like the Prince, who so well loved both nature

and art. "I am often quite intoxicated with delight," he
says, "when I come out of one of the galleries." The
country round Florence, too, possesses extraordinary
attractions. His great delight was to take long walks in
the beautiful country that surrounded him. It has
been noticed how much the aspect of the land had
changed when his son went through it after the lapse
of a quarter of a century. Old associations were gone,
railways had wrought a revolution, and sumptuous hotels
had taken the place of the less pretending Albergo.
Only in one inn did he find the name of the Prince in
the hotel books. If we have no account of the Prince's
own of his observations, we may profit by some letters,
written by an Englishman of great accomplishments, de-
scribing Italy as it was in former days. These letters
were revised almost at the time of the Prince's visit,
but they refer to two visits that had been paid long ago.
He was so much impressed with the beauty of what he
saw, that on his return to England he built a palace that
is only inferior in dignity to the finest in the Italian city.
Speaking of entering Florence at moonlight, he says, after
passing the plains, "continuing our route, we bade adieu
to the realms of poverty and barrenness, and entered
a cultivated vale, shaded by woody acclivities. Among
those we wound along, between groves of poplar and
cypress, till late in the evening. Upon winding a hill we
discovered Florence at a distance, surrounded with gardens and terraces rising one above another. The serene
light of the moon on the pale grey of the olives, gave
a visionary and Elysian appearance to the landscape;
and I was sorry when I found myself excluded from it

by the gates of Florence. I slept as well as my impatience would allow till it was time next morning to visit the gallery and worship the Venus de Medicis. I felt, upon entering this world of refinement, as if I could have taken up my abode in it for ever; but, confused with the multitude of objects, I knew not on which first to bend my attention, and ran childishly by the ample ranks of sculpture, like a butterfly in a parterre, that skims, before it fixes, over ten thousand flowers."

There is much in these few extracts to remind one of Prince Albert; and so closely do they describe some of his traits, that the following description of the "deity of sleep" might have come from his pen. After making the tour of the gallery, he says: "Having regarded these powers with due veneration, I next cast my eyes upon a black figure, whose attitude seemed to announce the deity of sleep. You knew my fondness for this drowsy personage, and that it is not the first time I have quitted the most splendid society for him. I found him at present of touchstone, with the countenance of a cowardly brat sleeping ill through digestion. The artist had not conceived very poetical ideas of the god, or else he would never have represented him with so little grace and dignity." One more extract will probably remind us of what any memoranda of the Prince's, now lost, might have been—though, in explanation of a former sentence, it should be added that the author quoted was nearly as strong an advocate of abstention as Prince Albert himself. "I returned home and feasted upon grapes and ortolans with great edification, then walked across one of the bridges over the Arno, and from thence to the gardens of the Boboli which lie behind the Grand Duke's palace, stretched out on the side of a mountain. I ascended terrace after terrace, robed by a thick underwood of bay and myrtle, above which rise several nodding towers, and a long sweep of venerable wall, almost entirely concealed by ivy. You would have been enraptured with the broad masses of shade and dusky alleys that opened as I advanced, with white statues of fauns and sylvans glimmering among them, some of which pour water into sarcophagi of the purest marble covered with antique relievos. The capitals of columns and ancient friezes are scattered about as seats.

"On these I reposed myself, and looked up to the cypress-groves which sprung above the thickets; then plunging into their retirements, I followed a winding path which led me by a series of steep ascents to a green platform overlooking the whole extent of wood, with Florence deep beneath, and the tops of the hills which encircle it jagged with pines—here and there a convent or villa whitening in the sun. This scene extends as far as the eye can reach. Still ascending, I attained the brow of the eminence, and had nothing but the fortress of Belvidere and two or three open porticos above me. On this elevated situation I found several walks of trellis-work clothed with luxuriant vines. A colossal statue of Ceres, her hands extended in the act of scattering fertility over the country, crowns the summit. Descending alley after alley, and bank after bank, I came to the orangery in front of the palace, disposed in a grand amphitheatre with marble niches relieved by dark foliage, out of which spring cedars and tall aerial cypresses. This spot brought the scenery of an antique Roman garden so vividly into my mind, that, lost to the train of recollections this idea excited, I expected every instant to be called to the table of Lucullus hard by in one of the porticos, and to stretch myself on his purple triclinias." Tourists and fashion have altered the Florence of the Prince's time, and that not for the better; but we can, from the description quoted, readily understand that to a well-stored mind and a lover of art and beauty, Florence was full of fascination for Prince Albert.

The country round Florence possesses extraordinary attractions; and Sir Francis Seymour—then a lieutenant in the 19th Regiment, who had, at the request of King Leopold, joined the Prince at Florence in February, and remained with him for the rest of his tour—mentions that his great delight "was to take long walks in the beautiful country round Florence. This he appeared heartily to enjoy. He became at once gay and animated. 'Now I can breathe! Now I am happy!' Such were his constant exclamations."[1] The words of the English gentleman, whose accomplishments fitted him so well to enjoy the scenes Prince Albert saw, would seem to reflect the feelings with which the Prince regarded them, and they are quoted again,— for the Florence of those days was very different from the Florence of to-day, when the railway-whistle and smoke intrude upon the Piazza Vecchia, and trains bring passengers from every part of the world. Like the Prince, also, he had no taste for company—that

[1] Life of the Prince Consort.

is, fashionable society—and gladly escaped from its obligations. "The woods of the Cascim," he says, "shelter me every morning; and there grows an old crooked ilex at their entrance, twisting round a pine, upon whose branches I sit for hours. In the afternoon I am irresistibly attracted to the thickets of Boboli. The other evening, however, I varied my walk, and ascended one of the pleasant hills celebrated by Dante, which rise in the vicinity of the city, and command a variegated scene of towers, villas, cottages, and gardens. On the right, as you stand upon the brow, appears Fiesole, with its turrets and white houses, covering a rocky mound to the left; the Val d'Arno, lost in the haze of the horizon; a Franciscan convent stands on the summit of the eminence, wrapped up in ancient cypresses, which hinder its holy inhabitants from seeing too much of so gay a view.

"The paved ascent leading up to their abode receives also a shade from the cypresses which border it. Beneath this venerable avenue crosses with inscriptions are placed at certain distances, to mark the various moments of Christ's passion,—as, when fainting under His burden, He halted to repose Himself, or when He met His affected mother. Above, at the end of the perspective, rises a chapel designed by M. A. Buonarotti; further on, an ancient church, incrusted with white marble porphyry and verde-antique. The interior presents a crowded assemblage of ornaments, elaborate mosaic pavements, and inlaid work without end. The high altar is placed in a semicircular recess, which, like the apsis of the church at Torcello, glitters with barbaric paintings on a gold ground, and receives a fervid glow of light from five windows, filled up with transparent marble, clouded like tortoise-shell. A smooth polished staircase leads to the mysterious place; another brought me to a subterraneous chapel, supported by confused groups of variegated pillars, just visible by the glimmer of lamps. Passing on, not unawed, I followed some flights of steps, which terminate in the neat cloisters of the convent, in perfect preservation, but totally deserted. Ranges of citron and aloes fill up the quadrangle, whose walls are hung with superstitious pictures most singularly fancied. The Jesuits were the last tenants of this retirement, and seem to have had great reason for their choice. Its peace and stillness delighted me. Next day I was engaged by a very opposite scene, though much against my will. Her Royal Highness the Grand Duchess having produced a princess in the night, everybody put on grand gala in the morning, and I was carried along with the glitterings of courtiers, ministers, and ladies to see the christening. After the Grand Duke had talked politics for some time, the doors of the temporary chapel were thrown open. Trumpets flourished, procession marched, and the archbishop began the ceremony at an altar of massive gold, placed under a silk pavilion, with pyramids of lights before it. Wax-tapers, though it was noon-day, shone in every corner of the apartments. Two rows of pages, gorgeously accoutred and holding enormous torches, stood on each side of his Royal Highness, and made him the prettiest courtesies imaginable, to the sounds of different bands of music, though led by Nardine. The poor old archbishop, who looked very piteous and saint-like, led the *Te Deum* with a quivering voice, and the rest followed him with thoughtless expedition. The ceremony being despatched (for his Royal Highness was in a mighty fidget to shrink back into his beloved obscurity), the crowd dispersed, and I went with a few others to dine at my Lord T——-'s. Evening drawing on, I ran to throw myself once more in the woods of Boboli, and remained till it was night in their recesses. Really this garden is enough to bewilder an enthusiastic spirit,—there is something so solemn in its shades, its avenues, and spires of cypresses. When I mused for many an interesting hour amongst them, I emerged into the orangery before the palace, which over-looks the largest district of the town, and beheld, as I slowly descended the road which leads up to it, certain bright lights glancing about the cupola of the Duomo and the points of the highest towers. At first I thought them meteors, or those illusive fires that often dance be-fore the eye of my imagination; but soon I was convinced of their reality, for in a few moments the lantern of the cathedral was lighted up by agents really invisible, while a stream of torches ran along the battlements of the old castle."

This extract has been given at some length, because the Florence of to-day is not the same as the Florence which Prince Albert saw; and indeed the same thing struck his son Prince Alfred when he visited it in after-years and found it so much altered from the city he had heard described.

There were also not a few points of resemblance be-tween the gentleman who wrote the above and Prince Albert, which would be apt to make them regard what they saw with somewhat similar feelings. A dislike for fashionable society, great culture, a knowledge of modern languages, and devotion to music and art: he was, moreover, an enthusiastic collector.   He complains also of a continual desire to sleep, and the trouble it often gave him to shake this off.   There was a similar love of the country and its delights; and the house he built on his return to England, for which he himself was the principal architect, bore some resemblance in plan to Osborne, which, as we read in the ' Life of the Prince Consort,' was designed by Prince Albert.

At Florence, amidst the engaging scenes by which he was surrounded, the Prince found abundant opportunity to pursue his studies.   He rose at six in the morning, and went very early to rest.   Music, in which he so excelled, was his great solace, and he could play equally well either on the piano or the organ.   The signal services that he and his descendants have rendered to England in music, and the hope which recent and present events hold out that these will extend to all classes, have suggested a special chapter on the subject. As to the present notice, it is enough to say that the Prince, when at Florence, resorted very often to the Badia church when the public were not admitted, in order to play on its fine organ.   Papi was the organist, and an excellent professor of music; he also was the instructor of Prince Albert.   When the music had fairly penetrated the stillness of the church, the monks would say, " That foreign prince plays as well as our own Papi."

From Florence the Prince went in March to Rome, where he spent three weeks, working hard from daybreak to sunset in seeing all that it offered of interest in art, ancient and modern, and in antiquities. He did not spare himself the tourist's accustomed penance of an interview with the Pope (Gregory XVI.) "We conversed," he writes, "in Italian, on the influence the Egyptians had on Greek art, and that again on Roman art. The Pope asserted that the Greeks had taken their models from the Etruscans. In spite of his infallibility, I ventured to assert that they had derived their lessons in art from the Egyptians." It was with sincere pleasure, if not surprise, that the writer read this in the ' Life of the Prince Consort,' as the subject has been one of absorbing interest to him for many years. Perhaps nobody doubts now that the Prince was correct. Every type of Greek architecture is to be found in Egypt, from the triglyph to the Corinthian column ; and indeed it is commonly believed by many, that traces of these are to be found in remains of nationalities still further east. Derived from the Etruscans ! Why, the Etruscans derived their arts from Greece. Yet, when Prince Albert ventured to express a difference of opinion from the Pope in this matter, his opinion would be but that of a small minority. The Romans were indeed indebted to the Etruscans for their models ; but the tombs of the Tarquins, some of which belong to the latter days of Etruscan independence, and were coeval with the Roman republic, display from first to last the most unequivocal marks of their Greek origin, and we can trace, in the vast number of vases that are often marked with strong conventional characteristics, the different epochs of Hellenic art. The vases that are found in the tombs of the Tarquinii, and at Volscium, may be counted by thousands. They present such different characteristics that there is no difficulty whatever in assigning to them very different ages ; yet about eight or ten years after the time when the extract of the Prince's memorandum, which is quoted in the ' Life of the Prince Consort,' was written, it was commonly agreed by all scholars that these Etruscan vases were the work of Greek hands.   Dennis quite disposed of this question in 1848.   We find in the Etruscan remains the conventional yet animated outlines of some of the early Greek marbles, and some of the best designs of the most graceful Athenian age.   The vases themselves are almost identical with those that are found in Campania and Sicily (two undoubted colonies of Greece), both in form and colour, and even clay.

The Prince, Stockmar, and Sir Francis Seymour, next went to Naples, and from there to Pompeii, where, of course, he was greatly pleased with all he saw, and returned to Coburg through Milan.   The circumstances of the Royal marriage were known beforehand in Coburg, where, as in other towns in Germany, public and private events are discussed in market-places and by the fountains.   These latter form a kind of public exchange for the humbler classes, and news, either past, present, or to come, is a general topic.   There are several picturesque fountains there, and one is given here, as being a characteristic of the smaller fountains of Germany.   " You receive these lines from dear old Coburg, where I have been received with all possible cordiality.   All are on the tiptoe of curiosity."

There was, indeed, an unusual feeling of regret in Coburg and Gotha that the Prince was about to leave the country; and this was greatly increased from the fact that the reigning family had made themselves so very popular, and had been on terms of almost intimacy with people of every rank in life. The circumstances of his leaving his native country, and the surroundings and events of unusual happiness that marked his connection with England, have been well described in the 'Life of the Prince Consort;' and nothing more can be

Fountain at Coburg.

said on the subject by the present writer. The private sources from which much of the deeply interesting narrative, with all the artless correspondence, has been drawn, are probably exhausted, at least as far as the public is concerned; nor would it be the writer's wish, even if it lay in his power, to add another word, except it might be to say that what will always commend this part of the history to the Anglo-Saxon race is, that the correspondence, if divested of the mere externals that we know surround it, might occupy a worthy place in "the short but simple annals of the poor." The Royal marriage and all its circumstances hardly belong to the present work, and they have been well described and often read before. Suffice it to say, that when the expected event was made known in the duchy that the Prince loved so well, there was, as is often the case in human affairs, a strange mixture of joy and sorrow.

> "Such welcome and unwelcome things at once,
> 'Tis hard to reconcile."

The Prince himself was filled with many emotions. The official declaration had been made with unusual solemnity at the palace at Coburg, and on that occasion there was great rejoicing; and, as the Prince says, the people kept firing guns and pistols all night through, so that it might have been supposed a battle was raging in the streets. The joy thus expressed was coupled with a widespread regret that the country was to lose the presence of a prince who had made himself no less beloved than respected throughout the country. He says himself: "I bade adieu to dear old Coburg; now it lies behind me, and we are at Gotha." An anecdote which appears at the beginning of the chapter on the game of the Thuringian revels, and which is perfectly accurate, will account in a great measure for the popularity of the Prince in his own country, and will easily explain the facility with which he reached the hearts of the English people; and I am assured at Coburg and in other places where he was known that the anecdote is most characteristic, and many more similar ones could have been collected. The justice, and the neat rejoinder are, to say the least, equal in the Prince's remark. How the Royal marriage was received in England it does not require a very old man to remember: there were demonstrations of joy not only in the metropolis, but in the remotest parts of the kingdom. In the city of Chester, where these lines are written—and surely it is remote enough, and even more remote in those days from any centre than it is now—the rejoicings were on a scale quite commensurate with the opportunities of the inhabitants. To say nothing of the profuse hospitalities of Eaton, the residents themselves put their shoulders to the wheel, and the mayor and the bishop each of them presided over meetings to devise the best means of expressing the loyalty of the ancient city —a city which indeed the Prince never saw, but one which would have delighted him possibly beyond any other in England. A very interesting account of the celebrations is given in a contemporary Chester paper which happens to be before me, and it would seem that even from Hawarden to Beeston, and probably from there to Yorkshire, the country was lit with bonfires. Doubtless similar demonstrations were seen in all other parts of England ; so that if, as astronomers tell us, a great conflagration would be distinctly within the range of Ross or Herschel's telescopes to an inhabitant of the moon, the loyalty of England would have been very apparent indeed.

H

CHAPTER XI.

IT was a little more than five years after the Royal marriage that the trip to Germany, in order to revisit the early homes of Prince Albert, was made. It had long been a subject of arrangement and discussion, and it is not difficult to understand what a mutual wish there must have been to visit or revisit the scenes that had been familiar to the Prince in his youth. The spring-time of life, the best wishes of all the world, and a little perhaps of adventure were before them, and there was not a single cloud in the blue sky. There was peace everywhere; and though some of the periodical eruptions of Celtic zeal had troubled England, Peel was able to say that Ireland was settling down to a state of quiescence. Prince Albert, it is said, had looked forward with great anticipation to the visit. He had, indeed, made a journey to his old homes in the previous year, but then everything was wanting to make it a pleasant one. It was in the depth of winter, and his mission was to be present at the funeral of one of the kindest and best of fathers. Now all was different. August is one of the most delightful months for visiting the hills and valleys of Thuringia and for sailing through Rhineland, and the visit was to be made with one who was so near to him. We all know how pleasant it is to visit the scenes of our early days, or places connected with the history of our friends and relatives. One of the most beautiful passages in Thackeray is in the first chapter of ' The Virginians,' where there is an account of the proposed visit of the two Warringtons to England to see the home of their ancestors in Hampshire : " Again and again Harry Warrington and his brother had pored over the English map, and determined upon the course which they should take upon arriving at Home. All Americans who love the old country—and what gently nurtured man or woman of Anglo-Saxon race does not ?—have ere this rehearsed their English travels, and visited in fancy the spots with which their hopes, their parents' fond stories, their friends' descriptions, have made them familiar." English history was as familiar to the brothers as the Thirty Years' War or the Life of Martin Luther was to the Royal travellers ; and as Thackeray so finely says of colonists, they long to stand before the " resting-place of Shakespeare, under the tall spire which rises by Avon, amidst the sweet Warwickshire pastures, before Derby, and Falkirk, and Culloden, where the cause of honour and loyalty had fallen, it might be, to rise no more. Before all these points of their pilgrimage there was one which the young Virginian brothers held even more sacred, and that was the home of their family——that old Castlewood in Hampshire, about which their parents had talked so fondly. From Bristol to Bath, from Bath to Salisbury, to Winchester, to Hexton, to *home*——they knew the way, and had mapped the journey many and many a time." I believe this to be a faithful picture of the way in which a visit to Coburg was regarded by the Royal travellers, but with this great difference, that poor Warrington had to make his journey alone, as his brother had unaccountably disappeared during the Indian wars. The Royal visit had long been a theme of conversation in England, and of expectation on the Continent. In a letter to the 'Franconian Mercury,' the writer draws a picture of the interest which it had excited at Coburg. The following is a translation : " Queen Victoria and Prince Albert will not arrive here before the 18th or 20th of August. Already, however, there are no more apartments to be had, and even the Ducal Court has been obliged to hire the best private lodgings for their friends' accommodation. The number of foreigners of high rank who are announced, and who are desirous of being presented at Court, is almost incredible. Not less than sixty-one persons belonging to Imperial, Royal, or Princely families are expected. The smallest dwellings are let upon truly English terms. One English family is paying £3 per day for three small rooms ; " and this letter was written nearly a month before the arrival of the Queen and Prince. Of course, in an unsophisticated town like Coburg, especially as it was in those days, this sum caused wonderment. A letter in the ' Journal des Débats ' from Cologne, which was published at the same time, speaks of the whole town being busy in making proper preparations for a regal reception.

A curious question arose as to the appointment of a
Regency during the absence of her Majesty. This was
raised in the Lords by Lord Campbell, and in the Com-
mons by Lord John Russell, and precedents were given,
though the journey of Queen Elizabeth to Kenilworth
was not quoted, as indeed it might have been,—for she
appointed the Lord Mayor of London, the Archbishop of
Canterbury, the Bishop of London, and others to fill her
place during her visit to Warwickshire. But the general
sense of England went with the Queen and Prince, when
they solved the question by weighing anchor in the Victoria and Albert, and not troubling themselves further
with so abstract a question. The squadron was composed
of the Royal yacht, the Porcupine, and the Black Eagle.
The Queen's journal, which is quoted from the 'Life of
the Prince Consort,' says: "It was a pouring, melancholy
evening when we went up after dinner, but nevertheless
the poor people have illuminated Antwerp with those
triangular illuminations on the tops of long poles as they
did when we were here before." The weather, as we
learn from other sources, was most unpropitious; and an
Englishman, who was a visitor to Antwerp, has given an
account of how things proceeded on shore, which I quote
from memory.

The rain, he says, had so damped people's spirits that
there was really no outward sign of rejoicing at Antwerp,
or, at any rate, none on such a scale as even the least
exacting could have looked for. He and many others
were contemplating the proportions of the grand spire,
with its network tracery, by way of solacing themselves
for the weather, when those of the expectant crowd who

had more acute eyesight than the others, were suddenly conscious of a ladder at the topmost part of the spire, and a tiny human form appeared to be in motion; and then, on what seemed no larger than a reed, but which was really a flagstaff, the Royal standard of England was unfurled. Even the good citizens of Antwerp assembled in groups at their doors to see the spectacle. Soon after this, a salvo of artillery announced that the Royal party had become visible in the devious channels of the Scheldt, and then the excitement in the city became excessive. The day had been raw and very gusty, but, as if by magic, the salvo drew men, women, and children from their abodes; and from every nook and quaint old street with which the city abounds, a picturesque crowd emerged. The saddest part of it was that they had all adorned themselves in their best attire; and picturesque lace caps, with thin high lappets, were put out of all form when met by the pelting rain; but the Scheldt itself was soon alive with gay holiday dresses, for the whole city was resolved to do what honour it could. Nearly opposite the landing-place the yacht slackened her speed, and then her paddles stopped, and the excitement on shore knew no bounds, as it was believed that the Queen and Prince would land at once; but the yacht quietly turned round under the guidance of the Dutch pilot, as her bows left the Antwerp shore, and the rattling of a chain announced that she was anchored in the stream. The standards of England and Belgium, which were raised on the quays, drooped side by side under the pitiless rain. Improvised bands, it is said, also struck up 'God save the Queen' everywhere in Antwerp, though the vessels of the Royal squadron lay on their moorings. But the most was to be made of the time, and, quoting again from the ' Life of the Prince Consort,' we read in an extract from the Queen's journal: " We got up at half-past five. The morning was cheerless, blowing, grey, and rainy. We breakfasted at six, and at half-past we left the yacht, and were amazingly danced about even for the few yards we had to go in the river to the landing-place. We were received by a guard of honour, and immediately proceeded in uncle's carriages to the railroad." This is the simple account which appears in the ' Life of the Prince Consort ; " but the same eyewitness who spoke of the pitiless weather adds some interesting details. The Burgomaster of Antwerp was M. Henry Tegrelle—the commander of the forces was Count d'Hane,—and these gentlemen, with Count Arnim, received her Majesty at half-past six on an August Monday ; and it is very well worthy of notice that, at the first entry of the Queen and Prince on the Continent, ceremony was at once dispensed with as far as possible, for the officials who received them were requested not to wear any official costume—a desire which probably would commend itself to the majority of Englishmen. The short passage from the river to the railway station is very interesting, and it leads through quaint, picturesque streets, with crow-stepped gables, like those we see in old Scotch buildings. Her Majesty and the Prince landed at the Quai Rubens, which is the river boundary of Antwerp, and forms so pleasant a promenade along the water-side. The quaint, grotesque, architectural combinations of the streets, in which there are houses almost as high as we find in Edinburgh, were passed, and the railway station was reached, from which the first part of the journey to Coburg and Gotha was made. There were not many people about, as the rawness of the morning and the earliness of the hour were against sight-seers. The regiments, of course, played the National Anthem, and everything was done that the very excellent regulations, for which the Belgian lines are justly praised, could accomplish. At exactly seven the steam whistle sounded, and the train went on its way towards Malines. The station is about five minutes from the town, and the town itself is one of the most picturesque of all the Flemish cities ; and its grand cathedral and curious old buildings have made it a favourite resort of travellers. The town was reached by about a quarter before eight, and here the Queen and Prince met their relatives the King and Queen of the Belgians, and instead of the accustomed " God save the Queen," the bands struck up the Annen Polka.

The King and Queen of the Belgians accompanied the Royal party as far as Verviers. " Every point of beauty or interest in the fine country through which the railway passes was noted." The country is more beautiful than we find in many other parts of Belgium, and Verviers, though not interesting in itself, is charmingly situated. It is full of industry, and has been called the Leeds of Belgium. " Guards of honour saluted at every station ; and the numerous tunnels between Liège and Verviers, through which the traveller is swept from one lonely valley to another, were lit up with lamps and torches." [1] Every traveller will remember this delightful drive.

[1] Life of the Prince Consort.

The railroad winds through beautiful glens, that remind us of Derbyshire. There are vistas of rock, and wood, and water; and there is many a trout stream—just as we see on the Midland line as it passes through Derby—which is either crossed over, or runs by the rails, or is lost in the woods. Perched in snug nooks in the hills, and surrounded with corn-fields and vineyards, we may discover chateaux pleasantly placed in groves of trees; and lower down we may find manufactories, principally of cloth, in the valley, but here the industry does not interfere with the picturesque surroundings. The mills are turned by water. When shall we imitate our German friends in this respect? There are rivers in England that could supply all the power which all the industries of the kingdom require.

The reception at Verviers was much more enthusiastic than at any previous place. Triumphal arches and tri-colours in great abundance were displayed; and one who had followed the route remarks, that the contrast was striking between the reception here and the phlegmatic orderly demonstrations that the Royal travellers had met with in the low-country cities. Part of this no doubt, as he said, was owing to constitutional differences, but much of it was owing to the circumstance that Prince Albert was approaching the country where he was still recollected. All Germany was in a state of excitement, and prepara-tions were made for one of the greatest receptions of the present century, equally due to the Prince as to the Queen of England. The next station which the train stopped at was Habersthal, where the territory ,of the King of Prussia commences; and here it was arranged that the Royal party should be received by the Crown Prince of Prussia, who was in waiting, and entered the carriage as soon as the train stopped. The reception here was quite as enthusiastic as at Verviers, and deafening cheers succeeded each other. At Aix-la-Chapelle there was a similar scene, and an equally demonstrative reception. Prussian troops lined the station, and the King of Prussia was in waiting to receive the Queen and Prince. "In the room of the station were assembled all the authorities, the clergy (Catholic and Lutheran), and a number of young ladies dressed in white, one of whom, a daughter of the Burgomaster, recited some complimentary verses." The receptions at each place increased in enthusiasm, but the one at Aix-la-Chapelle was very brilliant. Amidst the firing of guns and military music, they went to visit the cathedral, where Charlemagne, the founder of the empire, rests. A body of gentlemen, excellently mounted and uniformly dressed, had formed themselves into an escort, and they accompanied the Queen and Prince through the quaint picturesque streets of the city. They went past the Fontaines Chaudes, the theatre, and the principal attractions of the place, followed by an immense concourse in holiday attire. The Queen lunched with Mr Alleseen the chief Burgomaster, and a very large cloth manufacturer. He had made sumptuous preparations for the occasion. On leaving his house, a rush was made from all sides to obtain a sight of the Queen and the Prince. Up to this time the Royal party had used Belgian carriages, but now Prussian vehicles were attached to the train; and in one of these, which was a splendid carriage, the

Royal families of England and Prussia pursued their journey. At Cologne the reception was still more enthusiastic, and the authorities had "caused the roadway to be sprinkled with eau-de-Cologne—whether to disguise the proverbial fragrance of the place, or in honour of the great local manufacture, may be left to conjecture." "The King," his Majesty writes, "never has an escort, and the people are wonderfully well behaved."[1] As the train approached the famous city, it was noted that the country wore a richer aspect. Cottages arose on all sides, corn-fields and noble woods were passed, church spires towered up on each hand, as the train swept by; while a distant range of hills shadowed out the land of the Rhine. Suburban mansions and country *cafés* soon began to appear, and indicated the approach to a large and wealthy city. The cathedral seems to fill the sky almost as we approach the vast pile, though it is soon lost to view as we enter the streets. The Royal standard waved from the summit of the great building; and the train had hardly stopped before great salvos of artillery from the fortifications announced the arrival of the Queen and Prince.

"From Cologne the Brühl station was reached in fifteen minutes, and here the Royal party alighted and drove to the Palace. One drives into the hall, where a truly magnificent marble staircase begins, which, like the rest of the castle, is in rococo style. The Queen, Princess of Prussia, Archduke Frederick of Austria, the Duchess of Anhalt Dessau with her daughter, and the whole Court in state, received us, and showed us up-stairs. We went into

---

[1] Life of the Prince Consort.

one of the rooms to hear the splendid Zapfen‐streich
(tattoo) performed by 500 musicians (military), the place
being illuminated with torches and lamps of coloured
glass, which had a splendid effect.   The evening was
lovely, and the whole thing the finest of the kind I ever
witnessed.   They played 'God save the Queen.'   It was
better played than I ever heard it.   So too thought
Lord Aberdeen."   "Next day," the Queen's journal
proceeds, "we felt so strange to be in Germany at last,
and at Brühl, which Albert said he used to go and visit
from Bonn."   Brühl is itself a small town with hardly
3000 inhabitants, and the castle is opposite to it.   It is
surrounded with park-like grounds of great splendour.
Her Majesty and the Prince were received at Brühl
station with all possible honours, a torch-light procession and military music awaiting the arrival of the train.

"Immediately after breakfast we drove to the railroad,
—Albert with the King; the Queen, the Archduke (who
has been sent here to compliment me), and the Prince of
Prussia with me,—and went by rail to Bonn.   From the
station we drove to the house of Prince Fürstenburg, a
very rich and influential man, where we were received by
the Prince and his wife.   .   .   .   Many gentlemen connected with the university, and who had known Prince
Albert, were there, and were presented to me, which
interested me much.   They were greatly delighted to see
Albert, and pleased to see me."   The visit to Bonn was,
in the first place, to be present at the great Beethoven
festival, which occurred at the Beethoven Hall on Sunday
night, August 10; but beyond that, was the natural wish to
visit the place connected with Prince Albert's college life.

The Beethoven Hall has an arched roof, and from it were suspended about fifty brilliant chandeliers, with laurels and wreaths. Every part of the hall had some memorial of him. There was an oil-painting, with great decorations, in which he is represented as writing his " Missa Solemnis." The orchestra was not sufficiently raised, but the conductor's seat was correspondingly diminished. The arrangements for this festival, which is spoken of even yet in Germany, were simple and effective, and indeed resemble our own. Each seat was numbered, and no ticket given out which the building could not easily contain. The young lady singers wore white dresses, and as they were young and many of them beautiful, the effect was charming. Spohr, then advanced in years, conducted the orchestra of 500, and notwithstanding his age, he was erect and fully competent for the occasion. He was received with great applause, and saluted with a flourish of trumpets. Amongst other performers, Herr Staudigl was there. After cries of " Seats " and " Hats off,"—" Sitzen " and " Huten,"—a still silence prevailed as the grand strains of the " Missa Solemnis " were raised. There appeared to be but one opinion, and that was, that the " Crede " and " Benedictus " were the finest parts of the score.

Beethoven's statue was unveiled at Bonn, in the presence of the Queen and Prince. The face is full of inspiration ; in the right hand is a pencil, and in the left a music-score. The Queen's journal says: " We stepped on the balcony to see the unveiling of Beethoven's statue, in honour of which great festivities took place— concerts, &c. But unfortunately, when the statue was

uncovered, its back was turned to us," &c.   "From here
we drove with the King and Queen, only a few of our
suite following, to Prince Albert's former little house.
We all went over it, and it is just as it was,—in no way
altered. We went to the little bower in the garden,
from which you have a beautiful view of the Kreuzberg,
a convent situated on the top of a hill."   There were
two ladies from Cologne, who were known to the King

Prince Albert's House, Bonn.

of Prussia, in the garden
of Prince Albert's old
home, and they were in-
troduced to the Queen.
She received them cor-
dially, and made many
natural inquiries about
the way of life pursued
by the students.   The
house is a pleasant one,
and lies in University
Street, near the cathe-
dral.   There is a beautiful garden round it, and it
would seem to English students to be quite suitable for
the requirements of a collegian of any degree in life.
Not only is the high monastery visible, but, as the
Queen's diary adds, " the *Sieben Gebirge* (seven mountains)
you also see, but the view of them is a good deal built
out."   The house of Count Fürstenburg was occupied by
the Royal party, and the statue of Beethoven is there yet,
with his back turned towards it.   This mansion is a
quiet-looking residence, two storeys high, with rooms in
the roof, and nine windows in width ; but it does not

suggest more accommodation than the family of an English squire would expect. " At four o'clock the same day a grand banquet was given at the Palace, at which, in addition to numerous royal personages, all the most distinguished residents in Bonn and Cologne were present; " and the details of this banquet have been fully described in Sir Theodore Martin's work. In turning over the files of some French correspondents, we find several rather amusing accounts of this part of the journey; at least, we are indulged with the opportunity of seeing ourselves as others see us. One French correspondent says that the most pleasing circumstance of the visit to Brühl Palace was this: in going through some of the rooms of this vast building, the King of Prussia caused to be produced a portrait of the Prince of Wales, who was his godson. The French correspondent says that the portrait was a good one, and it was " suddenly displayed to the delighted Queen." The French had some excellent correspondents, and the one that has been quoted says that at Cologne, the Burgomaster, who has been alluded to, said, " The day in which your Majesty, by the side of our beloved and venerated King, placed your foot as a welcome guest in this territory, will live for ever in our memory, and history will hand down this happy event to posterity as one of its finest pages."

Another writer, who was the correspondent of ' La Presse,' has given a much more humorous account of his struggles on the great occasion to see the Royal family. He frankly admits that he lost his way often in the devious streets of Cologne, and asked his road an incredible number of times. He simply said that the general reply was *canif fourchette,*—which probably was *kan nicht verstehen,* or " I do not understand you."   He seems, however, to have been under many obligations to the editor of the ' Cologne Gazette,' who spoke French perfectly, and who found him a seat in the front parlour of the publishing establishment, — where, as he simply remarks, without encumbrance or fatigue, he had the pleasure of " assisting " at the Royal entry into Cologne.   This correspondent is very refreshing : he says that her Majesty was dressed *à la Parisienne* upon the occasion ; and enlarging from his lofty situation in the editor's window, he says, in speaking of the Queen, " Her charming blue bonnet was the cause of much covetous desire among many fair German damsels."   He further adds that the Queen of Prussia was " a model of dignified grace and beauty, and not awkward or stiff " as he should have expected in a northern sovereign.

" Cologne was now *en fête,* and illuminations on the grandest scale had been prepared.   Thither, accordingly, the Royal party went by rail, and embarked on a steamer to see the illuminations to the best advantage.   A constant blaze of coloured lights, rockets, and saluters of every kind, dazzled the eye and stunned the ear.   The houses were, many of them, lit up so as to appear red-hot, and the majestic cathedral seemed to glow with fire."[1]   The Rhine here, it may be remarked, is about as wide as the Thames at Westminster.   The passage across the bridge of boats was prohibited, and the navigation of the river was for a time suspended.   A dim line of lights showed the course of the stream and the direction of the bridge, which was left open

---

[1] Life of the Prince Consort.

in the middle part for the passage of the two steamers, which steamed slowly through towards the landing-place where the Queen and Prince were to embark. When the steamer passed the city on its upward course, it is said that a scene such as has hardly ever been witnessed took place. " A rocket was sent up for a signal," as an eyewitness says, " and a *feu de joie* commenced on a scale scarcely equalled. It extended for two miles on both sides of the river, and was kept up for more than half an hour, the men loading and firing in rapid succession : at the same time the Rhine was brilliantly lit up by port-fires burnt in boats in the middle of the stream. Above the Thurna-market showers of rockets were shooting up with boundless profusion. As the vessel glided down, the firing continued ; and the constant rattle of musketry, blending at intervals with the booming of cannon, gave the spectator the idea of some night attack. But the great spectacle was yet to come. As the steamer neared the opening of the bridge, the whole structure, if so a bridge of boats can be called, was lighted up by a line of fireworks, throwing up showers of brilliant sparks like fountains of brightness, the gleaming drops descending in a graceful form, and becoming quenched in the river, rolling darkly down beneath. At the same moment the exterior of the cathedral, which towers grandly over the whole city, burst into light like the dome of St Peter's in the Holy Week ; every cornice, buttress, and pinnacle gleamed in the flood of light, and the effect of the whole scene was at that instant the grandest and most magnificent of its kind that ever was beheld. The play of light and shade over the mass of Gothic architecture,

and the roofs and towers in its vicinity, was perfectly magical.   It was not the dim religious light that we associate with such structures, for which even the 'beams of the garish day' are held unsuitable; nor was it the moon, which softens all imperfections. . . . It was an artificial splendour, the brilliancy of a moment cast upon the dark pile on which rest the shadows of ages, chasing them with a fitful and transient splendour, and then leaving them in a deeper gloom than before."
It is hardly

Wine-Garden, Cologne, showing Spire.

necessary to say that Cologne Cathedral was unfinished at the time.   But exactly a quarter of a century after, almost to the day, it was the writer's fortune to see Cologne once more the scene of a brilliant reception. Many of the distinguished visitors who had been present to welcome the Queen and Prince Albert were assembled to celebrate the completion of the cathedral; and it was asserted very commonly that the Royal visit had given an impetus to a work which had occupied more than six hundred years in building, and that without that visit it would not then have been finished. Now the spires rise grandly over the town, and often combine beautifully with humbler surroundings. Of course all objects in Cologne were visited that possessed sufficient interest; and perhaps nothing was more pleasing than the old Romanesque church of great St Martin. In those days its spire made it one of the most conspicuous objects from the waters of the Rhine, but now the spires of the cathedral have reduced its comparative proportions sadly. This church has always been a favourite study for artists, and it is generally surrounded with picturesque objects.

On their return to Brühl, the King and Queen of the Belgians had arrived. "It seems," the Queen writes, "like a dream to them and to me to see each other in Germany." A great concert concluded the evening. Meyerbeer conducted in person, and a cantata composed by him for the occasion in honour of our Queen was sung by Staudigl, Pishek, and others. Among the performers at the concert were Jenny Lind, Madame Viardot, and Liszt; and this terminated the most brilliant scene, perhaps, that even Cologne ever witnessed. Our Gallican neighbours were not behind the English in sending special correspondents to inform their countrymen of the doings in Germany, and some of them appear to have had much success in picking up the more sensational items of news. It is sometimes interesting to turn to an old file of papers, and see how our neighbours regarded us; and the good people of Cologne would now feel some surprise at the report of the proceedings in the 'Siècle.' The enterprising writer seems to have gone into an estimate of the cost of the celebration, which, according to his calculations, amounted to £3000 sterling,—a sum which he says the city was quite unable to meet, and the King of Prussia generously came forward to help (!). The same correspondent says that the Royal bed in the grand apartments that had been prepared at Cologne covered 60 square feet; so that if it were, let us say, seven feet in length, which is a very ample allowance for any rank of life, it would have been nine feet in width. But the visit to Cologne ended, and a chilly wet morning augured ill for the journey up the Rhine; "but before the steamer in which the passage was to be made got under way, the sky cleared, and all that noble series of variegated and beautiful landscapes between Bonn and Coblenz was seen to perfection." Stolzenfels was reached the same day, and it is familiar to all travellers on the Rhine,—so familiar, indeed, that it is almost difficult to find anything new to say about it.

CHAPTER XII.

AMONG the guests at Stolzenfels was the venerable Prince Metternich. The Queen says—" The Prince I found much older than I expected, and laying down the law very much, yet very amiable." The view from the castle is spoken of by the Queen with great enthusiasm, even though seen through a mercilessly wet day. A well-informed gentleman who was present at the time says: "The Rhine is a puddle; the washings down from the valleys have quite discoloured it; and all the fine castles, and crags, and fortresses that looked so imposing and grand yesterday, are dimly seen through river-mist." On the occasion of her Majesty's and Prince Albert's visit there was an ovation in fireworks similar to that which has been described at Cologne, though it was not, of course, on so grand a scale.

Stolzenfels Palace was built by the Archbishop of Trèves, but it was sadly knocked about by the French, as indeed was its neighbour Lahneck. The latter has been restored by a private gentleman, who lives in it, and the former by the King of Prussia. Isabella, the sister of Henry III. of England, and the bride of Frederick II., was magnificently entertained here. A bill of fare is preserved, from which it appears that Rhine salmon, venison, and Oberweseler, formed part of the *menu.* It is here that many of the weird tales of alchemy originated. It was practised, or professed, by the Archbishop of Trèves and John of Baden who succeeded him. Stolzenfels came into possession of the corporation of Coblenz, and in 1802 they made a present of it to King Frederick. William IV. was at that time a prince. In 1836 he began to rebuild it in an expensive style, and employed Schinkel as his architect. Müller says : " It is indeed a real delight to see the castle with restored battlements, gates, and windows, looking down from its green summit into the beautiful Rhine valley. It has a noble and delightful appearance when the rays of the morning sun shine and glitter on its lofty windows. The rooms are arranged in excellent taste. The furniture carries us back to those bygone days of which we never seem to be tired of hearing and reading ; and the view of the Rhine is especially grand. There are many who consider that Stolzenfels commands the finest situation on the Rhine, though some would give the preference to Rheinfels. The beautiful valley of the Lahn is opposite, and down the stream the view embraces the town of Coblenz, with its fortifications, and the range of Andernach hills beyond."

Next morning (Saturday, 16th of August) a gleam of sunshine broke out as the Queen and Prince left

Stolzenfels, accompanied by the King and Queen of
Prussia, and the other Royal personages who were to
see them on board; but before they had reached
their yacht at Capellan they had again to " tax the
elements with unkindness. The adieus were made
under a violent shower of rain, which, however, soon
ended; and the rest of the panorama of ruin-crested peaks
and picturesque villages which skirt the river as far as
Bingen, was seen under the varied play of sunshine and
cloud which sets off such scenery to the best advantage.
. . . At Mayence the Queen and Prince were met
by the Governor, Prince William of Prussia; his son-
in - law, Prince Charles of Hesse; and the Austrian
commander. The Austrian and Prussian troops were
drawn up near the place of disembarkation; and after
a march past of men 4000 in number, and a dinner
with Prince William at his residence, Das Deutsche
Haus, the hotel was reached by 9 P.M. Soon after, the
Austrian and Prussian bands made their appearance,
preceded by bodies of soldiers bearing torches." [1] At
Mayence the Queen was much fatigued with the constant
demands that the receptions had entailed upon her, and
she and the Prince remained quietly at the Hotel
de l'Europe during the Sunday morning. Mayence is
very beautifully situated. The tall hills of Hochlinn and
the many vineyards that surround it overlook the con-
fluence of the Main and the Rhine. Many local steamers
ply across the river here, and in the distance we may see
the faint outline of the Platte, the hunting and shooting
box of the Duke of Nassau. Below we can clearly see

[1] Life of the Prince Consort.

the terraces of the vast vineyards of Rüdesheim, rising one over the other; and a field-glass will enable us to detect the white posts which indicate that it is Royal property.

The scenery at Mayence is beautiful indeed, but its chronicles are, like many others where all seems peaceful, sad enough. Legendary lore is very prolific here, and it is said that Mayence was built by some fugitives from the siege of Troy, led by one Moguertius, and that he gave the name to the town. There are many Roman remains of immense interest and value. Caius Drusus built a palace here, and spanned the Rhine with a bridge, but the piers which yet remain are used to anchor floating water-mills to. But there was a subsequent period which connects Mayence with the hierarchy in a way that hardly reads pleasantly in our days. Charlemagne built a palace here, and St Boniface became bishop, and abuses increased, until the notorious Bishop Hatto astonished the whole of Germany by his cruelty, and his shocking misuse of the power that had unhappily been committed to him.

With the country they were now travelling over Prince Albert was quite familiar, and it was most unfortunate that, until then, the weather had been so far from propitious. "Queen's weather" is proverbial for its brightness; but the writer can recall two occasions on which Royal visits of great importance were made, and the weather was so unfavourable that the days themselves, disconnected with the events, would have been long remembered. One was on the Queen's visit to Liverpool in 1851, and the other was at the great Volunteer Review in Edinburgh in 1881. Of course the inhabitants, and visitors, and newspaper correspondents all suffered equally. The fine temper of the gentleman who represented the 'Constitutionnel' seems to have almost given way at Mayence, and he began to take a most bilious view of things. He states, that on the platform where the Royal party landed, the carpet was of the most inadequate character, and full of patches, and quite worn threadbare. This was noticed in time, however, and the fragile covering was gathered up and stowed away, a new carpet having been sent for from the town. This one, however, he considered as much too good as the other was inadequate, for he profited by the opportunity to make some observations upon the platform, which he says was a shocking piece of hurried carpentry. He spoke also of the apathy of the good people of Mayence as our Queen passed them with the Prince, and says that even the latter failed to raise any enthusiasm. There probably was an absence of demonstration among the good townspeople, but a German resident writes to the 'Times' that it was from no lack of loyal feelings to the Queen and Prince; but he gives a curious account of the cause. The depressing weather may have had some little to do with the matter, but at any rate there were several collisions between the soldiery and the populace before the Royal arrival, and the latter were not in the most amiable mood, especially as the military had formed two dense lines, through which the carriages passed, and which, as the correspondent says, prevented the populace from even getting a sight of the Queen and Prince. He concludes with the following words: " I cannot imagine that her

Majesty, who in other places has shown herself so kind and condescending, should have wished us to be treated in such a manner."

The correspondent of the ' Constitutionnel ' sees, of course, a different cause, and says that if the rulers of France had been passing through, the people of Mayence would have rushed to a welcome. Yet our French friend was well able to write an interesting and indeed striking account of what he saw ; and if it had no other merit, it would at least show us how others see us.

" Queen Victoria saluted the public with a great deal of grace. She wore a rose-coloured dress, and a black silk cloak. She had scarcely sat down when she opened a white *gros de Naples* parasol, with fringes of the same colour. The Queen of Prussia sat by her, wearing a yellow bonnet of most equivocal taste. The King stood up at a distance of five or six steps from Queen Victoria, to whom he did not address a single word ('either good or bad,' as Corporal Trim would say) during the whole of the time they remained on the balcony. Prince Albert, in a Field-Marshal's uniform, stood at a respectful distance of about two steps behind the King and Queen Victoria, in the attitude of a timid, well-bred young man just on his preferment."

Of course the longed-for goal was Coburg, and the Royal travellers left the Hotel de l'Europe (which is a fine and comparatively modern building, that had been prepared for their reception) at 7 A.M. They had, however, in their short visit, seen the old Electoral palace, with the museum of Roman antiquities, the manuscripts of the tenth century, and the statue of Güttenberg, the inventor of printing, who was born in 1397. The statue is by Thörwaldsen, and stands in front of the theatre. "They drove through Hochst, Frankfurt, Offenbach, and Seligenstadt, to Aschaffenburg. Here they were met by a body of the Bavarian troops, and one of the King of Bavaria's gentlemen belonging to the post department, with instructions to precede the Royal travellers on their route through Bavaria."[1] The difficulties of the journey, as we learn from other sources, were greatly increased as they advanced further in the interior of the country, towards the early homes of the Prince. The travelling is graphically described by the correspondent of the 'Times' who had, of course, a *carte-blanche* for any kind of expenses. " In the last despatch we said that her Majesty had left Mayence for this place (Würzburg). It was an undertaking of no slight difficulty and magnitude even for one who had at command all the resources of royalty, and the especial aid of the Government in a country where its power is used to retard all locomotion of the people by refinements in regulation, and where, therefore, its assistance is more especially necessary if it is desirable to accelerate one's movements." But the gentleman who writes says that he found in Bavaria almost an organised defiance of anything like speed ; and it was not persuasion, or scolding, or even gold, that would induce the drivers of the *calèches*, to do more than five miles an hour; and even before they started at all, there was a very weary procrastinating preparation in such stables and sheds as they kept their vehicles in. He declares further, that the vehicles were

[1] Life of the Prince Consort.

not composed of as much wood as they ought to have had ; and even the wheels depended for their safety to a great extent on ropes, and, he says, on sometimes straw plats. The Royal party were able to command, of course, the best of vehicles and horses, but their progress was very slow compared to what they had been accustomed to in England. We learn from the Queen's diary how much the resting-place of their journey was desired. " Many miles of road had to be covered before Coburg, the eagerly expected goal of the day's journey, could be reached. Soon after three, Lichtenfels was reached, where horses were changed for the last time before leaving the Franconian territory, and the day, which had been lowering and showery, grew brighter and brighter. I began," the Queen writes, " to feel greatly moved—agitated, indeed — in coming near the Coburg frontier."[1]   This extract is introduced perhaps a little out of place, but it enables us to appreciate the eagerness that was felt to arrive at the early homes of the Prince—the great curiosity to see them on one part, and the pride and anxiety to show them on the other. From Mayence a long journey was before them ; but the anxiety to visit the old homes of the Prince is so natural, and so commends itself to the sympathies of every one in any rank of life, that it is certainly one of the touches of nature which has made the ' Life ' so welcome, and, as after an extended residence in the New World, the writer is able to add, has roused the feeling of "kin" all over the Western Continent among its readers. But Coburg was not yet.

The Royal progress, if not so rapid, was now very plea-

---

[1] Life of the Prince Consort.

sant, as the weather had improved. " Starting from Aschaffenburg, and traversing the beautiful woodland scenery of the Spessart, Würzburg and its magnificent palace were reached through Langfurth, Schweinfurth, ' where the air was exquisitely pure and delicious,' and Rossbrunn." Aschaffenburg was the first place at which the Queen stopped after leaving Mayence. She lighted for a short time, and rested at the inn for a quarter of an hour, but took no kind of refreshment except a glass of spring-water. The *cortège* consisted of six carriages and a *fourgon*. Some of the suite alighted, and partook of the celebrated Bavarian beer, which resembles Burton ale. The name of the inn is not given in any account I have seen, but it was probably the Freihof, the principal one, and a very comfortable useful house.

It may be interesting to mention here that King Ludwig caused a Roman villa to be erected exactly on the plan of one of those at Pompeii, and even the mural decorations were imitated,—so that we may see a Roman residence as it was. But forward was the order of the day, and twelve o'clock, or five hours after they started, the Royal party were once more *en route* to the ancestral homes of the Coburgs. They went at a comparatively rapid pace to Hessenthal, where a relay of horses were trimly groomed and fresh. These were attached to the carriages, and the next stage—Essebach—was reached. On leaving Essebach the country is extremely beautiful. There are rich woodland scenes all the way down to the lovely valleys, where the river Main flows through sweet meadows. The harvest was ripe for the reapers, and the crops stood in shocks on each side of the road.

Only a few veteran husbandmen were at their work, for nearly all the reapers had donned holiday attire to line the road where the Queen and the Prince were to pass. Some few details which have been gathered from various sources are curious here, and indeed they may illustrate the progress that has been made in the locomotion of this part of Germany. At Langfort the Main had to be crossed, and no railway bridge spans the narrow but pleasant stream, so that a ferry-boat was called into requisition. This was decorated with flags, and conveyed its Royal freight to the other bank of the Main. The road runs along the Main in the direction the carriages were going, and many are the beautiful views that opened out and delighted the travellers as they journeyed on under clear bright skies. Sometimes the Main was as quiet as the upper water of the Thames, and the purple hills formed the background, and often the stream was lost in dense woods, but it reappeared through them like a silver thread in broken lengths in the distance, as the height of some hill was reached. There were deep ravines that opened up on the roadside, and ruins of some dismantled castle whose records were perhaps hardly preserved in any archives, rested on hill-tops. Spires or stunted towers in some of the valley clearings indicated the site of a village, and every picture that has been indicated rose in rapid succession, as the *cortège* proceeded at a hand-gallop along the road.

But Würzburg was reached at last. Quoting again from Sir Theodore Martin's work: " Everywhere the harvest was in full progress, and gave life and interest

to the landscape, the pleasure of which seems to have been not a little dashed by the spectacle, never welcome to English eyes, of the burden of the labour being borne by the women. At the entrance of the palace, which greatly impressed the travellers by its vastness and the state iness of its elevation," they were received by Prince Luitpold of Bavaria; and they found at their disposal " an endless suite of very fine rooms," which they were able to enjoy, tired as they were with the long day's journey, and disconcerted, as even Royal tourists occasionally are, by the non-arrival of their luggage. The appearance of Würzburg is simply grand as we approach it from the Main. The Queen and Prince were received at the gates of the town by a guard of honour, headed by the King's third son, Prince Luitpold of Bavaria. The King himself was detained on business at Munich, which knew no delay, and which quite prevented him from leaving his capital. There was just light enough as they crossed the bridge to show the great towers of the Festung, and the quaint figures that are perched on the pedestals. The King's son, however, in the necessary absence of his father, did the honours well, and a magnificent banquet was served up in the great baronial banqueting-hall. The drawing shows the bridge with the figures and the great castle. Formerly this grand old town was governed by a bishop, who was the primate of the German Empire. It received its name from the gardens by which it is sur-rounded, as, if literally translated, it would signify " root or plant town." The cathedral and the fine church of the Augustinians are well worthy investigation; but time was pressing, and only a hurried visit was paid to them. Next morning the suite left Würzburg at four o'clock, and in two hours after the Queen and Prince followed them. Time, of course, was limited, and it was the especial desire to spend as much of it as possible in Coburg and Gotha, and their surroundings. In about seven hours they had reached Bamberg, which many persons would consider one of the most picturesque towns in Germany. The old cathedral is simply grand, and the palace and Rathhaus are quite among the

Würzburg Castle.

sights of Germany. "The town itself, rich in stately buildings, the remains of the luxurious splendour of the prince bishops, did not long arrest the travellers;" but after a series really of forced marches they arrived at Coburg on Tuesday afternoon, the 14th of August,

about half-past four. In the Queen's journal we read:
" At length we saw flags, and people drawn up in lines,
and in a few minutes we were welcomed by Ernest, the
Duke of Coburg, in full uniform.   We got into

Market-place, Coburg.

an open carriage of Ernest's, with six horses, Ernest
sitting opposite to us. The good people were all dressed
in their best—the women in pointed caps, with many

petticoats, and the men in leather breeches.   Many girls were there with wreaths of flowers."

The gateways of Coburg somewhat resemble those at Conway, and the former ones of Chester.   But in the middle of last century the Chester gates were destroyed, and modern ones, over which the wall is carried, were substituted.   At Coventry and various English towns are the remains of similar ones, but none of them are quite equal in size to those of Coburg.

The market-place, which is shown here, contains a fine statue of Prince Albert.   The town-hall occupies one side of the square, and is a very noble building.   The houses are high, and exceedingly well built, and they have in many instances the gable-windows, which are so rarely well managed in England, but they are models of proportion.   This is especially the case with the town-hall itself, which contains three dormer-windows of beautiful proportion and very fine design.   This building has also two oriel-windows, one at each angle, which add greatly to its picturesque appearance.   These are features, also, that English architects seem to have neglected.

As the Royal party reached the triumphal arch that marked their entry into Coburg, a number of girls, chosen for their beauty, approached the carriage, and two of them presented an address to the Queen in memory of her auspicious visit.   The day, which had begun in clouds and showers, brightened up.   On their visit to the market-place all the crowned heads and Prince Albert were received by the clergy of both the Catholic and Protestant denominations.   There was one beautiful feature in the decorations.   Temporary posts were erected, and from these garlands were festooned from post to post for nearly 300 yards. This, an eyewitness says, had a fine effect; and the posts themselves were decorated with fir boughs and streamers. From the tower of the gate through which the entry was made into Coburg, there is a grand view of Coburg and the surrounding country.

An avenue of trees on the Bamberg side of the road conceals the entrance to the tower, till the Roman Catholic church and the clergyman's house is reached. As might almost have been expected, the accommodation for the members of this creed in the land of Luther was humble; but that did not

Street in Coburg.

prevent a really tasteful decoration of everything belonging to the community, and pine boughs and garlands, the willing work of voluntary hands, made the plain structure look pleasant. There is a beautiful tract of country on the right; and on the left, just as we enter Coburg, there is a picturesque height, crowned by summer-houses and gardens, and below this are some fine mansions, belonging to residents who had thrown their soul into making arrangements for a proper reception—the house of Herr von Levenfells, of Herr von Lutz, of Herr von Paubel, and also that of an English gentleman of considerable wealth, who for two years had made Coburg his home.   This house attracted the interest and admiration of the Queen and the Prince.   It was beautifully decorated with flags, and the choicest flowers that the skies of Thuringia could produce were tastefully arranged in great profusion.   Costly banners floated over it, and there was a transparency with " God save the Queen."

The Royal party entered the town accompanied by the King and Queen of the Belgians, and the Duke of Saxe-Coburg.   The Prince's brother rode by them on horseback.   They went up the Ketchen Strasse to the market-place ; and thunders of artillery from the great fortress that has figured so often in the history of Europe, announced the arrival of the visitors.   They went then to the ducal palace, which faces a large square, and certainly has little architectural beauty to recommend it.   It is opposite the new theatre.   In the evening the ducal court visited the theatre at Coburg, which is a very nice building, about the size of the Haymarket Theatre in London.   The opera of the " Huguenots " was selected for performance, and admirably it was rendered.   The moment the Royal party made their appearance the National Anthem was struck up, and the audience rose to their feet by a single impulse.   The Royal box was opposite to the performers—a very excellent arrangement, and much

more convenient than the custom which prevails in London, where private boxes are by the side of the stage. The " Bride of Messina " was also performed on another occasion. The advantage of the Royal box being in front of the stage is that it presents so very much better an opportunity for the performance to be witnessed. One of the most accomplished reporters that accompanied the travellers was curious enough to remark that the front seat of the box was entirely devoted to crowned heads. Even, he says, Prince Albert, who may, in a sense, have been considered one of the lions of the day, sat behind

Court in Coburg Fortress.

when the performance was going on, which he supposes was one of the necessities of Royal etiquette. The weather was now lovely, and the out-of-door delights knew no limits. This was a real holiday; and though there are many that may smile at such a word when applied to

Royalty, it is only necessary to read the correspondence in the ' Life of the Prince Consort ' to be very well assured that a crown is, even in these days, but too often a

> " Polished perturbation, golden care !
> That keeps the ports of slumber open wide
> To many a watchful night."

The sympathy we so continually meet in the Queen's diary with the peasants and their families, as they crowded, in their holiday attire, to render their homage, almost reminds us of the memorable speech of Henry V., when he sadly compared the weight of a crown to the "homely biggin'," whose rustic wearer "snores out the watch of night." "A visit to the Festung or fortress, which overhangs the town of Coburg, occupied the afternoon of the first happy day. The fortress, of which part dates back from the twelfth century, had been admirably restored by the late Duke, and the interior arranged as a museum and armoury, which have since been largely augmented by the present Duke, and also by contributions from the Prince. Not the least interesting feature of the place is a room which was occupied by Luther, in which his chair and a portion of his bed are still preserved." [1]   The walk up to the fortress from Coburg is simply delightful. Nearly all kinds of trees flourish on each side of the ascent, especially the *Abele* and the birch and pine tree. As we continually rest or turn round to see the uncommon beauty of the landscape that is spread out like a map before us, we can well understand the feelings with which the Queen said, later on in the diary, that Thuringia had quite spoiled the Rhine. This great

[1] Life of the Prince Consort.

fortress, which has so long been associated with Luther and his memories, was almost allowed to fall into decay; but the father of Prince Albert had it put in thorough repair, and rebuilt some parts of it. There is a black and white façade, in one of the inner courts, which is shown here, that he built, and it is very characteristic of German architecture. This style is called "post and

petrel" in England, and the beams and standards are, as a rule, much more massive than we are apt to find in Germany among the ancient architecture. At the old castle of Coburg are some curious relics of the past, and many parts of the quaint building appear just as they were 200 years ago. There are portraits, of more or less merit, of princesses and princes of

Inner Court, Coburg Castle.

the house of Coburg. One room of great beauty is said to have interested the Queen very much. Its walls and ceiling are lined with oak, and different woods are curiously inlaid in a very admirable manner, representing incidents of the chase. It was built by Duke Casimir. In another room are portraits of heroes who figured in the Thirty Years' War,—Wallenstein, Tilly, and the Duke of Saxe-Weimar, Gustavus Adolphus, &c.   In another room is a splendid collection of old armour, quite unique in its way.   Then there is a large collection of Duke Casimir's carriages, of ponderous dimensions and quaint carving.   There is also a really good portrait of Bernhard of Saxe-Weimar, who greatly distinguished himself during the Thirty Years' War, painted by Schreder, an artist of Frankfurt.   Often, in the plateau, the Duke of Coburg, with his sons Albert and Ernest, used to breakfast in the pleasant open-air fashion that seemed to have exercised the fine temper of Councillor Florschütz, the Prince's tutor.   The Queen's diary adds: " From the bastion the view was glorious and most extensive,—Coburg below, with the Thüringer-wald and all the fine mountains toward Gotha in the background.   The effect of light was peculiarly beautiful, and there is such a constant movement in the ground it looked quite Italian.   Then those rows of poplar-trees are so picturesque."   A view is given (p. 154) of the prospect from the bastion, which so pleased the Queen.   It was sketched soon after the conclusion of the Franco-German war, and a sentinel who passed the writer many times seemed to hesitate whether official notice should be taken of the circumstance ; but he proved to be very polite, when a few inquiries were made at him that showed his questioner was a true man and " no spy."   This little bastion is very pleasant, and on a hot summer day it would seem, from its well-worn benches and doorway, to have been a welcome retreat in bygone times.   The view of the Thuringian woods and valleys and plains is very good ; and, as a daughter of Prince

Albert's who won the affections of the Queen's subjects in Canada could testify, it bears a singularly striking likeness to the grand prospect which meets the eye from the northern and western sides of the Montreal mountain.

Look-out Turret, Coburg Old Fortress.

In the room which is mentioned as containing a collection of Tilly and other great commanders, there is a curious assemblage of ancient drinking-cups,—vessels which would realise an immense sum of money if ever

Christie & Manson had to dispose of them. They are of many ages, and nearly of every possible shape and

Bastion of Coburg Castle.

size : some are broad in the top and narrow in the

bottom, and some are just the reverse. Many of the vessels are embossed with subjects taken from Scripture, and some of the most solemn parts are chosen for illustration. Some of them have ancient gold coins let into the sides, and others are carved and painted with dragons and Calibans. In one respect, however, they all agree, and that is in their amazing capacity. The old Dukes of Coburg seem to have held, with the Dutchman—

> " That a draught should be
> As deep as the rolling Zuyder Zee."

Some of the flagons could hardly have been intended to drink from, as they are almost too heavy to lift; the very smallest—the liqueur-glasses, as we might say, of the collection—would, however, require an English quart to fill them.

As has been said before, the landscape is one of the very finest in Europe. It reaches to the mountains of Bohemia and the nearer hills of Thuringia. Villages and hamlets dot the landscape, and just appear through the dense green foliage. The old Saxon Wittikind, when he surveyed the county, cried out, " It is fair "—and here he laid the foundations of the great castle. He is represented in the hall as the founder of the house of Coburg, and lies at the very root of the genealogical tree.

CHAPTER XIII.

ROYAL VISIT TO COBURG—RESIDENCE AT ROSENAU—GREAT WELCOME —ST GREGORIUS FEAST—GRAND SCENERY OF THÜRINGER-WALD— VISIT TO CALLENBURG—PARTIALITY OF DUKE FOR FIELD-SPORTS —DEPARTURE FOR GOTHA—NOTES ON THE ROAD—MEININGEN— GERMAN VILLAGES AND RURAL SCENES — ARRIVAL AT REIN- HARDTSBRUN.

THE Royal party took up their abode, during the stay at Coburg, principally at the Rosenau; and it is pleasant to be able to add that the proper feeling of the Germans prevented anything in the shape of pressure. This was remarked at the time by the correspondents of all the English journals who were present. Rosenau was re- spected; and as a gentleman said, "though it now lodges a Queen, there is scarcely a sign of that state which sur- rounds Royalty. The old Saxon colours, red and white, and a sentry or two lounging about, are all the tokens by which it may be known that Rosenau is the present abode of Royalty." Here, as the same observer truly said, when the highest rank walks abroad there is neither crowding nor obtrusive gazing, while with us a queen or prince could not outstep the palace confines without being subjected to the hustling of well-dressed vulgarity.

The country round Coburg is cultivated like a garden. There are no vineyards visible, but orchards, and cornfields, and meadows stretch away along the plain and cover the sides of the hills. When the visit to this part took place the harvest was nearly gathered; corn was still in shocks in many of the fields, but some of the land was cleared and covered with flights of birds as gleaners. What struck some of the Royal suite, as indeed it did the writer in after-years, was the very primitive and rude construction of the carts and vehicles that were employed to secure the harvest. Everything was as simple as it was when Virgil wrote his Eclogues. Everything looked like quiet labour, free from the strain of commercial complication; and though, indeed, the life was laborious, it did not seem as if the lot of the peasants was hard. The palace of Ehrenburg, which stands in the middle of Coburg, is much more suited for a royal visit than Rosenau; but the sylvan delights of Rosenau, and the unbounded affection that Prince Albert always entertained for it, made it a more welcome retreat.

While the Queen and Prince were at Coburg, the celebrated feast of St Gregorius was held. In the reign of our own Queen Elizabeth some kindly German left a sum of money to entertain the children of the twin schools, and this entertainment was held on the feast of St Gregory. That was the stipulation in the bequest; but probably the Germans have not always the fear of a Chancery suit before their eyes, for the time-honoured *fête* was held on the 22d of August, whereas our calendars tell us that the anniversary occurs on the 12th of March. "A procession of school children, about 1300 in number, from the different schools, was witnessed by the Queen and Court from the balcony of the palace.   All the children marched two and two into the courtyard, headed by their schoolmaster and a band—the boys first, and then the girls,—some in costumes as shepherdesses, &c., and a little boy in Court dress and powder.   The greater part of the girls were in white and green.   Three girls came up-stairs and presented us with a very pretty poem to the tune of 'God save the Queen,' and which they sang extremely well.   The children then marched off as they came.   After this we drove to Auger, a meadow close to the town.   Here were pitched two tents decorated with flowers, and open at the sides, under which we went to dine.   All the children were in front of us.   We walked round among them, and then sat down to dinner; a band of music played the whole time.   The children danced—and so nicely and merrily !—waltzes, polkas, &c.; and they played games, and were so truly happy—the evening was so beautiful, the whole scene so animated, the good people so quiet— it was the prettiest thing I ever saw.   We were all much struck with the number of pretty children."

This is from the Queen's diary.   A gentleman who was present says that shortly before three o'clock the children marched into the ground, which was marked out with pines and evergreens, and arranged in the same taste- ful manner that had elicited the admiration of every visitor to the city on previous occasions.   The ground was kept by the military, and there were, of course, the excellent bands in attendance that are never wanting in Germany on any occasion.   The girls, this same observer says, were generally in white, and decorated with ivy-leaves, the effect

being simple and very elegant. Fancy costumes were the rule rather among the boys than the girls, and these often assumed a form that caused great amusement; besides German courtiers of the olden time and the more common run of Greek brigands and soldiers, two miniature Napoleons put in an appearance, much to the amusement of the guests. This day is looked upon by the children as the great day of the year. A small sum of money is given to each of them, and also some cracknels of time-honoured make. Altogether it is said that a merrier day never closed over Coburg. In England such scenes have almost disappeared. The Eton "Montem," I believe, is almost a thing of the past; and the only resemblance to the one described at Coburg is perhaps to be found at the pleasant town of Knutsford, in the heart of Delamere forest in Cheshire—and, though it is perhaps not generally known, the May-pole on May-day still rears its head, and a May-queen is chosen. Like the *fête* at Coburg, this is attended by many of the gentry of the country and their friends. In an account of the German festival I saw in a French paper of the time, it is said that the Queen, or the Queen of the Belgians, sometimes called out a girl and praised her for something they had seen to approve of or admire about her, which, as a French correspondent benevolently states, " caused great envy among the others." The Royal party stayed at Rosenau for about a week, and enjoyed comparative rest and quiet, and explored some of the recesses of the great Thüringer-wald. " No one," says Sir Theodore Martin, " who has visited this beautiful region, in the heart of which Coburg lies, and of which not the least beautiful spot is the domain of the Rosenau, will be at a loss to understand the delight with which her Majesty speaks of it in her journal."

Nothing can be more charming than a roam in the Thuringian woods; and I have no hesitation at all in quoting a description of a ramble through a forest that quite corresponds with my own recollections. It was proposed to explore the recesses of a Thuringian forest, Ilmenau being the goal of the journey. " Thuringen is still little frequented by English tourists; at least, judging from the experience of three days' travel without encountering a single fellow-countryman, I must confess to no little astonishment. Here is all the traveller asks for—solitude, a wild and lovely nature, historic and poetic associations, past legend and present picturesqueness. But he should give much more to such a journey than three days, and take a sketch-book with him. We had started so early that by nine o'clock we were fairly in the forest. Oh, the wild flowers! who can describe them? who can imagine them? The valleys were a mosaic of blue, red, and gold, so thickly were the rye and oats interspersed with corn-flowers, borage, and others; and then the hillsides and hedgerows — what a splendour were they in this July verdure and fragrance! The sweet-scented cytisus, willow-herb, white and purple foxglove, meadowsweet, with abundance of ferns, clothed the walls of the mountain-roads through which we passed, now ascending a superb height, now dipping into a soft green valley, catching a glimpse of lovely scenery at every turn,—pine-forests, elder-trees growing beside noisy little rivers, blue hills, and yellow corn-fields. At midday we reached Rudolstadt, where we stopped to lunch.

The little town has a little castle, and a prince of its own, whose fortress-like Schloss stretches grandly along a bold mountain-ridge. From this point the grandeur of the scenery increases by degrees, till it reaches its height

Village of Neuses.

at Schwarzburg. That superb five hours' drive can never be forgotten. Now we drive along a smiling valley of corn-field and pasture, now we enter the solemn gloom of a mountain-pass or penetrate into the heart of a pine-forest, seeing the wild deer scamper away at our approach. Ever and anon we hear the rippling music of the impetuous little river Saale, or a burst of admiration escapes our lips as we reach some eminence looking over vast chains of pine-clad peaks, losing themselves in the purple distance.   In some places the character of the forest is savage, with wild gorges, and forest fastnesses, and tumultuous torrents; in others it is bright, peaceful, and playful, with sunny slopes, green as emerald, tall lovely alders screening one herd from another, and the river glances under their shadows; abundance of field-flowers shedding perfume as we go.   Such solitude I never before witnessed."   The villages, the same writer remarked, are small; and at the time of his journey all the people had turned out for the harvest.

A visit was of course made to Callenburg or Kalenburg, for in the maps it is spelt both ways.   It is situated about three miles from Coburg, and is placed in a commanding situation, though in this respect it is tame when compared with the fortress at Coburg, or the steeply perched castle of Wartburg, which is rendered for ever famous as the safe shelter which an ancestor of the Prince gave to Martin Luther.   The road to Callenburg is very interesting.   It passes by the old village of Neuses, which is represented on the preceding page, and is a perfect specimen of a German village.   There is the spire, the Lutheran minister's house, the schools, and a few villagers' cottages, all of which seemed to be well kept and comfortable.   Callenburg is approached through a magnificent avenue of Lombardy poplars, and the grandeur of these trees in a landscape has only been

properly appreciated by Turner. They do not flourish in
England quite as luxuriantly as they do on the Continent,
but the success that attends their cultivation is quite

Poplar Grove.

sufficient to encourage extensive plantation, especially
as they grow so very quickly. Near Windsor there are
some magnificent specimens which are only inferior in a

slight degree to those we see in Southern Germany. The delight of these tall trees, which are so utterly unlike anything else that we see in other flora that grow where they do, was naturally chronicled in the Royal journal. Callenburg Castle is about three miles from Coburg, and the road is the highway that leads to Rodach and Hildburghausen. Rosenau is left on the right hand, and the small county town of Ummerstadt is away on the left. Callenburg is more handsomely fitted up than most of the other ducal seats, and there are in it many remains of the chase. In one room the furniture is principally made from stags' antlers, and other significant trophies of sporting. The summer-house where the Princes and their father used to break-fast in the open air, which has already been shown, lies in the upper part of the park, not far away from the castle. The view of the castle which is engraved, is one of the many where it shows to advantage. In the park is the hospitable little refreshment-room where travellers of any class can obtain some sustenance on the pay-ment of a moderate sum which is duly advertised on a small board. It was an intensely hot day in August when we walked out there, and we looked forward naturally to having to reach Coburg again before we could rest, and this hospitable arrangement in such a quarter gave us great surprise. Architecturally speaking, Callenburg is more in accord with the Eng-lish taste than any of the other ducal seats; and though it would not be just to compare the situation with either Rosenau or Reinhardtsbrun, the architecture is more pleasing. There is another seat at Rodach on the same road, belonging to the Duke of Coburg; it is

Callenburg Castle.

also used as a shooting-box.
The Duke is a passionate
lover of the chase, and keeps
a small pack of hounds. His
private study is ornamented
with prints, both French and
English, of hunting and shooting scenes. Callenburg might
be regarded more as a summer palace than as a shooting-

box, and more nearly resembles the house of a midland county squire than any of the other places we may have to notice. The road up to it from the highway is very charming, and winds through pleasant foliage. There is a beautiful private chapel at Callenburg. The pulpit and its sounding-board, with its quaint niches and statuettes, fills a narrow wall between two tall Gothic windows, and it is approached by an external staircase. What might hardly have been looked for in a Lutheran chapel is a black crucifix with a white figure.

The 26th August was Prince Albert's birthday, and it was spent in the house where he was born. Twelve years had elapsed since he had passed his birthday there, and the Queen, in the extracts which have been published from the diary, says: "To celebrate this dear day in my beloved husband's country and birthplace is more than I ever hoped for,—and I am so thankful for it." There was, of course, a ball and festival at the Rosenau, and another for the good citizens at Coburg. This was just outside the gates of the ancient city. There was a play at the theatre of Coburg in the evening, at which the Queen and Prince attended. The theatre is a good substantial building two storeys high, with a directory, and is well arranged. A comedy was played in which the peculiarities of Frederick William, the eccentric father of the great Frederick, were admirably shown. Real pipes and beer-flagons were brought on the stage; and though the acting was more refined than the boisterous mirth of the Prussian King, it was a very fair representation of the Court.

The weather at the Rosenau had been charming all day, and a rural *fête* was held : that is not a common sight. A number of rustic dancers had been selected from among those in the Thuringian villages and towns who had any extra skill in dancing, and who were possessed of good looks. These were dressed in the most pronounced costume of the day that pertained to the peasantry; and after the military band had performed, they danced with great vigour before the Residence to their own band, which, of course, was excellent. But afterwards, according to ancient German usage, and a custom that yet prevails in some old-fashioned estates on certain rent-days in England, the aristocratic part of the assembly joined in the dance—the ducal ladies being partners with the rustics, and the gentlemen with the damsels—an arrangement which gave, it is said, much opportunity for mirth, owing to the very different styles of dancing which each class practised. But the pleasant days of Rosenau were now over, and it was necessary to leave this beautiful place the day after the Prince's birthday. The road runs through a charming country : it is a continuation of that which goes from Coburg to Callenburg. The Duke of Coburg's shooting-lodge at Rodach was visited on the journey—for here Prince Albert had spent many quiet happy days in his early years. At every part of the road girls and rustic youths were drawn up in holiday attire to welcome the cavalcade. They were still on the Duke of Coburg's territory, where Prince Albert was so well known ; and days had doubtless been spent by these artless people to appear in gala-dress before a cavalcade that swept by them in a moment ; and they had their reward.   A bow was appropriated by a hundred spectators ; and then, at least, they had seen the Queen and the Prince, whose memory they all so loved.   The Meiningen frontier was soon reached, and here demonstrations as enthusiastic as anywhere else greeted them.   Only a few villages and quiet hamlets are passed between Rodach and Hildburghausen.   There are two little pleasant market towns or villages—Adelhausen and Steinfeld—on the road, but they are hardly marked in any English map we should be likely to find at even a first-class map-seller's. Hildburghausen, through which the cavalcade passed, deserves a notice, as also do the quiet streets of this old capital.   The deserted palace has already figured in these pages ; and of course the whole town was *en gala.* The clergyman, however, laid his heavy hand upon the travellers ; and, without the fear of *clôture* before his eyes, he delivered himself of a lengthy and confused speech to a wearied audience.   At Hildburghausen there is a fine old Rathhaus, which seems to carry all the peculiarities of German architecture to the furthest degree.   The crow-stepped gables and the dormer-lights in the roof are quite remarkable.   " At Themar, the next halting-place, the same ordeal had to be gone through," and the clergyman made another confused and discursive speech. The journal says : " He called me ' Die herrliche Britten Königin ' (the noble British Queen) in such an extraordinary way, that we had great difficulty to keep our countenances."   The Royal party, it is true, was kept waiting in Themar, and the day was wearing on ; but the dignity of the place was not compromised— the clergyman had made his speech.   Themar is a small pleasant German town, about seven miles from Hildburg-

Meiningen—Duke of Landburg's Castle in the distance.

hausen. It is situated on the Werra river, where it is

joined by a brook that runs past the little hamlet of
Leugfeld, over rocks, and is said to contain many fine
trout after a shower of rain.   The speech, however, came
to an end, and the journey was resumed to Meiningen,
which is about twelve miles further along the road.   A
short way out of Meiningen the travellers were met by
the Duke of Meiningen, who accompanied them to the
capital, where again the clergyman, and young ladies with
flowers and lyrics, awaited them.   In consequence of the
detour to Meiningen, some of the towns and villages on
the ordinary Coburg and Gotha road were left on the
right-hand side, and this caused some disappointment at
such towns as Eisfeld, Schleusingen, and Suhl ; for arches,
and flags, and flowers had been prepared in vain.   One
feels, indeed, sorry that such preparations should have
been useless, though this was entirely unavoidable by the
Royal travellers.   All the towns were proud of the Prince,
who had been born in their midst, and all wished to see
him once more and give him a welcome.   It must be
confessed, however, that it would require a large amount
of charity to extend the same sympathy to the various
pastors, who were obliged to relegate the MSS. of the
respective speeches to their several drawers.

Meiningen Palace closely resembles Hildburghausen in
outward appearance, though, of course, it is kept in perfect
order.   The front is about 500 feet in length.   The inhabitants of Meiningen were, at the time of the Royal visit,
about 4500 in number, and the majority of them were
occupied in some way about the Court and the public
offices.   Since that, however, it has increased ; and there
are many good shops.   I was a little surprised, in going

A. Rimmer

into a stationer's to make some purchase, to be addressed in English by the shopkeeper—and the more so, as the English bore a very decidedly American accent. He told me that he was an American citizen, though why he had cast in his lot in Meiningen is not apparent. In passing so rapidly through the country as the Royal party did, much of the interest in small towns and villages is unavoidably lost. Even among the visitors who accompanied them, either as correspondents of journals from various countries, or only as tourists and sightseers, there was no opportunity for judging of the country in its normal condition. The fronts of the smallest houses were commonly hidden by decoration, and all was in holiday attire.

As a rule, German villages, in the parts we are now considering, are built in a massive style, and almost every house has its circular-headed doorway, suggesting, as has been observed, a fond regard for the old style of Saxon architecture; or, at any rate, the huge round gateway bears distinctive evidence of the origin of its builders. "All German houses are large — space seems no object. Through the whole place there is a curious mixture of rudeness and attempt at ornament. Most houses are heavy, and rude, and weather-worn; but others, again, are light and neatly painted, and their upper windows are filled with bright flowering plants. Here and there is a house painted up in a tawdry manner, in imitation of red and yellow marble and of Corinthian columns." Now, if this description were applied to French-Canadian towns, nothing more accurate could be written; and indeed we are reminded by it of the frequency with which these countries were overrun by the French, who in their turn copied German village architecture, for the old French architecture is of a different type.   The great feature, however, in all German towns is the fountain; and this is found not only in large cities, but in villages.   Sometimes, as at Nuremberg, a fountain of exquisite beauty is erected (though, indeed, this one stands quite by itself); and sometimes there is a broad basin with a grotesque figure rising up from the centre, and distributing clear streams of water through wrought-iron pipes, which are held in their places by many twisted devices.   In the smaller villages, of course, no such elaboration is attempted, but a conduit supplies the country maidens. In all instances these fountains are a rendezvous for the neighbours, and round them they gather to discuss each other's affairs, which they continue to do long after the clear cold water is flowing over their pails.

The village churchyards in this pleasant country are peculiar; and for long before the custom prevailed in England, flowers of various kinds—roses, carnations, and others—were planted.   At the head of the graves is a cross generally, which is constructed of wood; sometimes this is triangular, as at the Roman Catholic graves, but generally plain wooden crosses prevail.   The epitaphs in these old churchyards correspond very closely with many we see in our own.   We often find inscriptions that might be translated—

> " Weep not for me, my husband dear,
> I am not dead, but sleeping here ; "

and the old one about life being but an inn, is not uncommon.   The trade a man followed is frequently recorded on his tombstone, and ingenious comments follow

Reinhardtsbrun and Chapel.

in verse of more or less excellence; but one of the

favourite epitaphs is a German rendering of a very common one in our own churchyards—

> " As I am now—so shalt thou be ;
> Therefore prepare to follow me."

After dinner at the palace, the journey was resumed, and by 6 P.M. Schmalkald was reached, " where there was an amazing crowd, and a very ridiculous postmaster." We are not further informed in any contemporaneous account of the details of this halting-place ; but a dreadful vision of the postmaster undertaking the rhetorical part of the reception is present to our eyes, and we are involuntarily reminded of Henry V.—

> " Alas, your too much love and care of me
> Are heavy orisons."

" A little stream runs through the street, which has a very good effect," the Queen writes. There is indeed nothing more pleasing than a combination of old buildings and water. We see this in Wrexham, and Wells, and Salisbury, and some other places—a stream of fresh water running through a town,—and the effect is always pleasant, if the most ordinary care is taken of such an inestimable boon. " Soon after Schmalkald, the most beautiful scenery begins,—fine mountains covered with spruce fir, like Scotland, but much more wooded, and then we have very little spruce fir,—valleys and meadows, with little houses, and smoke rising from where the charcoal-burners are ; so solemn, wild, and impressive, and such pure, cool, mountain air." The Thuringian villages are exquisitely beautiful ; they nestle in openings of mountain-ranges, and the cottages are more picturesque even than those of Wales or Scotland. Then the groups

Reinhardtsbrun from the Lake.

of peasants seem to be almost arranged for Harding, or Prout, or Stanfield. They are so unstudiedly picturesque, and they move about in new combinations so often, that we continually wish for an instantaneous photographic machine to record them. We see in the little farmyards the peculiar breed of Itz valley cattle that is beginning to lose its individuality through mixing with other herds. The Itz valley it is where Rosenau is situated, and there can be no doubt that the value of this breed of cattle was well understood by the Prince and his ancestors. The homesteads are neither worse nor better than we commonly see in England, but there is one thing the Thuringian farmer understands the value of, and that is poultry; every cottager has his fowls, and capons and turkeys are seen in farmyards. The modest residence, also, can boast of a flower-garden, and a neat vegetable plot for home use. "At Klein Schmalkald Ernest's territories begin. It was getting dark here, and still more a little further on, where on the top of the Thüringer-wald were a number of people." There was a triumphal arch, and everything was done that could show the enthusiasm of the populace as Reinhardtsbrun was slowly approached. This was, indeed, an early home of Prince Albert's, and many were the sketches he made of it. In every respect the situation differs from that of Rosenau. The latter is on a gentle height, but Reinhardtsbrun is precisely like that of a Cistercian convent. It is in a lovely valley with hills on all sides, and it much resembles, in situation, Combermere Abbey in Cheshire, only that the sheet of water is not so extensive. The Queen speaks enthusiastically of the beauty of the place: "The trees with their great branches sweeping the ground, and the deep rich green, the luxuriant flowers, the wooded mountains that surround the house, make it one of the most beautiful spots imaginable." Perhaps the façade of Reinhardtsbrun would be considered rather formal, and indeed it does not suit an English taste. It was built just at the time when in England an attempt was made to revive Gothic houses. There was a belief that an Italian façade could be adapted to Gothic details. This in no way, however, affects the great beauty of the scene, and it is just a matter of individual taste whether the situation of Rosenau or Reinhardtsbrun is to be preferred. But all the residences of the German princes are situated in spots of signal beauty.

CHAPTER XIV.

ARRIVAL OF ROYAL PARTY AT GOTHA — RESULTS OF VISIT IN RE-
MOVING ERRONEOUS IMPRESSIONS — RESIDENCE OF DOWAGER-
DUCHESS OF COBURG-GOTHA — ART-TREASURES AND MUSEUMS OF
GOTHA — 'ALMANACH DE GOTHA' — MUSEUM BUILT BY DUKE OF
COBURG — ANNUAL SHOOTING FESTIVAL — PROCESSION OF PEAS-
ANTRY BEFORE QUEEN AND PRINCE — BATTUE OF DEER — FINAL
PREPARATIONS FOR DEPARTURE TO ENGLAND.

IN the afternoon the Royal party arrived at Gotha, the limit of Prince Ernest's dominions; and the various travellers who had followed their route, but were left behind in the race, were able to arrive. Different and often graphic accounts of the journey had been sent home to France and England and to other parts of Germany, but the remarkable fact is that people in England had been so ignorant of the resources and the social life of the inhabitants of Southern Germany. I copy the following extract from one of the most influential journals of the metropolis; it appeared the same month that the Queen and Prince returned to England from their Continental tour. The editor in his leading article asks, What is the effect or result of the Royal visits? and he answers his question by saying that they have no political results, and are not intended to have any; but the effect on the

Restauration
A. Rimmer

opinions and knowledge of the people is very important. " Vast masses of the English people read nothing but the newspapers; they have little time, often less inclination, for anything else. Books must be sought for; the newspaper is like the Sibyl's leaf, and is borne as it were on the winds to the hands of almost every man. . . . Our insular position has too long preserved among us a vast amount of national prejudice, which knowledge of other countries alone can soften; and it will be of advantage to learn that England does not possess exclusively all the wealth, greatness, and power of the world—that social happiness is not always found in proportion to political freedom—that we might borrow much from our neighbours with great benefit to ourselves—and that it is quite time to dismiss the idea that everything foreign is contemptible." After speaking of the singular errors that obtained credence even during the present century about Napoleon and his family, such as would be " laughed at by every schoolboy," the writer proceeds to say that the visit of the Queen and Prince to the early homes of the Prince have had the further effect of dispelling many more common illusions, and these we can now smile at. " Thus there is almost a universal belief in England that the minor sovereignties and principalities of Germany are exceedingly despicable—that as Powers they verge on the burlesque of monarchies. Till her Majesty's visit, no popular and generally read description of them had been brought so forcibly before the public as the late accounts in the papers; and these descriptions cannot but abate very considerably the disposition to sneer at the ' petty German Courts.' . The Duchy of

Coburg - Gotha does not number more than 150,000 inhabitants ; but the land is well cultivated, and the people are well fed and clothed ; and there is scarcely a beggar to be seen in the whole territory. We with our greatness and wealth are now daily reading an exposure of the poor-law system. . . . We laugh at the small revenues of the German States ; do we manage our own immense resources half so well, or in proportion do with them one-tenth as much for the good of the people ? . . . As to Royal residences, the Queen of Great Britain has cause to envy the Duke of Gotha, at whose petty State it is the pleasure of Englishmen to laugh. He has three palaces superior even in architectural effect to Buckingham House, and seven or eight residences, any one of which would be preferred to the Pavilion at Brighton." This article at the time it was written was not at all out of date, and even now many men of reading and culture have very inadequate ideas of some of the more remote Continental towns. I have spent a number of years in collecting drawings and little historical sketches of the old county towns of England, and I can say that I know of no county or country town at home that is as large as Coburg, or that musters say 10,000 inhabitants, which would cost as much to build in a similar style as the German capital. Coburg of course musters rather more inhabitants now,—they number 12,819 ; but at the time of the Royal visit they were below 10,000 in number. To continue the narrative, however. In the afternoon the travellers arrived at Gotha and were met by great crowds. "The peasant-women not only wear a different costume, but look quite different—have longer faces, and are dark and handsome." The entry into Gotha was quite as brilliant as that into Coburg—wreaths and garlands were extended in every direction. Pine-trees, which are very abundant, were laid under heavy contributions, and the dark green relieved by the red berries of the mountain-ash, had a beautiful effect. The good citizens had subscribed six thousand crowns for the great occasion.

The Queen and Prince were the guests of the Dowager-Duchess of Coburg, who lives at the Palace of Friedrich-stahl. This is a very pleasant residence, consisting of a centre part with a pediment, and two very extensive wings ; there is a wrought-iron railing that extends all along the front, and a beautiful fountain rises up through the bushes. It requires no very vigorous imagination to paint the enthusiasm with which Prince Albert was received at Gotha, accompanied as he was by the Queen of England. The citizens felt, and felt truly, that he was one of themselves, and his even features and clear blue eyes were perfectly familiar to every one there. From six in the morning, a gentleman who was present says that perhaps every vehicle that could hold together, and that lay within reach of Gotha, had been brought into requisition, and the collection of vehicular antiquities that crowded the highways and the byways was something to wonder at. Arrivals of such interesting carriages, with, of course, great numbers of smart waggons and omnibuses, continued through the whole course of the day. The road from Gotha to Reinhardtsbrun was full of pedestrians and horsemen, who remained all day to obtain, if possible, a sight of the Queen and their beloved Prince.

Her Majesty spent the first day quietly, while all Gotha was in a ferment, " the Burger guard mustering and doing their best to look as little like respectable tradesmen as possible." At two o'clock, the same gentleman says, they took up their ground, lining the roadside from the city gate to the *aide*, " and here they stood for four weary hours under arms, relieving the tedium of delay by smoking profusely and drinking beer extensively, for the day was hot and the road dusty. It must have been a great support under their arduous duty, but detracted somewhat from their martial appearance. It is beyond the power of belt and buttons to make a respectable middle-aged gentleman look like a hero, if he mounts guard in spectacles and a pipe, a combination of which there were several instances." All those who were in Gotha, and who were in expectation for the arrival of the Queen and Prince, were delighted to hear a distant gun in the direction of Reinhardtsbrun—and there were many speculations as to whether it was a gun or not; but the cavalcade was fairly *en route,* and the sound soon came in once more, and " nearer, clearer," though happily not " deadlier than before." Salvos were fired along the route, and at a hand-gallop the Royal cavalcade entered Gotha through a temporary gateway which was made to resemble in some degree the arch of Titus. To the Prince, of course, every stone was familiar, but to the Queen every scene was new. Gotha, the capital of the State, was reached at last. It was little known at the time of the Royal visit, to Englishmen, and indeed is rarely visited now by them. Even by the aid of rail the journey is a long one—and before this mode of travel, the diffi-

culty of reaching it, and the cost and discomfort, made
Gotha still more a sealed book ; but the ingenious gentlemen who are alluded to in an extract at the beginning of

the chapter, would have been surprised to learn that (Oxford and
Cambridge, possibly, apart) Gotha
contained a finer library, more
scientific appliances, grander collections of articles that are only
within the reach of wealth, than
any town in the United Kingdom
of twice its size, or even twice
that ! A brief description of this

*Gotha, showing Royal
Palace.*

beautiful and interesting town is given, and though its
population may have increased since, it numbered at the
time of the Royal visit rather less than 18,500 inhabi-

tants. The only building that has been added since then is the magnificent museum in the palace grounds; but the collections it contained were at Gotha very long ago—only the building is new.

The town of Gotha is the capital of Saxe-Coburg-Gotha, and is situated in a district of exceeding beauty, on the left bank of the Leine, by the Thuringian railway. It is handsome and well built, quadrilateral in form, and was once surrounded by walls. The street here shown is a steep one, and near the top is a curious fountain with dolphins and faces. This is a favourite meeting-place for the townspeople, and many are the picturesque groups that appear and disappear on a summer-day. On each side of this street are substantial dwellings, and at the top are some fine residences. The extremity is blocked by the noble ducal residence called the Frieden-stein Palace, which is the finest of all the palaces in the duchy. The principal building at Gotha is the palace. It contains a picture-gallery, in which are splendid speci-mens of Rembrandt, Rubens, and Holbein. There is also a very valuable collection of engravings, and a library con-taining 150,000 volumes and 6000 manuscripts, and one of the finest collection of coins in Europe. One is apt not to realise the magnitude of such a collection of books, but it might startle any one who had not con-sidered the subject to learn that, if we allowed each book only a single inch in thickness,—and how inadequate that is their own library will tell them,—no less than two and a half miles of shelving would be required to contain them. There is also a Japanese and Chinese museum. Gotha contains an arsenal, and an old and new town-hall,

Kuhn
Reinhel
A. Rimmer

and it is the seat of many industries, such as the manufacture of muslins, porcelain, coloured paper, cloth, linen, and tobacco, &c. &c. There are several hundred designers and engravers in Justus Perthes' geographical and printing establishment. The street on the opposite page shown is remarkably picturesque, and at the end it turns up on the left to the royal palace. The gables rise quaintly over each other and form groups of great beauty. The buildings are of stone, and very substantial; the masonry is like that which we see in the old parts of Edinburgh, but the architecture is even more picturesque. A waggon with two horses had stopped in the position shown, and I hastened to commit it to paper; but, fortunately for me at least, though the driver might have thought differently, there was a slight breakdown in the harness, and some friend came out to condole with him, and discuss the demerits of breakdowns in general, and this one in particular.

Mention has already been made of the imperious sway of Napoleon in these parts during the first years of the present century, and the straits to which the royal Germans were for a time reduced. But there is an amusing incident which occurred in 1757 at the palace of the Duke of Gotha, which well deserves recording. Of course the alliance against Frederick the Great was overwhelming, but his genius always rose with difficulty. The German allies were the Landgrave of Hessen and the Dukes of Brunswick and Gotha. The latter Duke was defeated by the French; and when the troops occupied Gotha, this palace was the scene of a curious occurrence, which is described in the history of the Seven Years' War, before the decisive battle of Rossbach. " Gotha had been chosen by the French as a luxurious retreat, where the general and the *élite* of the army might recruit themselves after the fatigues of the campaign. To this Capua, Soubise the general-in-chief, with his staff, and about 8000 men, repaired, and great preparations were made at the ducal court to receive the guests in due form. It was just dinner-time,—a splendid banquet had been ordered. The tables were already spread, and the company were about to seat themselves, when tidings arrived that Seidlitz the Prussian general had suddenly made his appearance at the gates with 1500 cavalry. The 8000 French never thought of resistance. They hurried out of the town, leaving the luxurious fare and smoking dishes untouched." This is extracted from a diary written in the early part of the present century. By the most singular and grim law of rotation, it may be remembered that in the Franco-Prussian war the French troops, round their camp-fires, were grouped picturesquely together, and had a most warlike appearance. The mustachioed soldiers, full of energy and life, discussed the chances of the day, and indeed some of the more reflective might have bitterly thought of the morrow ; but they presented a wonderful contrast to the Prussians, who in their tents were silent, and not very warlike-looking, but intent on cleaning their arms and accoutrements. The Germans in Napoleon's time had, on the contrary, all the proper orthodox appliances of war, and indulged in much more than orthodox language——with what result let Jena tell. (!) But in 1757, when the French army was before Gotha, they in their turn were the luxurious and idle, and Arch-

enholz gives a very humorous account of the spoil found
in the tents of the French general officers.   There were
chests full of pomades and perfumes; there were wigs of
various cuts and styles, according to the present necessities of the wearer; and there were powders, puffs, and
parasols to shade off the rays of the sun, as well as
parrots to cheer the warriors with their *naïve* remarks
after the toils and dangers of the battle were over.

The celebrated 'Almanach de Gotha' is published here.
It is a very remarkable production indeed, and has been
established for more than a century.   It was originally
written in the German language; but when Napoleon
became Emperor, he had it published in French, and it
has continued to be issued in French ever since.   It is
a little pocket volume of about a thousand pages of small
type, and it records the sovereigns and families of every
civilised country.   It also gives the various officers—civil,
diplomatic, naval, and military,—together with a great
amount of statistical information, and a compact and
comprehensive summary of historical events, obituary
notices of eminent persons, and other matters of political
importance.   No book ever published contains such a
mass of information in so small a compass.   The revenues
of states are given, the populations and their religions, and
the boundaries according to the latest treaties.   The
'Annuaire Diplomatique' contains the names of every
diplomatic representative and *attaché* in Europe and
America.   The pay of the officers of Government, the
national expenditure and debts, with the interest, are
stated; and in representative Governments, the number
of representatives and their proportion to the popula-

tion are also recorded. In some instances, to show the exactness of the editors, a page is dated to indicate that changes may have occurred for which they are not responsible. There was only one republic in existence —Switzerland—when the almanac was first commenced. It was indeed a register of crowned heads, and the Royal families of Europe ; and for years after the French Revolution, it continued to print, under the head of France, Louis XVII. as reigning monarch. It was only after Napoleon became Emperor that his name was recorded, and then his whole family and their connections were given, as with other Royal houses. Napoleon regarded this work as very important, and he exercised a rigid supervision over it. Indeed, in 1808 an entire edition was suppressed after it had been worked off; and when the editor hurried to Paris, he found that his error had been his adopting the alphabetical arrangement of Ernestian princes, by which the Anhalt line took precedence of Napoleon, who of course claimed the right to be the head of the Rhenish nobility. To secure the rearrangement of the alphabet, the edition of that year was published in Paris. The same energetic supervision also prevented such untoward events as the battle of Trafalgar from being recorded among the historical events of the year. On the restoration of the Bourbons, however, ample amends were made for this in a *résumé* in which not only the great sea-fight was duly set forth, but many other successes of the allies, which had been considered as hardly important enough by Napoleon to chronicle.

There is another establishment in Gotha which is worthy of all honour, and which is owing to the enlightened public spirit of the Duke of Saxe-Coburg-Gotha, and that is the magnificent museum which he built. In this he collected the vast stores of art and curiosity which were in the ducal palace of Friedenstein, and has made one of the most complete, and certainly one of the best contrived, museums in Europe. The designs for this admirable building were made by Mr Franz Neumann, who was the architect for the Duke of Coburg-Gotha and H.R.H. Prince Augustus. Some other designs were sent in, but this one was selected. The castle of Friedenstein stands on elevated ground, partly natural and partly artificial, and it commands a magnificent view over the surrounding country. A terraced garden surrounds it, and the first level, which is about 600 Gotha feet from the castle, leads to the beautiful Reinhardtsbrun road. In the middle of the space before the castle is a plateau, which was used as a ride; this was thirty-one feet lower down. The kitchen-garden was still further from the castle, and on a lower level. Mr Neumann has extended the plateau before the castle towards the kitchen - garden, and on the newly made ground the museum is built. Advantage was then taken of the different levels, and so a considerable saving was effected by the architect being enabled to build rooms of different heights on the ground-floor. The museum was arranged for the following objects: A picture-gallery, a collection of plaster-casts, a collection of engravings, a collection of Chinese objects; and also the usual collections of fauna, mineralogy, and conchology, &c. &c. It was considered best to build the structure in three storeys to lessen the cost, which was necessarily great. And this gave the architect a little extra difficulty, as he had to provide for some articles that required large wall-space, and others that needed floor-accommodation ; and besides this, he had to adapt his plans for workshops for repair, and also for curators' rooms. The systematic arrangement of the great collection was also placed under his charge, and the connections of the different sections with each other. In the basement, the rooms, as before said, are of different altitudes to accommodate the plaster - castings and the specimens of the museum that stand highest — all of which is easily done by taking advantage of the different levels of the ground. The system of separate recesses formed by large openings has been adopted, by which the different objects are divided into their several classes, and yet the collection may be viewed as a whole. The windows in the basement are raised high above the floor, so that there is an available wall-space of eight feet below them. Space has been reserved for attendants and a restaurant. The ground-floor has often filled me with admiration as a perfect model of arrangement. The four principal rooms which, as will be seen, occupy the centre, are placed here to avoid the direct rays of the sun, and so to escape the ravages of moths. There will, however, as we can see, be quite sufficient light for the collection, as the side and end windows are large, and shine straight through the corridors. The birds are exhibited in the left wing round the mammalia, and in precisely the same manner corals and skeletons will be distributed around the mammalia of the right wing ; the department for reptiles and conchology also, and studies of horses, will be arranged round in the same manner. A glance at the plan will show how complete these arrangements are, and the light streaming in on the four sides will enable the specimens to be inspected and examined thoroughly. The octagonal vestibule which connects the wings is very elegant, and leads directly from the principal staircase to the vestibule. The staircase is of stone, and is situated on that side of the building which looks over the park. The floor is reached by a flight of steps from the outside, and this flight leads into an open colonnade which communicates with the octagonal vestibule; and so the principal ground-floor apartments are entered. Of course, from the many lights in this floor, it would be impossible to show pictures, so these are reserved for the first floor, which is lit by a skylight, and is admirably fitted for the purposes of a gallery. The collection contains amongst other things a series of portraits of the principal sovereigns of the country, and some of the most interesting events in history. The foundations of the building have been carried down below the newly formed earth to a solid footing, and nothing has been left undone to complete the edifice in the most solid manner. Complete plans, and a perspective of the exterior, were given in the 'Builder' for July 1867.

At Gotha, of course, all was now enthusiasm; and as it so happened, her Majesty's visit fell in with the celebration of the "bird-shooting," which is a festival held annually for practice in rifle-shooting. We may see from "Freischütz" what importance is attached to winning a prize as a marksman; and when her Majesty and the Prince arrived, the annual festival, with which he was so familiar, was at its height. There is a large building at Gotha, and a garden attached to it, which is the scene of the sport. Rifles are supplied, though it is perfectly free for any one to bring his own piece, with which he may be better acquainted, and he may also load for himself in his own way. But what strikes one as peculiar, is the rest which is constructed for the rifle, and which can be raised or lowered at pleasure. The targets are birds or animals, which can be set in rapid motion with pulleys and cords, according to the nature of the shot required ; and they also represent still animals. Any one may shoot by paying for his shot, and the money is paid into a common fund which is given in prizes—either plate or money. Of course we had somewhat similar festivals in England, such as shooting at the popinjay ; and even now our own rifle-matches are only an advance in point of arrangement upon this one. The *fête* was proceeding when her Majesty arrived, and it was resolved to make the most of the occasion. There was a dais raised in front of the shooting-house. The Queen and Royal party took their seats at two o'clock ; and shortly after, a singular procession passed them which occupied nearly two hours, the like of which, perhaps, never was seen by an English crowned head before. The farmers were mounted, often on good horses, and the peasantry rode in the long waggons which are peculiar to the country, all gaily dressed, and in holiday attire, and wearing boughs and green wreaths. The dresses were of the most diverse description, as often the same long cart contained ladies of different positions in the villages they hailed from. Not a single break or delay occurred while the long line filed past. As each vehicle appeared in sight there was great speculation among the girls as to which was the real Queen (" Königin "), and if it were the lady in the pink or the blue bonnet. This was set at rest only when the dais was passed, and a kindly bow and smile removed all uncertainty.

The procession was on the 30th August, and on the following day the notable *Treibjagd*, or battue of deer, was held for the amusement of the visitors. Again and again we have read of the great hunting scenes of Germany, and the mighty Nimrods of the chase that killed great store of game and venison, and we are apt to associate all this with exciting and dashing scenes; but the reality was quite different. The deer were driven to be slaughtered without the least fatigue to the sportsmen, and the latter simply sat down to their work of destruction, "while a fine band of music mingled with the intermittent crack of rifle-shot. Battues of this description, lacking as they do the elements of personal effort in the sportsman, and of reasonable chance to the game, which alone justify the chase, can only be viewed as a barbarous relic of a period when cruelty entered largely into the pastimes of the great." The Queen, even though she admitted that there was some interest attaching to it as a relic of the past in the Saxon forests, records the following in her diary : " As for the sport itself, none of the gentlemen like this butchery." If the object of a *Jagd* were to supply a larder or market, no exception could be taken to it, but it is as far from sport as anything we can imagine. On the occasion which is now spoken of, the site selected for the battue was the top of a low hill, surrounded by hills of greater altitude on all sides. An enclosure was made here, and the beaters, assisted by peasants, were assembled in great numbers for the " drive." All this was arranged by the head gamekeeper, who marshalled his men in a ring of great magnitude, to drive the deer from distant parts of the forest. The only thing the men had to do, in the first instance, was to advance towards a common centre, and keep within hail of each other. As they closed in, the deer became more packed, though some of the older ones would turn round and break through the line, as sometimes the more knowing grouse will do on a drive; but a large number, for all that, sought the enclosure. At first, as an eyewitness said, a few stragglers appeared, and when they bounded into the enclosure, they timidly looked round as though they feared all was not well. More came in, and finally the beaters closed up the entrance to the pound, and shooting commenced. The deer became frantic and rushed about in all directions, and then rapidly in a long line across the enclosure amidst a volley of rifle-balls. Only three fell dead, which is a fair indication that the sportsmen's hearts were not in their work; but at the same time many were fearfully wounded. The keepers despatched them; but for all that, there were a large number that were mortally hit, and hid among the bushes. What seemed most incongruous in it all was, that while all the slaughter was going on, a splendid band performed light strains of sweet music.

When the animals were laid out in rows they num-

bered forty-eight, all told, though the keepers brought in
more afterwards. It is significant of the way in which
such sport is regarded by the people, that when a stag
broke away and escaped there was a loud cheer. I do
not remember to have seen it noticed that this was probably something like the hunting of Chevy Chase. The
account of the latter is, of course, confused, and some
parts of it almost contradictory; as, for example, where
it is said that

> "The gallant greyhounds swiftly ran
> To chase the fallow deer."

It is certain if dogs had been allowed to roam about with
the bowmen the deer would have soon left that part of
the Cheviot Hills; for they were well acquainted with the
ground—better, indeed, than their southern pursuers.
Then again, even though Earl Percy had men to assist
him in his unwarrantable poaching raid, who numbered
fifteen hundred, and

> "Who knew full well in time of need
> To aim their shafts aright,"

this could not have helped much to bring down a stag
as it bounded through the forest. Scottish stags then
were almost as careful of themselves as they are now;
and ask the owner of a Westley Richards if the best
archery shot would bring down a stag by fair means in
a century. The key to the "hundred fat bucks slain"
is the fact that they were driven with system.

> "Then having dined the drovers went
> To rouse them up again."

Any uncertainty as to the nature of the chase is set aside

by the amount of game that was killed when Earl Percy
" to the quarry went ! "   The hunting began at daylight
on Monday morning—

> " And long before high noon they had
> A hundred fat bucks slain."

Of course such a " bag " could only be made by driving
into some enclosure of an extemporised kind.

This is alluded to merely to show that deer-driving
was common to England and Germany in old days.   A
quiet Sunday succeeded this day of excitement, to be
followed again by fresh festivities and ceremonials.   " All
Gotha was in turmoil to be at the *Liederfest;* and we be-
times went up-stairs after breakfast to see the procession
walk round the orangery—numbers from each town, with
their banners and excellent bands.   But now princes and
princesses without number—numberless"—had flocked to
Gotha to do homage to the Queen, and to welcome once
more their early friend Prince Albert.   At a grand concert
given at Gotha was one interesting item.   A piece was performed called " A Greeting to my Brother."   The words
were composed by the reigning Duke, and the music by
his brother the Prince.   The National Anthem was sung
in conclusion by a chorus that was supposed to consist of
700 singers; but in reality there were about 1000 voices,
as many of the company, though not enrolled, had procured copies of the music and the words, and joined in
the celebration.   But the genial holiday was to end.   On
Tuesday, 2d September, the Queen and Prince visited
Obershoff, which is one of the Duke's shooting-boxes, and
is grandly situated in one of the gorges of the Thüringer-
wald.   It crowns a sort of abrupt spur, something like

Rheinfels, and on each side are dark woodland dells. It seems almost hopeless to reach it; but the road winds pleasantly and easily enough, just as is the case at Rheinfels, and the summit is attained without much difficulty. Obershoff lies on the highroad between Coburg and Gotha. From here the Royal party paid one more visit to Reinhardtsbrun; and after wandering over the delightful grounds they returned to Coburg, in order to be present at a grand ball given by the Duke to a very large assembly in the theatre. There were a thousand people there, and many crowned heads. Besides the Queen and Prince there were the Queen and Prince of the Belgians, the Prince of Leiningen, Duke Alexander of Würtemberg, the Grand Duke of Mecklenburg-Schwerin, and many other personages of high degree. This was, for the Royal party, the last day at Coburg-Gotha. The homeward route was to commence the next day; and at eight o'clock on the 3d September, the Royal party started for England through Frankfurt and Fulda. The interest of the road, however, was not abated at all; and they were about to be for a time the guests of the Duke of Weimar, and to visit the scenes of Luther's captivity, if so it can be called, at the castle, which once was a residence of an ancestor of Prince Albert, and where the great Reformer was in reality an honoured guest.

CHAPTER XV.

FROM visiting the castle at Gotha, the Royal party returned to Friedrichsthal, and there they found the Grand Duke of Saxe-Weimar and his son the Hereditary Grand Duke, who had arrived from Weimar, and were awaiting them at the Dowager-Duchess's palace, as has been said, and it was agreed that the Queen and Prince should halt on their road homeward at Eisenach. On Wednesday, the 3d September, her Majesty and Prince Albert started on their homeward route; and the 'Life of the Prince Consort' says, "Next morning broke in gloom, sad as the hearts of those who were about to part. 'The breakfast,' writes the Queen, 'with dear grandmamma, Ernest, and Alexandrine, was sad. Dear grandmamma was so grieved at the parting, her dear kind face looked so

AUG ROTHBCHUK

plaintive.'" She took a most affecting farewell of Prince
Albert—a farewell, which, as it happened, was to be
the last. As the Royal party drove along the road—and
a pleasant road it is that leads from Gotha to Eisenach—
they had many English companions in the shape of railway labourers, who were constructing the line of railway
which connects the two towns. This railway runs parallel with the highway for a considerable distance, and at
the time of the visit it was fast approaching completion.
The distance it traverses is nineteen miles. It goes
through the pleasant little town of Frottstedt; and soon
after leaving it, the Duke of Saxe-Weimar's territories
commence. In Gotha, the toll-gates, and post-houses,
and all public buildings are marked by green and white
stripes, and as soon as the frontier is passed these give
way to orange and black. At the frontier the Queen
and Prince were met by the Grand Duke, and were
conducted to the palace in the large square of this delightful town. The bridge here shown crosses the Hörsel;
and the quaint combination of cattle in the stream, and
large public buildings beyond, was very curious and picturesque. Eisenach is so full of interest, and it further-
more is so intimately connected with the house of Coburg
that it would require a separate notice, at greater length
than could be afforded here. The great castle that looks
over the town was the abode of Prince Albert's ancestors,
and here, by their sheltering care, the great Reformer
was able to finish his work, and strike off the shackles
of religious freedom from Europe. It is quite an error to
suppose that Charles V. rendered any assistance to the
cause. He gave, as we know, a safe-conduct to Luther

when he went to Worms, and he respected it as a matter
of course; but his sympathies were against Luther, and
we are entirely indebted to the house of Coburg for the
part which Luther was enabled to play in the great
question of the time.   His residence, and all the circumstances connected with his friendly incarceration by the
Saxon Elector at Wartburg are romantic to a degree; for,
while all Europe was in a ferment, Luther, in an almost
inaccessible eyrie, was advised of the doings of the outward
world, and of the many multitudes who firmly believed
that he was dead.   The State of Weimar is within the
Thuringian forest, if in this we include the spurs that
shoot out to the east and west.   It is considerably larger
than Coburg-Gotha, indeed it is nearly twice as large,
and its surface presents many of the same appearances.
There are the dense pine-forests, and hills, and valleys
that characterise Gotha, and it is equally true that there
are pleasant valleys in which the husbandman can look
forward with some assurance of certainty to gathering
in his crops; but the weather, as a rule, is cold in this
part, and the snow lies long.   Game abounds in the
woods, and as many as 20,000 hares and 1400 deer
have been killed in the ducal woods in a single
season, besides wild boars, and literally thousands of
pheasants.   The rivers are very picturesque, and would
afford unlimited subjects for the pencils of Cox or
Harding.   The Werra, the Saale, and the Ilmenau are
the principal streams, but Eisenach is situated on the
Hörsel.

Sebastian Bach was a native of this place, and his
memory is greatly cherished here.   Eisenach was also,

like Gotha, quite familiar to Prince Albert, and of course the heads of the ducal houses had been familiar with each other for generations.

The market-place, which is here shown, is very characteristic of those which are found in and around Coburg-Gotha in the larger towns. The church has no architectural features, and indeed pretends to none; but at the same time there is a "presence" about it, if one may use the word, which is extremely picturesque. When the Queen and Prince visited the city, there was an immense concourse to see them,—the Queen, of course, as the Queen of England, and Prince Albert, because his face was very familiar to almost every one who was ten years of age. The market-square was filled, and the town had been *en gala* for the whole day. The Royal party stayed at the palace for more than an hour and had luncheon, and then they proceeded on their route to the castle of Wartburg, which is situated even as grandly as that of Coburg. In the market-square there is a noble fountain, with a group on the top that looks very like George and the Dragon, and from a centre column the water-pipes emerge. There is a stone block on the lower side of the fountain, carved with quatre-foils, and opposite to this is a long narrow wooden trough, which is balanced so as to fall towards the fountain; but when the narrow trough is pulled down by any one outside the fountain, the further end meets a pipe that supplies the basin, and diverts the stream of water, which is deliciously clear and pellucid, to the thirsty wayfarer. Saxe-Weimar is about the size of Shropshire, or nearly twice as large as Coburg-Gotha, and it has always been a State where the reigning monarchs have commanded respect.

After luncheon, the Royal party went to the great fortress of Wartburg, and the town was literally filled from all directions—indeed the inhabitants speak of the rejoicings even yet. The travellers walked through the principal apartments and the rooms that have been immortalised by Luther. All was of course familiar to the Prince, and of the greatest interest to the Queen. They did not return to Eisenach, but went by a cross-road towards Fulda. This road lay toward Marksuhl, which is embedded in lofty pine-trees, and resembles in appearance some of the towns in the Highlands of Scotland, nestling in dark olive-green backgrounds. Soon after this it is evident that we are in a Catholic country. The Bavarian frontier is reached, and then crosses and chapels appear on each side of the road, and crown the crests of the hills. When the Royal travellers reached Fulda they were welcomed by the Grand Duke of Hesse-Cassel, and were received at the Electoral Hotel. The whole of the troops were turned out, and the town was brilliantly illuminated as the Queen and Prince drove through. Dinner was served immediately on their arrival. Fulda is one of the oldest towns in Germany, though now it is modernised beyond recognition. The old Prince Bishop's palace is apparently not much more than a century old, and it is of enormous dimensions; courtyard follows courtyard in endless succession, but these are now grown over with grass, and cottagers dry their clothes in the deserted squares. The cathedral and the church of St Michael were duly visited. The former

contains the tomb of St Boniface, and the latter has a crypt that, it is very generally believed, among those who are well able to judge, dates back to the ninth century.

The Duchy of Saxe-Weimar, which the Royal party left before they arrived at Fulda, should hardly be dismissed without some further notice. It is certainly one of the most representative of all the German Duchies.

After leaving Weimar, the change in the occupation of the inhabitants is very apparent. Agriculture is quite as prosperous as in the Thuringian States, but the holdings are somewhat larger. We see, also, long rows of vines; and at the time when the Royal visitors passed, many of the bunches of red grapes had been cut too soon to ripen, though here, as elsewhere, they desire the fruit to be very well matured for the vintage. The change of scenery also, as we proceed to Frankfurt, is very marked. The Thuringian land is seen behind us in great dark-peaked ranges, and the hills of Rhineland begin to reappear.

We leave the thickets and woods of the wild boar and stag, and the thousands of acres that are preserved for the ducal sportsman and his friends; but before leaving Saxe-Weimar we may revert to the capital of the well-regulated State as it was in the early years of Prince Albert.

Saxe-Weimar is cut in two by his father's Duchy of Gotha. Eisenach lay in the western, and Weimar lay in the eastern division of the State, and both of them were nearly equally distant from Gotha. The following remarks were written by an English gentleman who visited the Duchess when Prince Albert was in his fifth year; and these, which may be depended upon for correctness, will illustrate the greatness of the people by whom at that age the Prince was surrounded. We see in the Court of Saxe-Weimar the first-fruits of the national revival to which Germany was stirred by such heroic souls as Arndt, and Steffens, and Immermann.

These, when all was despair and gloom in their country, and the insolent oppression of Napoleon had crushed down nearly all that was of good report, never lost heart, and never tired in trying to rouse their countrymen to gain back their freedom. Here is a picture of the Ducal Court of Saxe-Weimar as it appeared to perfectly unprejudiced eyes fifty-five years ago. Weimar was then the capital of a State which at the time numbered within its limits only about 200,000 souls. (Now it is more than 300,000.) This town is a Royal residence. The inhabitants call it, and justly call it, the Athens of Germany, though it is hardly more than a large village, and as such they prefer to consider it. There was not a large house in the whole town, but it was, as indeed it is now, a quiet, old-fashioned, academic-looking place—a happy hunting-ground for the artist and lover of the picturesque. The palace and the place where Parliament assembled were the only public buildings, and in three minutes any one could be completely in the country; and though the railway has completely changed this, rural delights are not far to seek in the present day. The palace was unfinished, for, as the writer said, the Grand Duke was too careful of the money of his subjects to involve them in anything but necessary expenses, and his great desire was to let the treasury recover from the misery and exhaustion which commenced with the battle of Jena, and only ended at Leipzig. He had enough of the building completed to accommodate himself and Court, and the establishment of his eldest son. Close by Weimar is the river Ilm, which joins the Saale, and empties its little stream hundreds of miles away into the North Sea, through the river Elbe. It is not a very picturesque or pellucid stream, and Schiller has said of it right well—

> "Though poor my banks, my stream has borne along
> On its still waters many a deathless song."

But since the above remarks were inspired a great improvement has taken place on the shores, and woods that had just been planted along the river have grown up into respectable proportions.

The simplicity of the daily life at Weimar was very singular in 1825. "It is not in Weimar that the gaiety, or the loud and loose pleasures of a capital are to be sought; there are too few idle people, and too little wealth, for frivolous dissipation." The little place had neither police nor spies, but everything, as it were, was under the notice of the Court; and the lofty tone of the Grand Duke, in all his relations of life, was an abundant safeguard and example. The nobility were sufficiently numerous, but they were men of moderate means, and "many of them would find it difficult to play their part, frugal and regular as it was, were they not engaged in the service of the Government in some form or other,—as ministers, councillors, judges, or chamberlains. There is not much dissoluteness to be feared when it is necessary to climb the outside stair to the routs of a minister, and a lord of the bedchamber gives, in a third floor, parties which are honoured even with the presence of princes. The man of pleasure would find Weimar dull." In those days the forenoon was devoted entirely to business of some kind, and even the few, the very few, who had no occupation, did not show themselves till the approach of a very early dinner-hour seemed to justify a walk in the Belvidere. At six o'clock nearly all the population find their way to the theatre, and they were little more than a large family gathering, except that, of course, the ducal party had a separate box. It is really delightful to learn that the performance was over by nine; and at ten o'clock, though there were no police regulations, the streets were quiet and empty. There was less parade and pomp at the Court parties of Saxe-Weimar than was to be met with in a private nobleman's house in London, and only the best bred and the best informed society was to be found there. The Grand Duke Charles Augustus was deservedly the most popular prince in Europe, and right well he deserved the praise that was lavished upon him by his people.

The visitor who wrote this account of Weimar spoke of the way in which English people were accustomed to wonder at the smallness of the German princes, and to make almost disparaging remarks about them, when compared even with an English squire of broad acres and untrammelled estates; but he says that Englishmen little understand the amount of happiness which a prince, even if he is not among the wealthy, can diffuse. The mere pride of sovereignty, which is often most prominent in the smaller realms, was quite unknown to Charles Augustus during his long and his more than eventful reign; and though he was said to be the most affable man in his dominions, this affability was not the result of lofty condescension, but of real goodness of heart. Much of his reign had fallen in evil times. He saw his principality overrun by greater devastations than it had ever known since the Thirty Years' War; but whatever was the vicissitude, or indeed whatever was the indignity inflicted by an arrogant conqueror, he never lost the respect of himself or his subjects, or even of Napoleon.

During the whole of his long reign, the conscientious administration of public money, the great anxiety for the impartial deliverance of justice, and the kindly ear that was always open to individual misfortune of any kind, never tired. Then his efforts to elevate the political character of his people, and to give them a representative government, are too often forgotten; and, to quote once more the words of an English visitor to his country, who, more than half a century since, had a good opportunity of judging, "ought to make him rank among the most respectable princes, in the eyes of foreigners, as far as respectability is to be measured by personal merit, and not by square miles of territory, or millions of revenue." To this I could heartily say Amen! if, instead of "respectability," "greatness" was the word used to express the efforts of the Duke of Weimar to advance his subjects in honour. His efforts, Mr Russell adds, were justly regarded by his subjects as having raised them to an eminence from which their geographical position and their political importance would hardly at first seem to have entitled them. He was educated by Wieland; he grew up for the arts just as the literature of Germany was beginning to triumph over the obstacles which the indifference of the people and the naturalisation of the French literature had thrown in its way. "He drew to his Court the most distinguished among the rising geniuses of the country; he loved their arts, he could estimate their talents, and he lived among them as friends. In the middle of the last century Germany could scarcely boast of possessing a national literature. Her very language, reckoned unfit for the higher productions of genius, was banished from all cultivated society and elegant literature. At the beginning of the present century there were few departments in which the Germans could not vie with her most polished neighbours. It was Weimar who took the lead in working out this great change. To say nothing of the lesser worthies, Wieland and Schiller, Goethe and Herder, are names which have gained immortality for themselves, and founded the reputation of their country among foreigners. While they were still all alive and celebrated in Weimar, the Court was a revival of that of Ferrara under Alphonso; and here too, as there, a princely lady was the centre round which the lights of literature revolved.

"The Duchess Amelia, the mother of the present Grand Duke, found herself a widow almost at the opening of her youth. She devoted herself to the education of her two infant sons. She had sufficient taste and strength of mind to throw off the prejudices which were weighing down the native genius of the country." Wieland was intrusted with the care and education of her son, who early imbibed an attachment for genius, and the delights that surround it. If he could not make his State important in its political relations, he could at any rate make it the abode of German genius. His revenues were small, but he took care that such men as Schiller should have ample leisure. "Schiller could not have endured the caprices of Frederick for a day," and Goethe would have pined away at the Court of an Emperor who publicly said in a seminary, "I want no learned men; I need no learned men." The fostering care was given just at the hour of need. There was a widespread belief that France contained the genius of Europe, and her vanity fostered this belief. "It is difficult to conceive," the same acute observer adds, "that a monarch like Frederick, who possessed some literary talent himself, and affected a devoted attachment to literary excellence, should have adopted so mistaken an opinion of a country which he must have known so much better than his Gallic retinue. Yet he had taken this view in its most prejudiced form. Instead of cherishing the German genius that was beginning to develop itself, he amused himself with railing at the language, and laughing at the 'erudite obscurity' of its professors, and excluded from his library everything that was not French, except the reports of the universities and the muster-roll of the armies."

Napoleon conferred the Cross of the Legion of Honour upon Schiller and Wieland, which was a significant acknowledgment of the exalted place they held in public esteem all over Europe, for he certainly had never read a single line that either of them ever wrote. At some length the account of Weimar has been dwelt upon, because it encircles the Prince's early home of Gotha. The reigning families were on the most cordial of all terms, and the journey from Gotha to Weimar through Erfurth is only a little longer than to Eisenach, and must cut through Gotha.

Frankfurt was reached by the Queen and Prince Albert at half-past three in the afternoon, after a journey from Fulda which occupied about eight hours. Not within the memory of any one living had the city presented so gay an appearance. The house of Coburg was well remembered here. The Prince and his family had, in fact, to pass through Frankfurt nearly every time they went to Brussels or to any part in the west. The Hotel d'Angleterre was selected for the reception of the travellers, and the suite of rooms was very complete and elegant. M. Gouvernon, the proprietor of the hotel, received them. The Englishmen who joined in the reception were few,—Mr Fox Strangeways, the Earl of Westmoreland, Colonel Wylde, and Mr Kode the Consul, being the principal ones. Precisely at seven dinner was served, and shortly before, the King of Bavaria and his suite arrived and were received with Royal honours. Frankfurt was certainly in holiday attire, and was doing all it could to welcome the illustrious visitors. Every one was on the alert to see them, but no one caused more interest than Prince Metternich, the veteran statesman. His step was firm and steady, and his eye was bright, and years seemed to rest lightly upon him. He had come over from his estate of Johannisberg to meet the Royal strangers. It has been recorded that at the dinner-table at the Hotel d'Angleterre M. Gouvernon was able to produce some of the finest Johannisberg that was ever known, which he purchased from Prince Metternich at one of the castle sales for almost a fabulous sum.

In the evening there was a brilliant levee, and the two burgomasters of the city were presented, as also Count

Munich, the Austrian envoy and minister to the Diet. Frankfurt is strangely altered from what it was when the Prince used to pass through it on his way to Bonn. It is now almost a city of palaces, and the hotels are among the finest in Europe, not even excepting those of Paris. The Hotel d'Angleterre, though still a very fine first-class hotel, has been eclipsed since the Royal visit by larger and more imposing ones. Though Frankfurt wears now a modern appearance, and the buildings, tall, bright, and cheerful, rise up in all directions, it was even in the present century almost as antique-looking as Munich or Nuremberg. The Domkirche, or cathedral, is a very ancient building, and the original Golden Bull is preserved here. Frankfurt fairs still exist, but they are the tamest of institutions if compared with those which it is quite possible the Prince may have witnessed in his early years. These were indeed festivals such as would startle quiet Germans out of all propriety; but an exceeding graphic and quaint account has come to hand, which was written by an eyewitness within the lifetime of Prince Albert. It is too long, and has been slightly condensed to admit of insertion.

The fairs of Frankfurt are still held, but steamboats and railways have robbed them of much of their ancient glory, and shorn them of nearly all their picturesqueness. It was well worth any one's while, if staying at Darmstadt, or any of the courtly capitals of the surrounding Duchies, to visit Frankfurt at the Michaelmas fair, where he would have seen such a sight as perhaps all the world could not equal. For miles before the great emporium was reached were trains of waggons, and pack-horses, and vans, driven by people of every nationality of Europe, and perhaps some of Asia. The improvements and new buildings which meet us everywhere now, had not been commenced, and the streets of the city were narrow and sombre, deeply sunk between high-gabled houses. The drawing of Luther's house, which appears in the chapter on Martin Luther, conveys a good idea of Frankfurt of fifty years ago; and in the Jews' quarter there are similar ones yet, though many of them are doomed. If the visitor entered Frankfurt from the bridge over the Main, he was soon in the middle of hopeless confusion. The narrow streets were altogether too small for the commerce of the occasion; and on every available spot where some sort of refuge could be found from horses' hoofs or chariot-wheels, booths were pitched, and bargaining was carried on in every known language. The outside walls of the shops, and in many cases, of the first floors, were covered with gaudy pieces of cloth, on which were written the names of merchants, and the nature of the wares they had to sell. These superscriptions were in French, Italian, German, Russian, and sometimes, though not often, in English. There were many signs in Hebrew; but as that is a language not commonly understood by the outer world, they were translated into other tongues, as the Israelites found it more to their advantage to try and sell with the stranger than with each other.

The squares, of course, were soon filled, and the thoroughfares followed their example, until even the lanes and alleys contained their share of merchandise. Under gaudy booths were displayed the most motley and incongruous wares, and these were in the most motley juxtaposition. There were wooden platters and clogs, butter-moulds and dairy utensils; Manchester goods and Lyons silks, and every variety of glass-ware from Bohemia; pipe-heads from Vienna, and all kinds of musical instruments; saddlery in all its branches; of course toys, and even surgical and mathematical instruments, round which strange groups were bargaining. In the words of a witness of one of the assemblages of old—" Parthians, Medes, and Elamites were speaking in their own tongue." He further says that some Lancashire spinners tried ventures, but any clerk they could find to place in charge of the consignment, was rather too much like the Vicar of Wakefield's son at the fair. If any one could have returned with a good account of the consignment to his master, he would have been too valuable a man in a Manchester counting-house to have been spared. When a traveller arrived at Frankfurt during the fair he had to be content with a cellar or a garret, as all hotel accommodation had long ago been secured; but if he were content with this, he saw wonderful sights. For weeks the cooks and butlers had placed their commissariat on a war footing; and Frankfurt was provisioned in a manner that would have enabled a beleaguered city to hold out during the longest siege. The large hall reserved in general for civic feasts or civic balls was thrown open for the daily *table d'hôte*. A hundred and fifty people managed to live in a single hotel, and that, of course, one of the quaint old kind that bears no possible resemblance to the magnificent ones that we find on the Ziel or round the Parade Platz; and the evenings were as gay as the day with balls, and orchestras, and suppers; for wives and daughters used to insist very commonly on accompanying the merchants to the fair. A witty Englishman who visited the city in 1820 has left an amusing account of the Jew dealer of that period: "They inhabit," he says, "chiefly a particular quarter of the town, which, though no longer walled in as it once was to separate them from the rest of the community, repels the Christian intruder at every step with its uncleanness. In driving their traffic they are as importunate as Italian beggars. Lying in wait in his dark little shop or tattered booth, or if these be buried in some sickening alley, prowling at the corner where it joins some more frequented street, the Jew darts out on every passenger of promise. He seems to possess a particular talent for discovering, even in the Babel of Frankfurt, the country of the person he is addressing, and seldom fails to hit the right language. Unless thrown off at once, he sticks to you through half a street, whispering the praises of his goods, mingled with your own; for, curving the spare insignificant body into obsequiousness, and throwing into the twinkling grey eye as much condescension as its keenly expressed love of gain will admit, he conducts the whole negotiation as if he were sacrificing himself to do you a favour of which no one must know. When all the usual recommendations of his bargains fail, he usually puts on the climax,—'On my soul and conscience, sir, they are genuine smuggled goods.'" This same observer remarks that the Jew of Frankfurt seemed to be almost a more complete separatist from the world than many of his brethren, and kept himself distinct, not only in his creed and appearance, but in

his way of doing business ; and even where one of his fraternity
has become wealthy, and adopted Gentile ways, and calls in the

Rheinstein.

services of a
barber, or even
becomes a customer
to the dealer in West-
phalia hams, he is looked
upon as a shocking backslider.

Next morning the journey
was made by railroad from
Frankfurt to Biberich, from
which a Rhine steamer took
the royal travellers down to
Bingen, where they embarked in her Majesty's yacht Fairy,

which carried them as far as Deutz, opposite Cologne. "Strange to say," writes the Queen, "the Rhine, fine as it is, has lost its charm for us all. First of all, the excitement of novelty was over, and then we were spoiled by the Thuringian forest. Stolzenfels looked very well, and so did Ehrenbreitstein, and those fine *Sieben Gebirge;* but after passing Bonn we went down below, and Albert read to me." Doubtless, if the Castle of Rheinfels had been restored, it would have been visited; but its restoration has taken place subsequently, and it has received one of our own Royal family since. As it at present stands, there is perhaps hardly a residence in Europe that equals it for picturesque beauty. It is not very large, but exceedingly commodious. The rooms are shadowed with a dim religious light of stained glass, and furnished with antique chairs and tables and cabinets. All is quaint and old, and when a window is open, the Rhine at a great depth below is winding along through castles and vineyards. A visit was made on the homeward route to Wiesbaden and Biberich, the chateau of the Duke of Nassau. The morning was magnificent, and the fine forest scenery and ancient castle and lichen-covered ruins all showed to great perfection. St Goar, which is one of the most attractive towns on all the Rhine, shone out in beauty as it was passed. The glorious skies were in singular contrast to the leaden clouds that cast a gloom over the ascent of the river. Luncheon was served under an awning on deck by her Majesty's command, that no part of the scenery might be lost. Cologne was reached amidst rejoicings similar to those which before had welcomed the Royal party. Rail was now taken to Antwerp. At Langerwehe, about forty miles from Cologne, a short stoppage was made. Antwerp was reached about half-past five on Saturday afternoon: at nine the Royal yacht was under way; and the visit to Prince Albert's early homes was over.

St Goar.

CHAPTER XVI.

THE COBURGS AND THE CHASE—SHOOTING-BOXES OF THE DUKE'S
FAMILY—ANECDOTE OF PRINCE ALBERT AND HIS BROTHER WHEN
IN EARLY LIFE—GAME COMMONLY FOUND IN THURINGIAN WOODS,
WINGED AND "FOUR-FOOTED," CAPERCAILZIE, ETC.—WILD-BOAR
PRESERVES AT ROSENAU—PRINCE ALBERT'S RULES AND HABITS
IN SHOOTING.

THE Saxon race has always been noted for its love of
sport, and for its exceeding keenness in following the
chase.   Old Saxon manuscripts represent huntsmen, and
hawkers, and fowlers of every kind, besides sportsmen with
bows and spears who followed larger game.   The house
of Coburg is no exception to the general rule; and from
Duke Casimir, and even for long before him, the scions
of the house have been sportsmen.   Of course the deer-
chase at Reinhardtsbrun was only an excrescence, if one
may so say, and it was organised probably to concentrate
the excitement of the chase into the limited period that
was at the disposal of the guests.   The bands and surroundings had also, perhaps, a little more prominence than
would have been the case under ordinary circumstances,
and indeed the shooters themselves seem to have entered
into the work with but half a will.   The Coburgs, however, are real thorough sportsmen, and can hold their

own anywhere. There must be about seven shooting-boxes in Coburg-Gotha, exclusive of palatial residences, and all these are substantial mansions, not, of course, large or extravagant, but comfortable, and always splendidly situated. It may excite a little surprise that so many should be required; but it must be remembered that Thuringen is a land of high mountains and steep ravines, and only roads along the valley are possible. The snow comes down with great severity, and these roads are often blocked up. It may not, indeed, fall with such terrible weight as it does in Canada, but it is severe enough, and sometimes it is necessary in winter to find a shelter nearer than the home that had been left in the morning. But the shooting-boxes had other uses. The Thuringian forest was free at all times for the reigning house to shoot over; and as game might be plentiful in one place and not in another, the shooting-boxes were erected for a party to spend a few days in, and they were abundantly convenient for guests.

An incident connected with Prince Albert and his elder brother is spoken of yet in the place where it occurred. There is a small hamlet called Limbach in the middle of the Thuringian forest. It is finely situated, and possesses a humble country inn. The Princes were on a ranging excursion for shooting, and were overtaken by the dark. The weather was cold, and they resolved to spend the evening at the little inn. Such refreshment as was possible was provided, and as the day had been an arduous one, they retired early to rest. Ernest called his dogs to follow him up-stairs; but the landlady objected strongly to this arrangement, and said that her rooms were for Christians and not for sporting dogs, suggesting also a stable outside as a more appropriate place for them to sleep in.   Now, about Limbach many of the byres and stables are more suited to furnish studies for Morland than to serve as resting-places for any but the most hardy animals.   The village is almost on the top of a hill, and stands 1000 feet higher than the castle at Coburg. The ground gradually rises, indeed, all the way from Coburg, which is about twenty miles distant.   The elder Prince was inflexible; but the landlady stood up for her rights like a sturdy Saxon, and said the rooms were hers; and she was finally reminded by Ernest to remember who he was.   But Prince Albert completely reversed the argument by quietly saying to his elder brother, " I think you are forgetting that yourself."   A compromise was at once effected, and the tired dogs slept quietly by the kitchen-fire.   The old lady was exceedingly proud of the tale: if she is alive now, which is quite possible, she must be very advanced in years.

The conditions under which game are kept together in the British Isles and in a European State are different; for on the continent of Europe, which is so vast, animals and all kinds of birds have a much better chance of preserving their species than they have in Great Britain.   There are, for example, parts of Scotland and Wales, and certainly of Ireland, where wolves might even yet find a resting-place; but the hand of every man has been against them for so long, that it is more than a century since the last one, as far as we have any record, was killed.   The islands are so sea-surrounded that wild animals have a limited area, and unless they are in some way protected they become extinct. The more formidable ones like the wolf have long ceased to be, and the badger, the polecat, and the otter must soon follow in their wake. But in the Thuringian forests the case is widely different. Their roamings are not cut off by water, and the birds and animals can range without let or hindrance from the furthest extremity of China to Paris. This circumstance will account for continuance of species which have long disappeared from our island. The capercailzie again, the king of the grouse tribe, was formerly common in Great Britain, but its peculiar habits and its great size made it an easy prey, and it disappeared from the scene about the same period as the wolf. It has indeed been introduced into Scotland once more by wealthy proprietors, but this is recently; and it is very satisfactory to be able to add that it has taken to its new, or perhaps its old, quarters very kindly. This bird is the pride of the Thuringian forests, and though it is easily shot, it is always looked upon as a prize. It is often shot sitting in trees, even by sportsmen; and much care is required to approach one so as not to be heard. The keepers are generally to be depended on thoroughly, and if we follow them they are sure to stalk one, if there is one about. Capercailzie delight in the depths of the forest, and they will often establish themselves in such fastnesses that the stillness which generally reigns in these places is broken by the treading on dry twigs, and so notice of the approach of an intruder is given. The German keepers, however, are very dexterous in avoiding this, and step firmly on the debris to prevent sound. Some of them are very knowing at finding out the haunts of the capercailzie, and can imitate the call so perfectly as to disarm suspicion of an intruder. Indeed there are times when the cocks are so truculent that, if a call is imitated, the male bird will come out to give battle; cases are recorded of their even making some sort of attack upon a human trespasser. I do not know how far this is true, though it is related by excellent authorities, but it is certain that bustards have been known to attack pedestrians even in England. An English gentleman who obtained permission to shoot in the Thuringian forests, describes the way in which he stalked a capercailzie, with the aid of a very able gamekeeper, and the bird fell from a pine-tree like a black mass into a deep ravine on the edge of which the tree was growing. In the Thuringian forests, and, indeed, in all places where capercailzie are numerous, they will pack, at the beginning of winter, in droves of fifty or sixty, and then they are very difficult to approach. It is said that they can be easily domesticated, and if there are a few of their favourite pine-trees on the farm, they will build in them and rear their young. They lay some eight or nine eggs, and are good sitters. For such large birds their flight is not heavy, nor is it noisy, like that of a pheasant. These birds have again become tolerably abundant in Scotland, owing to the efforts of the Earl of Fife, and the Marquis of Breadalbane, and the Duke of Athole. We may see capercailzie in the English markets at a moderate price, but these birds are probably sent by steamer from Norway, where they abound. From Rosenau to many of the depths of the Thuringian forest where capercailzie are found is not a long journey; but the probability is that, when shooting them, the sports-

man went somewhat further from the towns towards
Limbach.

In winter, capercailzie leave the heights, and descend to
more congenial quarters on the plains. There are said to
be some birds in Africa that resemble the European
species, but the latter are almost *sui generis.* The stork
is also found in the Thuringian forests, and is true to
his times of migration, just as all of the species are in
every part of the globe; nor are they only true to their
"appointed time in the heavens," but they are true to
their mates, and many pages have been filled with accounts of their devotion to each other. In this part of
the country they live very much as herons do; but in
America they light on fields of Indian corn, and literally
devour them when in a succulent state. The consequence
is that, in the latter instance, the birds, though they seem
to differ but little in kind, are very excellent for the
table. The stork, however, is scarcely the bird that
sportsmen would follow in Thuringian covers when
there are others of so much greater merit. Quails
sometimes appear in considerable numbers, though these
have of recent years decreased; still, the immense flights
that have been so often noticed farther east, sometimes
send stray flocks into Thuringian forests, and these afford
the gunners excellent sport. Wild ducks also are found
along the river-courses, and they breed in some of the
swampy parts; but they are not very numerous, except
in some of the most inaccessible parts of the marshes.
Sometimes at the beginning of winter, if there has
been a flood in the rivers, immense numbers settle on
them as they pass from the northern lakes and marshes

to more congenial quarters further south; and indeed, all through the winter, wherever there is an unfrozen rapid, an early visitor may startle a teal or widgeon from the rivers of Saxony. Nearly the same species of ducks are found in these parts of Germany that we meet with in England or Scotland, excepting, of course, sea-ducks, which are never met with, such as scoters and mergansers. Geese also, and sometimes swans, come from the north and rest for a little in their southern migrations. Snipe —both jack-snipe and common snipe—are quite common, and it is said that double snipe have been met with. Woodcock are far from uncommon, and they breed here; but towards the end of the year they arrive in considerable numbers from the north, and rest for a time in the congenial wilds of Thuringia. As they fly south, other flocks come from the north, which, after recruiting, go on to milder lands. There is one singular circumstance connected with these migrations which, strangely enough, pertains to the American woodcock, a bird which, though it is said to differ from the English species, certainly differs no more than the American salmon or wild duck differs from the English salmon or wild duck. After the American woodcock has settled and become in good condition, another change comes over it, and it disappears, only to reappear, however, in the same place later on, and not nearly in such good condition.

But the most interesting of all the game that is found here is the wild boar. About two miles from Rosenau the Duke of Coburg has a Thiergarten or preserve for wild boars. The Duke of Westminster procured, through the Prince of Wales, some fifteen wild boars, and made a strong stockade for them, enclosing a little park of about seventeen or eighteen acres. Some brushwood was left growing in it, and he had dens made for them, but they did not seem to like the look of these, and avoided them; they were too shapely-looking for their tastes. Three of these dens they tore down, and with the materials constructed others. They have taken to their captivity, however, very kindly, and have bred in the enclosure. These animals are of very great size and prodigious strength. They weigh several hundred pounds, and the white tusks look most powerful weapons of offence. Inside the enclosure at Eaton Park the ground is torn up in places like as if a subsoil plough had been at work for a rut of twenty feet, reminding one of—"The wild boar out of the wood doth root it up, and the wild beasts of the field devour it." This Thiergarten at Rosenau always had a weird interest, it is said, for Prince Albert and his brother; but it might surprise a stranger to find that such powerful animals are so wild and fearful of man, for a man would be annihilated before one if it turned upon him. No visitor to Coburg should omit making a visit to the celebrated Thiergarten. There is not any difficulty in obtaining permission; indeed, what strikes a visitor to these parts is the facility with which access is obtained to almost anywhere; and one cause is, that the exceedingly well-behaved people never abuse their privileges. I did, indeed, see one or two names cut at Rosenau, and those Saxon ones too; but I blush to add they were Anglo-Saxon. A keeper, especially for some small fee, will willingly show this curious place to any stranger. It is enclosed like a deer-park, but it has ample limits, and the country is left, of course, in its wild state. Were they not so circumscribed, the crops in the neighbourhood would show but a poor return. Inside this enclosure are small pens for feeding; and here the keepers, at regular hours, scatter potatoes, and heads of grain of different kinds, and roots. The wild boar is much cleaner in his habits than the domestic one. I noticed that turnips were often broken and the best parts eaten; but the enclosures at Eaton and Rosenau prove a perfect paradise for rabbits and hares, who can demolish what the wild boars have left without much fear from the *chasseur*. The visitor is concealed in a little hut, from which the herd can be observed as it approaches the enclosure, but he is cautioned not even to cough if he wishes to see them. These animals are very regular in their habits of feeding, and they know well the time when they are likely to find their rations. At first a few young porkers, who know nothing of a rifle, put in an appearance, and without much fear commence their attacks upon the roots and grain; very soon some larger ones, with sooty coats, and little uncanny eyes, and huge ivory tusks, appear on the threshold of the enclosure. Here they stop, and with pricked ears and uplifted snout they scent the air to find if danger lurks in the thicket, and then they retire; but affectionate recollections of potatoes and Swedes and grain bring them back again to the entrance, till at last they take courage, if all is still. The scene is very amusing, and, if everything is quiet, the great tusker enters at last.

> " Ter limen tetigi, ter sum revocatus, et ipse
> Indulgens animo pes mihi tardus erat."

This preserve is only one of many that belong to the Duke of Coburg. There are about 190 head kept in it, and when one is required for the table, it is shot in one of the inner enclosures. It had been my hope to have recorded an opinion about the merits of the wild boar as an adjunct to the table, but no such opportunity occurred all the while I was in Thuringia. It is said, however, to differ much from the domesticated animal, and to be much more delicate.

Thuringia, therefore, as will be seen, is a country abounding in game,—and game, too, of a more diversified character than is found on English manors,—so that, as the author of the 'Life of the Prince Consort' has truly said, "it was natural that the Prince should be taught to take his part in shooting expeditions." In October the water-courses abound in some parts with snipe, and the covers not only with partridges and other of our best game-birds, but even more worthy quarry are not far to seek. Besides these, the wild boar, the deer, and the wolf, as the year draws towards its close, are to be met with by the adventurous sportsman. Prince Albert's father and his brothers, we are told, were much more enthusiastic in their pursuit of the chase than he was, though it is said that they were not more accurate shots. His system and his rule was to use this mode of enjoyment only as a diversion and as a means to health, and beyond this, he said, he could not understand why it should be followed. He used to wonder why people in England should devote so much time to it, almost to the exclusion, during the shooting season, of other pursuits; and I have it from head-keepers of some of the largest estates in England that his short-hour system has been adopted to an extent that could not have been credited in the earlier part of the present century, when it was common to start at nine or ten in the morning, to work hard till lunch, and then to commence again and shoot until the sun disappeared under the long grey bank of western clouds : and in reading this paragraph in the delightful memoirs which Sir Theodore Martin has compiled, I was reminded of a sentence in a quaint old angling book written by Barker, who lived shortly after Walton, though he was not equal in style to that incomparable master of the English language.   After giving many recipes for making pastes, and telling the learner where to get baits, and how to use them when he has got them, and supplying him with maxims of more or less value, he concludes by saying that " the wit of man is given him for higher purposes than to match them against foolish fishes ; and I can hardly say he spends his time well who uses angling for other than his amusement."   Of course in shooting, as in fishing, we are brought into contact with Nature in her most beautiful forms, and in the Thuringian valleys there are many brooks where trout and grayling of the finest kinds are caught.   If we wander up a stream with a fly-rod, we are attracted to the windings of the stream,—the network shadows that flicker on the gravel in the shallows, and the dark-coloured pools into which they flow.   The very colour of the pools is interesting—sometimes inky, sometimes brown, and sometimes olive ; but unless attention is directed to them by an artificial fly, one is apt to miss half their beauties. Then, as for the picturesqueness of shooting, there is quite as much of it, though perhaps in a different form, as we find in following the river-side. In the early season the covers differ little in appearance from summer-time, when the woods are full of bright flowers, and the many-coloured butterflies enliven the roads. These, of course, and many other pleasures, belong to September shooting, even though the sportsman has not considered that his day has come. Later on in the year, when northern regions begin to close up, the birds which have spent their summer months in them feel an inclination towards milder regions; and then along the banks of the Thuringian streams, wherever there is a slight show of marsh, most interesting birds are found, and woodcock, and snipe, and plover of many kinds may be sprung up from the reeds and rushes. Nothing can exceed the beauty of an October morning, when the sun rises in a clear sky and dispels white mists, exposing hedgerows and long spider-webs glittering with diamonds of dew. At a still later period the Thuringian chases begin to close in, and flocks of wilder and larger fowl make it for a short time a temporary resting-place.

The same keeper who told me about the Prince's skill as a shot, and the rules he followed in pursuit of his amusement, gave me a few other interesting details. His father had been head-keeper at Windsor for twenty-one years, and possessed the confidence of the Prince, while he himself had filled an office of under-keeper at the same time. The keepers and beaters, he said, always had abundance of fare if they required it during a morning's shooting, but Prince Albert made a rule of never touching anything in any form; and when the two hours and a half to which he limited his sport were over, he entered the carriage that was in waiting either at the Bagshot or Windsor covers, or wherever else they might be shooting, and drove rapidly back to Windsor. If, in the course of the day, any beater or keeper was wanting in his duty, he was quickly reminded of it. A man might lag behind the line, or get in advance, or use the dogs in an unmannerly fashion ; but whatever was the shortcoming, it was noticed at once by the Prince, and the man was advised of it in clear language. But then, as the keeper said, all was over, and he heard no more of it. Indeed there was one trait in the character of the Prince that used to delight the men, and made them so fond of him that, in the emphatic language of the keeper, "any one of us would have walked into Virginia Water, and stood an hour in November there, to please him." It was the rule for the men to pass in line when the Prince left, and raise their caps. This salute the Prince of course acknowledged by raising his ; and he always looked along the line to see the man he had reminded of his duty, and gave him a pleasant smile and nod. Can we see in this any trace of the genial bringing-up under his father's care at Rosenau, and Gotha, and Callenburg, where the rules were so lax that the good tutor used almost to fear that his pupils were being spoiled by the kindly education of the old Duke of Coburg ?

The days spoken of are the days before breech-loaders, and when it was customary to have a loader or two behind to keep all ready. The Prince generally was attended by four loaders, one of whom he brought from Coburg. The principal one, named Lawley, fell ill, and had to go to Old Windsor in his sickness,—a sickness he does not seem to have survived; but when the Prince came to the shooting-ground, wherever it might be, his first question was, " How is Lawley, has any one heard ? " and of course every one had heard the latest news, for they naturally made it a point to answer the question so as to speak to the master they all were so devoted to. Lawley was supplied with everything he could possibly require. Turner, my informant's father, used to carry an old double-cased silver watch, of the " verge " mechanism, but it kept good time, and often the Prince would say, " What time is it, Turner ? " This watch was secured by a double whipcord, and when the weighty horologe was drawn out he informed his Royal Highness what the hour was. Something about the matter seemed to strike the Prince's humour, and one year at Christmas he presented him with a gold watch, which of course is the pride of the family, and is yet at a cottage in Bedfordshire, where a daughter of the keeper lives. In the second visit to Germany which the Royal travellers made, Prince Albert found game more worthy of his rifle than the deer-drive we have spoken of; and at a boar-hunt in 1860 he killed three large tuskers with his own rifle. One is considered a very good day's sport; and one was all that so skilled a sportsman as Colonel Ponsonby secured on the same day that the Prince killed three.

CHAPTER XVII.

FARMING IN THURINGIA—PRINCE ALBERT AS A FARMER—WINDSOR
AND ISLE OF WIGHT—RECOVERY FROM THE THIRTY YEARS' WAR
— EFFECTS ON AGRICULTURE — SYSTEM IN COBURG AND GOTHA
OF PEASANT PROPRIETORS — BRANCHES OF FRANKFURT BANKS
IN THURINGIA—INTRODUCTION OF SOCKET-PIPE DRAINING BY
PRINCE ALBERT ON DUKE OF COBURG'S FARMS — CONDITION OF
COBURG FARMER — NOT A WINE-GROWING COUNTRY — STEAM-
MACHINERY INTRODUCED BY PRINCE ALBERT — INUNDATIONS
FERTILISE MEADOWS ROUND COBURG—OVERFLOW OF ITZ ABOVE
ROSENAU—EMIGRATION—EFFECTS OF WAR ON AGRICULTURE—
GERMANS, LIKE ENGLISH, LOVERS OF PEACE—COBURG CHURCH
AFTER LAST WAR.

FROM early youth Prince Albert had taken a great
delight in all that in any way pertained to agriculture ; many were the improvements he suggested at Windsor in his farm, and many were the improvements he
introduced into Coburg-Gotha.

Of course when Lutheranism had obtained a strong
footing in Germany there was a deadly strife between
its followers and the adherents to the old religion. The
Pope and the Catholic dignitaries began to fear that the
days of their ascendancy were numbered. During the
enlightened reigns of Ferdinand I. and his son Maximilian II., Protestantism made great progress ; but the

son of the latter, Rudolf II., was a very different man from either his father or grandfather. He had been brought up in the gloomy Spanish Court, and, as the Protestants had feared, he wished to restore the supremacy of the Catholic religion ; but all dissensions culminated in the reign of Ferdinand II. There can be no doubt that the summary treatment of the Catholics by Henry VIII. of England, not only exasperated, but also alarmed their co-religionists of the Continent; for it was only fifteen years after the appearance of Luther at Worms that he dissolved the monasteries and seized their vast possessions, and hanged the abbots who refused to call the " defender of the faith " their lord and master in spiritual affairs. How high animosity ran may be judged by the fact that one wealthy nobleman, Wallenstein, raised an army of 30,000 men at his own cost, and lived avowedly, and by an open arrangement with the German Emperor, upon the plunder of the conquered provinces. The " Protestant union and the Catholic league fought out their differences in what is known as the Thirty Years' War; and though the latter were superior in strength, the former were joined by hordes of free-lances, who cared more for plunder than the general cause they happened to have espoused. The weight of these terrible wars fell heavily on Coburg and the rest of Thuringia. It was then that the grand old fortress of Coburg was besieged by Wallenstein the Catholic leader, and a rusty chain and links are still shown as marking the place where the body of a man, who had recommended a capitulation, was hung out to show Wallenstein the spirit that was actuating the defenders of the castle. From this Thirty Years' War the district of Thuringia has not yet recovered, though more than two centuries have elapsed since it was ended. The peace of Westphalia restored the country to quietness, but not until a half, or as others compute, two-thirds, of the population had perished.

Mr Scott, in his interesting report on the manufactures and trade of Coburg-Gotha which he prepared for Parliament, in some preliminary remarks on this subject says that the records of Thuringia from early times describe the inhabitants as being above those of nearly all other countries in industry, and very successful in agricultural pursuits. The farmers were exceedingly skilful in rearing cattle and sheep, and the finest vegetables were grown that those times knew. The Bauer's homestead and his daily way of life were very superior to those of even the best farmers of the present day, and Freytag has selected the Thuringian country homestead of the sixteenth century as the model of quiet comfort and content. But it must be remembered that Wallenstein was to be paid by the plunder of the countries he overran; the farmers were gathered together to resist the invader, and they left homes and belongings an easy prey behind them. Their successors were too often military adventurers, who had neither character nor industry, and they were for the most part a thoroughly demoralised class. In the words of Mr Scott, " The fearful ravages of the seventeenth century, the traces of which are still observable, swept the whole race of these typical farmers, with their improvements and their gains, from the face of the land.

This war lasted, it may be remarked, for the same period as our own Wars of the Roses. These latter swept away, it is computed, more than half the fighting men of England; but they were nothing at all in intensity and ferocity if compared with the terrible Thirty Years' War. The seaport towns, and the wealthy trading classes, cared little about the civil wars of Henry and Richard; they were waged and carried on by men who were considered to be part of a country estate, and who had to fight as their lords demanded of them; and we do not read of the pillage of towns. Shocking as the slaughter of Barnet was, it was less terrible than the sacking of Magdeburg. Men-at-arms alone fought in the one case, but in the other the inhabitants were sacrificed without reference to age or sex; and indeed it is said that a more shocking or cruel destruction never disgraced Europe than the sacking of Magdeburg by Tilly. This part of the account has been somewhat enlarged upon, because it will more easily be seen why a new state of things came over Germany; and the present system of agriculture and agricultural tenure that prevails in Prince Albert's early homes is of especial interest now in our own country.

It is very generally said that only at the commencement of the present century did the agriculturists of Thuringia begin to recover from the dreadful effects of the Thirty Years' War; houses and substantial farm-buildings had been demolished, and there was not sufficient capital in the country to commence farming again. The condition of the farmer was far from being an enviable one. He was subjected to many vexatious feudal services, not at all unlike those we read of in old times in England; and though it is true that he had a vested interest in his land, and could not be dispossessed so long as these services were performed, yet they ate up a large portion of his earnings, and left him with but little for himself: these went to a privileged class of landed nobility that held almost unlimited power over their dependants. But during the time when Prince Albert wa. at Bonn University a strong reaction towards reform had commenced, and it was encouraged and forwarded by many of the distinguished professors of that university. This reaction resulted in freeing the land from almost the whole of the feudal imposts that had weighed it down for so long. Where the Crown was the proprietor of these dues they were abolished without compensation; but where lords of the soil held them, a more tedious process was necessary, and a time was fixed for the farmer to redeem them. This time was about eighteen years, during which a gradual redemption fund was paid, and then the farmer had his land free. The capitalists of Frankfurt and Hamburg were not slow to see that an opening was offered for safely investing their deposits, and banks were established all over Thuringia; an easy rate of interest was charged, and very generally the amount advanced for redemption was repaid before the stated time. The banks of Coburg and its surroundings were often quoted as a precedent for similar banks in Canada, but in fact the circumstances were widely different. These loans were required by the French Canadians, who, by reckless neglect of every rule of economy in farming, had become impoverished in order to restock their farms, and purchase artificial manures to make up for those they had neglected to economise—and this only meant a little more idleness, and the falling in of the farm to the State. In Coburg and Thuringia, generally, the advance was only to free the land from burdens which were none of their own making—and right loyally it was repaid. These banks remained to receive and invest the savings of their thrifty customers, and, where it might be needed, to advance money for improvements. Thuringia is now, therefore, as we may say, a country of peasant proprietors, and perhaps, in some instances, what we should call in England yeomen. It is sometimes termed Little Germany, forming, as in Mr Scott's language it does, "a watershed between north and south Protestant and Catholic Germany, where we may find, collected in the very centre of German fatherland, specimens of every different variety of its soil and race." Often have I thought that in Coburg we see perfect specimens of what our old Saxon forefathers were; and a stroll along the lanes near Rosenau or Callenburg will remind us vividly of the figures we see in the old Cottonian manuscripts. In these we find figures of the most pronounced Thuringian type. There is an angularity about their movements at times, that is singularly like the attitudes we see in the old Saxon MSS. I remember especially one day when I had wandered among the Thuringian pine-trees, and had lost my way in some newly cut roads, I asked a very respectable middle-aged man if he could direct me to Rosenau, where I wished to go and make a sketch; and it was curious to see the angular movements of his body. He was lost himself, but his destination was the same as mine, and his anxiety to find it for both of us was curious.   When we came to a lane-end he put up his right or left hand in a rectangular position, and the other arm was in some equally geometrical direction.   At first I almost thought he wished to be peculiar; but the visions of Cottonian manuscripts flashed across my recollection, and I saw in a well-bred and intelligent farmer, a perfect specimen of our Saxon forefathers.   Other resemblances were not far to seek; the plough and the harrow and the rake have differed but little for very many centuries, and the yokes of oxen add to the completeness of the parallel.   When speaking of yokes of oxen in this particular chapter, which deals with the tillers of the land, it may not be uninteresting to note that in Coburg and Gotha, and indeed throughout Thuringia, the beef is excellent; and I learned the cause from an old London detective policeman, whom I met as he was taking some discharged prisoners to a home.   He had been a farmer in Northampton, and he said that yoke-oxen were still in use there, and they made the finest of beef.   Open exercise kept them in robust health; and when it became time to slaughter them they were turned out in rich pasture, or stall-fed for only a short time, and then with perfect quiet they fattened up in a very short time.

But to return to the agriculture of Thuringia.   As has been remarked, there is a strong desire on the part of the inhabitants of this region to be landowners, even if only to a small extent; and clothiers, or brewers, or tradesmen of any kind, are always anxious to become proprietors, even though they do not cultivate the soil.   There is no limit to subdivision, and a farm may be cut up into any number of proprietorships. It has been said that another quarter of a century may produce evils in this system that are not now very apparent; but then it must be remembered that for every wrong there is a remedy, and the moment this arrangement becomes an inconvenience it will probably cease, or be gradually superseded by some other condition that will be more for the public good.

It will readily be understood that when the land was freed from all restraints or complications of transfer, and was made almost as commutable as any other species of property, it rose in value enormously, in many cases as much as 60 per cent, and that within a short period. Tenancies are the exception, and not the rule, in Thuringia, the largest number being found in Coburg; but even here, only one tiller of the soil in twenty is a tenant! In the report already borrowed from, is a slight analysis of tenancy and its conditions. There was a farm in the Duchy of Coburg that belonged to Duke Ernest. It consisted of 112 hectares, or about 260 English acres. The greater part of this farm was laid out in fields and meadows, and the rest was in gardens, and ponds, and uncultivated land. The stock on the farm was valued at 1500 guldens (say £128). The lease was for twelve years, and the annual rental was, in English money, about £181. This was payable in three instalments each year. Perhaps for the quality of the land the rental would be considered reasonable enough; but though there was a sufficient living for the farmer, the terms in which it was held were, to say the least, stringent. The tenant, in this instance, had to deposit £180 caution money, and he had also to give a bond on all property of every kind that either he or his wife possessed.   He was bound to return the farm in the best possible condition at the end of his lease, and all the stock he found was to be returned as he got it, or replaced by other stock of equal value; all this, of course, in accordance with the inventory which he signed when he entered upon possession.   Then he undertook every risk of weather, or accident, or fire, and paid the taxes, dues, and rates himself.   But what we in England would consider a greater hardship, he was obliged to forego his own judgment as to the best manner of farming his land, which might vary according to circumstances; and he engaged to follow some prescribed rotation of cropping, or else to substitute any other which the Department might have adopted in its place, for the Duke's domains.   Should he fail for two terms to pay his rent, then, as seems reasonable enough, he lost his interest in the farm; and though it is only the law in England, it does seem a little harsh that he lost also all interest in any improvement, however real or costly; and he engages not to submit his case to any tribunal.   When his lease has expired, all surplus stock or farming material not enumerated in the inventory may be claimed by the Crown or the incoming tenant at the market value of the day; and, of course, any damages the farm or the buildings may have sustained must be made good at his own cost.

The soil of Coburg is generally much lighter than that of Gotha.   There is also a considerable mixture of marl with it, and hence irrigation and drainage are matters of vital importance to the farmer.   Irrigation has been extended to the upper lands, and a complete system of drainage to the lower ones. Formerly, these drains were open water-courses which formed the boundary of the farms and fields; but Prince Albert was so thoroughly impressed with the superiority of the English system of stoneware socket piping, that he had it introduced into his native country with the best possible results. It was tried first upon the property of the Duke of Coburg, and then it was gradually adopted on the larger holdings. In the case of the farm alluded to, the lease could be extended by any tenant who, at his own cost, laid down the drain-pipes. And when a holding was put up at auction, the Crown always gave the preference to any farmer who undertook to effect better drainage. So fully is the Crown Office impressed with the necessity of good drainage, that they offer to advance money for the purpose, either in whole or in part. If they advance the whole, 10 per cent is charged; but if only a part, the rate is 4 per cent.

At the same time that the great reforms were made, and that, as has been said, banks were started to enable the tenants to take advantage of the changes, other reforms of perhaps an equal amount of importance were projected, and facilities were given for farmers to acquire their holdings. Money was easily procured on the security of the farms, and the landed proprietors—who seem, perhaps, more to have resembled the French seigneurs than the English squires—were enabled to dispose of their estates. The consequence was that Thuringia was soon cut up into small holdings; though still, even now, farms of 72 hectares, or 168 English acres, are seldom farmed by the proprietors, but are let to tenants, and the rental is as much as £1 an acre. But even at this high figure they are greatly in demand, and easily bring thirty years' purchase, or sometimes more. In the case of the peasant farmer, as Mr Scott terms him, he says that the smallest amount of land that can be made to support life in any degree approaching to comfort is 12 hectares, or about 29 English acres. Now, in a good season, the amount of produce that can be gathered from this, whatever may be the nature of the crop, will not average more than £180. But he is subject to heavy taxes: there is a land-tax to the State, which averages 3 per cent of the value of the land; there is also a land-tax for the *Gemeinde*, or for the maintenance of roads, schools, poor relief, and other local objects; then there is a 4 per cent income-tax; and it may be said that in such a farm the taxes alone would be nearly £15—perhaps quite that sum; and if we deduct the amount he has to pay for labour, and seeds, and keeping up his stock and plant, we shall find that only about 35s. per week is left for him to spend; and he would welcome with delight any relaxation of the imperial taxes, especially those that concern the vast military expenditure. He and his family work on the land with the greatest assiduity, and the labourer lives in some very humble cottage hard by. He earns about 9s. per week, and pays his master about 25s. per annum for his cottage and cow's grass; and when this is found for him, he does not receive more than about 9d. per day.

There is no doubt that the state of Coburg, if not of all Thuringia, might be profitably studied with reference

J.C.OORK.
A.HENNAKKER
A.Rimmer

to changes which are sometimes proposed nearer home. The peasant proprietor has his farm of thirty, or even twice as many acres, and in the most favourable condition (which is the best one to study the working of the system) it is quite free from debt or mortgage. A family grows up and must be provided for on the death of the proprietor. There may of course be cases, and doubtless there are not a few, where the landowner can fairly say that he has, by saving and otherwise, started all his younger sons in life, and he is able to hand over his property to his eldest son. But these cannot compare in number with those who leave nothing behind them except their lands, which have to be subdivided among their families. Even here, however, compensation comes in, and the readiness with which lands are transferred greatly increases their market value, and brings bidders into the field. In England I have known instances of persons with moderate means, and very anxious to invest in land, who have been frightened away from their intention by spectres of parchments, and lawyers, and wigs, and disputed titles, and very general ruin—and these by no means among the ignorant; so that those who, as in Germany, would have become customers for a property a landlord desired to sell, often feel themselves, whether rightly or wrongly, shut out from the list of purchasers. Still, the peasant farmer has much to contend with, and, as Mr Scott has said in his report, " From sunrise to sunset the small farmer may be seen daily with the male and female members of his family toiling in the fields; and yet his gains are but meagre, and his diet poor — generally a vegetable one. His dwelling often presents an appearance of squalor.

The silver ornaments that used to deck the persons of every *bauer's* wife and daughter at the village festivals in the seventeenth century, and which were religiously handed down from mother to daughter for many generations, have long disappeared ; the goodly store of coppers, the pride of every *bauer's* kitchen in those days, has long found its way into the smelting-pot ; and few peasants' households are to be met with now which have not some experience of the misery of galling debt impending over their small farms, and making inroads into their scanty returns.

" But the cottager of to-day is, at any rate, from a moral and intellectual point of view, far in advance of his fore-fathers.   He is, at least, warmly clothed, and comparatively contented, taking no small pride in his independence and rights of ownership.

" And after all, he is not so much worse off than his neighbours in the social layer immediately above him ; for simple living—except on high days and holidays, the village fair, or the anniversary of the consecration of the village church—is the rule of the land; and even the well-to-do farmer would consider himself guilty of unpardonable extravagance were meat, except in the shape of the ubiquitous sausage, to appear every day on the family table.   Compared with his neighbour in the towns, while the dwellings of the small tradesman and artisan may possess a few articles of luxury unknown to their country cousins, I doubt very much whether their daily lives would present any greater appearance of comfort ; and if the peasant has a life of hardship and drudgery, it is, at any rate, not aggravated by his having to contrast it with any glaring prosperity in his immediate neighbourhood.

In the Duchy of Coburg, especially, wealth is more evenly divided—more so than in Gotha, where there are a few large incomes, but more poverty in the lower classes." Thuringia is not a wine-growing country, and the clear bright streams form the principal beverage of the farmers, who in general live on milk, and flour, and butter, and eggs, and cheese prepared in different ways; but whatever their diet may be, the fresh mountain air makes ample amends, and braces up their energies. Indeed, if we look at the converse of the picture and see the Scottish Highlander, whose diet is much more exceptionable, and is often milk and oatmeal-porridge—or at least it was till recently—the clear mountain air was even more necessary; " nothing so foreign but the athletic man can labour into food." The cattle in Coburg farms are generally stall-fed—land is too valuable for them to roam over, as we see them roam in the pastures of England. But roadside growths and weeds are carefully gathered. We see the Thuringian peasant and his wife and family cutting down thistles and rank road-side grasses, which in England are allowed to waste, and bundling them up for fodder. At the stepping-stones over brooks the children wash them, and clear them from the dust, and carry them to the byres. Often have I thought what a wealth of pasturage is lost in every parish in England, simply for the want of economy. The annual waste of roadside growths in England would build many palaces, and sustain them in luxury! " The land is ploughed," Mr Scott says, " four or five times for rape, three or four times for rye or wheat, and twice for barley and oats. Light ploughing, to a depth not exceeding from 3 to 6 inches, is the general rule in Coburg, and the plough in common use was, till lately, the old Franconian head-plough, with a straight share; but this is gradually giving way to the Schwerz plough. Some of the old Thuringian ploughs on wooden wheels are still to be seen in use on the small farms, together with the Bohemian and Saxon horse-rakes. The plough is drawn more frequently by two oxen or cows, sometimes by two horses, or even by a horse and a cow yoked abreast." This has, to English eyes, a most singular effect, though not quite so singular as we sometimes notice in Naples, where nearly every-thing but poultry may be seen harnessed to a cart. Mr Scott says that a strong pair of cattle can plough from one to one and a quarter Coburg acres in a day. Plough-ing begins usually about the first week in April, and in autumn it lasts until December. Steam-ploughs are not in use in either Coburg or Gotha; but on some of the Duke's farms steam thrashing-machines have recently been introduced, and it is pleasant to be able to add that they do not seem to interfere with the picturesqueness of this pleasant land. Reaping-machines are nearly unknown, and the old sickle retains its place on all of the smaller farms; on the larger farms we may see the labourers with scythes cutting down oats and barley, and sometimes even wheat and rye. Farmers prefer the sickle to the scythe for many reasons: male labour is much more scarce than female, and it is, of course, necessary for the scythe; and then there is an irregularity in the shape of the small fields which makes a sickle a more convenient instrument to use. Besides this, there is a well-founded belief that a sickle used with skill saves the grain and the after-crop of clover, so precious to Thuringian farmers. In the neighbourhood of Coburg the farmers cut clover about the middle of May for fodder, and it stands to reason that there must be economy in their system of cutting, instead of pasturing. Cattle trample down much more than they eat, and every member of the farmer's family is of use in carrying fodder. The rule generally followed in Coburg is, to manure the land with stable-manure every three years, and they apply eight cart-loads to every acre. In addition to this they use liquid manure and soap-ashes; carbonate of lime and sulphate of lime are also very generally employed for clover and grass lands. But the rich meadows we see in the vicinity of the town of Coburg owe their fertility chiefly to the overflowing of the beautiful little river Itz, which runs past Rosenau, and forms many a bend and nook that are a paradise for the angler or the artist. These inundations occur almost as regularly as the overflowings of the Nile, and they leave behind a rich deposit on all the low meadow-lands. A great portion of the Coburg farms are cropped with potatoes; and it may well be believed that the terrible blight which overtook this system of cropping, caused some few years ago great distress, though now — if, indeed, the good seasons are permanent—the excellence of the yield has placed the farmers in comparative comfort. The report so often quoted says that 42 per cent of the entire population live by agriculture. One thing may be noticed. The refuse of the scullery, such as cabbage-stalks and potato-peelings, where not used for fodder, are dried under the kitchen fireplace and used for fuel,—an excellent example for small English householders in towns. In England they are commonly thrown into a heap, and left to ferment and spread typhoid, besides being at the cost of the tenant to remove.

Let us consider, again, the condition of the farmer who owns a moderately-sized farm, and has a family of five or six children, which is perhaps a fair average to take for a German household. These would seem to be more numerous than the French, but less so than the English. Now, if he has fairly good seasons and good fortune, his profits will perhaps average about £170 or £180 per annum,—that is supposing, of course, that his land is quite free from debt of any kind. It is true that his wants are not many, and his moderate diet of milk, and eggs, and flour, and cheese, is grown at his own door, and schooling is cheap enough and good enough to satisfy much more than the most exacting school inspector in England would look for; and the farmer's lot at the present day is very far from a hard one. But the day of reckoning must come at last; and when he dies, even if he lives to the allotted age of man, he must either cut up his forty or fifty acres into smaller holdings, or else he must make a special favourite of one son. The case is wholly different from a stock-in-trade, where the value can be realised, and all members of the family equally apportioned to push their own way in life, with the country from Vienna to Berlin before them. But it is difficult to see how equal justice can be done to all members of a family, unless what it has been a lifelong wish to avoid is resorted to, and the property is sold. In English estates, which descend generally to the eldest son, the difficulty is less; for the revenues are sufficiently ample to pay for a life assurance, or in other ways to provide for the younger members of a family, or at least to start them fairly for the battle of life. Often has the military service been urged as the cause for the great emigration to America which set in in 1871 and 1872, and even before and after; but in all probability it was as much in consequence of the subdivision, or the settlement in some form, of small landed properties. As far as the military service is concerned, our own representative at Coburg has grave doubts if it does really affect agriculture very materially. "The cry that has been raised recently in many German newspapers, that increased emigration to the United States is withdrawing a very large proportion of the well-to-do population from the country, and is a proof of the unsatisfactory state of the agricultural class in Germany, is met by the fact that during the last five years the number of emigrants to America decreased considerably;" and indeed, if it has increased again, the increase only represents the classes that would, under any circumstances, have left the country for their fellows on the other side of the Atlantic; and no one can have passed through America without being struck with the enormous German population that they meet with, drinking and brewing lager-beer, and speaking their own language. Our representative at Coburg also says that another cry which has been made that military service must end inevitably in ruining agricultural interests, is not quite correct, or at any rate the evil effects are much exaggerated. In times of war it need not be said that the evils are terrible, but then they touch all nearly alike. We in England do not know what war is, because we have never heard the roar of the cannon round our homes;

but even where, as in Germany, the battle is sometimes not on their own soil, the strain is sorely felt,—much more so, indeed, in Germany than here. In England, it matters not what the war is, any one is quite at liberty either to fight or leave it alone,—he has no one to consult but himself; in Germany, however, as in other lands, the cases are different, and a man must go to the wars whether he likes it or not. But it is said that there are some contingent advantages. The State takes a certain percentage annually of the population by ballot, and gives them a military training. Exemption can be bought, so that in reality the service falls very much upon the same class at last as it does in England. It would be wholly unjust to an English soldier to say that he is " one whose necessities have made him what he is," but at any rate he belongs to the more adventurous classes which are found in every community. The only real hardship, it would seem, is where skilled artisans are enlisted or drafted, who cannot procure a substitute; and there are in this part of Germany not a few branches of industry where skilled hand-labour is required. Here the apprentice goes from his years of training to follow up his trade, and acquire more experience and dexterity. But if he is called away when he has mastered his art, and if he must serve in the army, the skill soon leaves his fingers. It may indeed not have left his knowledge, but his term of service has roughened his hands. Tent-pitching and throwing up earthworks have hardly improved him for china-modelling, or locksmith-work, or chiselling a scroll on a sideboard.

But it would seem that military service conveys some

advantages. The conscripts are generally those who are not very comfortably placed. It would be, of course, most unjust to say of them, as Falstaff said of his recruits, "No eye hath seen such scarecrows; I'll not march through Coventry with them, that's flat;" but our consul at Coburg says "they are generally underfed, and imperfectly developed both morally and physically; and thanks to the excellence of the military schools, and to gymnastic training, combined with good food, the military service restores to the country the same material, after a few years' service, highly developed, and in an incomparably better condition to use its labour than when it was withdrawn from the soil." If the recruit has only availed himself of the many advantages that were offered to him, the time he has spent will not have been lost, for the education in many branches has been of the best, and habits of regularity and order have been acquired. Sometimes he remains in the ranks as a non-commissioned officer, or if he has sufficient address and ability, he may rise to a high position in the army; but as a general rule he returns to his village. When he does so, if he has filled his time of service without reproach, he is considered to have a sort of claim on the State. The railways, the telegraph, the post-office, and the customs are open to him, and if he can only qualify, he has the preference over all civilians. Should he not succeed in obtaining an appointment in any of these services, he generally loses little time in returning to his native village. Mountainous countries have a proverbial charm for those who in childhood called them their homes. We remember the eloquent passage in

Byron where the gladiator thinks of his home; and how many gladiators came from Saxony! How often in wars after the servile war, even to the present day, the combatants must have felt like him whose dying hours Byron so pathetically describes!

But even where the soldier's life has been spared, or indeed where he has not even seen active service, he is looked up to in his native village. The deep attachment of the Thuringians for their native country brings the young warrior back; and it is his sole ambition to acquire even a few acres for cultivation, in the land of his childhood. He is almost sure of good employment there, even if he has not been successful with the Government.

After all, though the Germans have so astonished all Europe by their military power, and though the country seems almost to be a camp when the Landwehr are out, they are not a military nation, as the French are, or were. They love war no more than English people love it; and though indeed they seem, in the chances and changes of life, to have had more than their share, peace was always more welcome even than the most glorious campaign. A quiet life in the country, or a vineyard or farm, is their delight; or if they live iu a village or town, a shop that descends from father to son, and that does not know what debt or embarrassment means, pleases them almost as well. A strong love of their Fatherland and its beautiful surroundings is their chief characteristic. Often have I talked with them both in Canada and in the United States, and they, one and all, hope to have made enough money before they die to leave the country of their adoption, and return to end their days in Fatherland. To speak to them of any part of the Rhine or Thuringia, or of the Hartz Mountains, is a sure passport to their friendship; and if you have visited it since they left it, every word you can utter about it is precious. So little are the Germans fond of war and its grim accompaniment, that when the French war was over in 1871,—and, contrary even to their own expectation, their triumph was one of the most complete on record,—they did not take very kindly to the triumphal entry of their troops when they returned in victory. Let us take Weimar, for example, and Coburg presented a similar picture at the *Friedenfast*. This *Friedenfast* took place on a Sunday, and all the town was decorated; banners were hung out from windows, wreaths were suspended on cords across the streets, and garlands and emblems, most of them in excellent taste, were seen on every side,—while at an early hour, young girls, dressed in white as an emblem of peace, found their way to the Stadtkirche, with branches cut from the adjoining woods, and with bouquets of flowers. So many of these were there that an English spectator happily remarked that it was like holding church in a forest. Through all the branches, however, the bright caps of the girls, with their roses and flowers, were very visible, the white lily being a very favourite emblem. I do not know if the contingent had suffered less than some of the others that were engaged in the war, but it is certain that there was not much mourning,—gala-dresses seemed to be more the order of the day,—and that which was donned appeared to belong to the elderly ladies, or the middle-aged ones, who had lost a son or a husband, or some relation that was closer than a brother, and to whom the glory of war, and the expected arrival of the victorious regiments, were vanity.

I arrived, after a long residence abroad, in Europe just as the troops were returning to their homes, and as the Germans were entering Paris; but some letters written by a resident have reminded me of several things which I made no note of at the time. The sermon in this Thuringian town was not a very good one, or calculated to leave a pleasant impression on the hearers. The glory of war and the grandeur of victory were too much dwelt on; the magnificence of emperors, and princes, and generals was preached to many an aching heart. It is true the familiar members of their homes may have fallen in a cause which, if there can be justice and right, was indeed a just and a righteous one; but this, even with all the glory added, could hardly fill the aching void in their lives, and there was a settled melancholy in the congregation as they left the *kirche:* and one could not help thinking that this very picture had been often seen before, even with the same surroundings, and in the same building, and in nearly similar habiliments, in the times of Gustavus Adolphus and Friedrich the Great, and the many other battles that had happened between these dates. Speaking of Weimar, again, a traveller chronicles the triumphant entry of the soldiers. But what an entry! True, indeed, they were almost covered with flowers and wreaths which a sympathetic populace had showered on them; but there was not a man, probably, among them that could not have said how often his heart had warmed towards his home and his Fatherland, and how often in the intervals of his night-watches he had been there.

> " Methought from the battle-field's dreadful array
> Far far I had roamed on a desolate track,
> Till autumn and sunshine arose on the way
> To the home of my fathers, that welcomed me back.
>
> I flew to the pleasant fields traversed so oft
> In life's morning march when my bosom was young ;
> I heard my own mountain-goats bleating aloft,
> And knew the sweet strain that the corn-reapers sung."

But as often as he dreamt it the voice of his dreaming ear melted away at the summons of the batteries of Alsace or Metz ; and the drooping figures and scarred faces, with the worn-out uniforms and boots, told a sad tale of suffering. Many of them had only come to their beloved Fatherland to be cripples for the rest of their lives ; and some, indeed, to find an early grave. But Weimar was there, and they had found their home at last ; and it was singular to think that all through Thuringia scenes and events of precisely a similar character were proceeding, and that at the same time. The parade was over, and crowds of youths were listening intently to some returned hero as, at the street-corner, he was relating his adventures to an old companion ; or at a window a returned warrior was the centre of a fond group of friends he had left behind. But all the merry-making was quiet. There were dancing and music, of course, and sausages and Rhine wine and beer ; but the readiness with which old pursuits and trades were again followed, and that in a day or two, showed that the returned soldiers were only too glad to beat their swords into ploughshares and their spears into pruning-hooks.

CHAPTER XVIII.

LUTHER — EUROPE INDEBTED TO THE HOUSE OF COBURG FOR THE
PROTECTION OF MARTIN LUTHER — PRINCE ALBERT A GREAT
ADMIRER OF LUTHER — SKETCHED MANY OF HIS FAMILIAR
SPOTS — BRIEF SKETCH OF REFORMER'S HISTORY.

IT is unnecessary now to say how much Europe is
indebted to the house of Saxony for the conspicuous
share that the Electors took in defending Luther from
the Pope, and his many enemies besides. The early
homes of Prince Albert were the early homes of the Protestant religion, and the preaching of Luther preceded the
Reformation of our own country. It has been recorded
how the Queen and Prince made a detour to the Duke of
Saxe-Weimar's territory, in order to see the great castle
where Luther was held by the Elector of Saxony until
the work he began had prospered and borne good fruit.
His history there, under the friendly captivity of the
Elector of Saxony, is extremely romantic and interesting,
and unlike any other authentic story that we know of.
The rooms where Luther found refuge are so quaint, and
so safe from outward attack, that we can understand the
security he felt under the sheltering care of the Elector.
Saxony was the kindly home of the early years of the

Reformation, and Coburg, Erfurth, Eisenach, and Wittenberg were identified with it in its early struggles. A history of England that brings its events down to the middle of the present reign has said that if England had no other cause to welcome Prince Albert to its shores, the fact that his family was so intimately connected with the circumstances of the Reformation should be enough to make his arrival welcome among us. He was an admirer of the great Reformer, and an ardent student of his history and his various localities, and his sketch-books were filled with careful drawings of the scenes and the buildings which were identified with his name. At Augsburg

Window at Augsburg with Coburg Arms.

there is a fine oriel corner window which is commonly
connected with the celebrated diet that Luther attended
there.   It is a noble specimen of architecture, and that of
a kind that has not been successfully attempted in England. The date corresponds exactly with Luther's appearance there, and the arms of Coburg are chiselled in a
panel ; and it is not a little significant that he went there
under a powerful escort of the house of Saxony. The
sacrifices that the house of Coburg had to make were
very great, and they were long and lasting. Wallenstein
was one of the results, and the cruel Tilly ; and, as has
been stated in the paper on agriculture, the consul at
Coburg, in summing up a few of the results of the war,
says that they were visible even till very late years.

The castle of Wartburg, which figures so conspicuously
in the following sheets, has the very air of romance about
it.   It was long famous as the most impregnable castle
in those parts ; and the hard, almost igneous-looking
rocks that we see all round it, are not suggestive of a
desirable place to try to take by mining.   Its legends are
curious, besides anything connected with Martin Luther ;
and, indeed, just as at one time we were beholden to
France for our lighter dramas, so we might bring from
Thuringia many a pleasant tale, and even monthly
magazines could vary their literature with one legend
or history from the exhaustless stores of Thüringer-wald
and other of the great German forest-ranges.   In the
archives of Wartburg are deposited many interesting
narratives of events that date far back into antiquity ;
and though some little of the marvellous may have found
their way into the oak chests, the facts that they chron-

icle are correct enough.   Among the records is one of Lewis

Wartburg Castle.

IV. of Thuringia, who married Elizabeth of Hungary, and lived at Wartburg about 1216; and the history of their early lives is very beautiful. They were brought up together in this lovely country, and formed a strong attachment from their earliest years; and the sufferings of Elizabeth are recorded when Lewis was obliged to absent himself from the castle of Wartburg.   In these annals it is said that she used to take her abode in a tall turret in the castle, and there watch each bend of the road as it opened to view in its windings through the woods, waiting anxiously for a first sight of Lewis and his retinue. Elizabeth was married in her fifteenth year, and great were the rejoicings at Eisenach. The Princess was a strict Catholic, and conspicuous for her deeds of charity and her piety. Her demeanour was characterised through life by kindness to all, and great humility and self-denial. Indeed, few such worthy saints have ever found a place in the calendar. All this is within the region of actual fact; and she moreover visited the poorer subjects of her husband, inquired into their merits, was always ready with kindly counsel, and relieved their necessities, whatever they may have been, with her own hands. She built hospitals and refuges for the sick and infirm at Eisenach, and her memory is held in reverence there even to the present day. Lewis, it is said, found that her charities, which expended very large sums, were rather costly for his exchequer; but he made little complaint, and even raised fresh supplies for her, so great was his devotion to her, though he hardly sympathised quite so strongly as she did with the objects of her benevolence. Indeed it would seem that the only grievance Lewis had was her over-strictness of life, for in dealing with herself she had none of the benevolence that it was her meat and drink to show to others. She fasted and denied herself nearly every pleasure. Her husband gently chided her, but could never alter her conduct. Finally, she appointed one of her ladies-in-waiting to rouse her in her first sleep each night, that she might resort to the chapel and there spend an hour or two in religious exercises and prayer, which Lewis said was really too much. Still, beyond chiding and a little coolness, all went on well.

Now in Wartburg, as in all other castles of the period, there were at least some bravos who did not quit the region of the castle, and longed for some excitement, and especially would have liked a different disposal of the revenues of Lewis. They could not, of course, find any possible charge to bring against Elizabeth, and they used to hint that the great amount she was spending was spent on unworthy objects, who battened on his resources. A name would be

In Wartburg Castle.

mentioned, and a knowing glance cast round would be taken, and then left to work its end.

> " I'll put the man
> At least into a jealousy so strong
> That judgment cannot cure."

And finally, Lewis was led to believe that the sacrifices he had made were for no really worthy object, and he became quite a changed man.   One day, indeed, he was ascending the hill from Eisenach to his castle, when he met his wife with a basket over her arm, and he was so altered as to ask her roughly what she carried there. She was so terrified at the change, that she did not admit it was some few delicacies from the castle for a poor invalid, but said "flowers;" and for the rest of the narrative, we must depend upon the most reliable monkish chronicles of the period.   He took the basket and pulled off the covering while she gently looked on, expecting to be upbraided every moment.   What was her delight and relief, however, to see that her delicacies had been changed into roses and violets! and the reflections of Lewis must have resembled those of Mr Ford when he saw the buck-basket carried out.   "If I suspect without cause, why, then, make sport of me; then let me be your jest; I deserve it."

Elizabeth was canonised, and her remains were interred in the magnificent church which was built at Marburg in Hesse-Cassel in her honour, and which still bears her name—the Church of St Elizabeth.   It was commenced about the year 1235, and in the transept there is a small chapel called the Chapel of St Elizabeth. This contains a carved representation of Elizabeth reclining in her coffin, surrounded by the objects of her many bounties—the maimed, the halt, and the sick; and the chapel floor is worn away in many places by the knees of pilgrims.

Another occupant of this castle is recorded among many others that appear in the archives, and his career has much less to admire in it than that of Lewis, whose fault seems to have been that he lent a too willing ear to the swash-bucklers of the age.

In 1270, Wartburg was the residence of the Landgrave Albert and his wife Margaret. She was amiable and excellent, and, it is recorded, very beautiful; but her wedded life was never, as it would seem, so happy as that of Elizabeth. Indeed it is sad to chronicle that the Landgrave found the society of one of her own maids of honour quite as attractive as her own, and this naturally led to much heartburning. It would be well if we could think that the maid from Eisenburg was content to rest satisfied with the knowledge that her beauty was appreciated by the Landgrave; but unhappily she thought she might herself be the Landgravine, and she plied Albert well with motives to this end. For long he would not listen to her suggestions. At length, however, she acquired so great an influence over him that he consented to compass the undoing of his excellent and beautiful wife. To this end some one was procured, and he was instructed to dress himself like an evil spirit, and strangle the Landgravine in her bed; and by this means Cunegonda of Eisenburg hoped herself to become Landgravine. When he reached the chamber the man felt awe-struck, and, it is said, stood motionless at the door, not daring to disturb the sleeper; but the commotion of the serf with his habiliments awoke the lady, and he was so overcome that he entered into the chamber and confessed the whole affair, so much was he subdued by the dignity of her manner, and her beauty and innocence. But the sound of voices awoke the chamberlain, who was in the next chamber. He was at once alive to his duties, and soon apprehended the danger that threatened his mistress. This chamberlain, whose name was Schenk, at once called in the few inhabitants of Wartburg who could be relied on, and after a long deliberation, it was resolved upon that the lady could no longer remain in safety there. Her children, to whom she was devotedly attached, were collected quietly for her to take a last farewell of them—and she took almost a passionate leave. Over and over again she embraced them, and clung to them, until, as it would appear, not only from records but pictures, she became too impulsive; and when her favourite Frederick—her best-beloved of all—had to be parted with, her reason seemed to have gone, and in a paroxysm of grief she bit his cheek. Frederick always bore the mark of his mother's excessive affection, and went by the name of "the bitten one," and his portrait at Wartburg shows a scar on the cheek. There are in Germany several portraits of Frederick, who seemed to be a man of great resolution and prowess, and these all have a scarred cheek. He was buried in the aisle of the church at Meissen, not far from Dresden, and his grave is still pointed out to visitors.

It was at Erfurth that the change came over Luther's life which was destined to play so remarkable a part in the world's history. Luther was intended by his father for the law, and he studied it for some time in the university. There is no doubt that had he remained at this profession, abundant success would have waited on him. It is not only his energy but his perspicuity that would have stood him in good stead, and his luminous and judicial mind would have placed him easily among the foremost lawyers in Europe. The accident, however, of seeing a Bible when he was only twenty years of age, opened up for him a much more brilliant career, and his name is the one

Luther's House, Frankfurt.

solitary star that stands above all others as the hero of the great Reformation. And it never must be forgotten what this "Reformation" really means. The state of things which in Luther's early life existed has passed

away so thoroughly that we can hardly recall it; and
some have even confused it with a protest against the
points wherein the tenets of the Protestants and the
Romanists differ at the present day. But this it had
nothing to do with; and the men who constitute the
hierarchy of the Romish Church, and number among
them characters quite as lofty and single - minded as
can be found in any other Church, would be quite as
much shocked at the scandals Luther protested against
as he was himself.   If we take even the monasteries
of England: in the reign of Henry VIII., two commis-
sioners, Legh and Layton, were appointed to visit the
religious houses, and to report upon their condition.
They seem to have done so fairly enough, and they
report that some of them were tolerably well conducted;
but the bulk of them, they say, were chargeable with
simony, great excesses in eating and drinking, and very
general immorality. In fact, the monastic houses had out-
lived their day.   At one time they fulfilled a useful and
important mission, and they were seminaries of learning and
instruction.   The members of each fraternity went about
doing what good seemed present to them to perform; but
in Luther's time their only aim seemed to be to contract
their corporations, to raise as much money as it was possible, and to do as little as they could in the way of duty.
This of course refers to the English houses; but those on
the Continent were almost worse.   Luther was contemporaneous with what is called the "Spanish Inquisition,"
which punished even a suspicion of free thought with
a barbarous death, and which, for cruelty and simple
wickedness, has never been even approached by any

institution of which a record has been preserved in history. Some estimate may be formed of the grasping power of the unreformed Church when it is considered that nearly half the wealth of the kingdom had under it been appropriated on every possible pretension, and even fraud, by the clergy, and this in England. How the property was divided on the Continent I have no data at hand to show; but when we consider how much more easily Rome was approached, and how prince - bishops lorded it, we may fairly conclude that the worldly affairs of the Continental church were as prosperous as those of England.

The immediate cause of Luther's action was the attempt of the Pope to sell indulgences for money. Leo X. had sent messengers to Germany to raise resources by an extraordinary sale of indulgences, and it is recorded, though it may be, indeed, by a cynic, that ingenious arts were used to enhance them in value. As for example, it is said that on one occasion, where scepticism was rife, a pronounced unbeliever made himself conspicuous, and jeered openly at indulgences and the power of the Pope to grant them. The Pope's vicar with much feeling and kindliness remonstrated with him in private and in public, especially the latter, and received nothing but taunts and flouts from the sceptic. The other finally threw every appearance of reserve aside, and openly proclaimed in the market-place that indulgences were a delusion and a snare. It came to pass that a sermon was preached about indulgences, and the unbeliever was there. He even went so far as to interrupt the service, and the good vicar stopped, on which the peccant unbeliever fell down in a fit, and was soon surrounded by the congregation. The clergyman pushed his way through it, and held up a crucifix and an indulgence before the apparently dying man, and the effect was really marvellous. In fact he revived almost at once, and recanted his unbelief. It is said that he was seen to enter the clerical residence after dark; and though, of course, an immense impetus was given to the merchandise in indulgences, there were not a few who openly said that the whole business looked very like complicity.

It was indulgences that first brought Luther to the front. He had studied the Bible as best he could at Erfurth, and when it was taken away he found where it was deposited in the library. He entirely repudiated the whole system of fraud, and nailed at great length his reasons on the door of the church. For these indulgences not only freed men from purgatorial torments for sins already committed, but if they only paid a sufficient amount of money, each as he could afford, according to his prosperity in life, he might have the Pope's sanction to continue to plot and to commit as many more as he desired with perfect impunity, if only his purse was deep enough, and his gifts towards the Church militant on a proportionate scale to his wealth. The most active party in pushing the sale of indulgences was a Dominican named Tetzel, and he seems to have been at any rate no hypocrite. His rhetoric became so audacious at last, that it defeated his own ends. He used, for example, to narrate in taverns and at market-places how many evils indulgences had cured; and finally he invented unheard-of crimes of such monstrosity that his hearers were horror-

struck; but when he had worked upon their feelings sufficiently, he suddenly produced his indulgences, and said,
—" Well, never mind ; if the money rattles in the Pope's
coffers all will be right." Now when Luther, as an influential professor at Wittenberg, heard and saw such things
going on, and considered also that he was the vicar-
general's substitute in the pastoral charge of Thuringia,
he felt he could be silent no longer. He applied to his
own diocesan, the Bishop of Brandenburg, to silence
Tetzel ; but the latter replied that it would be quite impossible to move, as it would be to attack the power of
the Church, and involve him in much trouble. On this
he wrote to the primate the Archbishop of Maintz, and
Prince of the house of Brandenburg,—a house, it may be
remarked, that was hostile to Luther's generous and
powerful friends, the Electors of Saxony. Luther wrote to
this magnate on 31st October 1517 :—

" Venerable father in God, most illustrious prince,
vouchsafe to cast a favourable eye on me who am but
dust and ashes, and to receive my request with pastoral
kindness. There is circulated throughout the country, in
the name of your Grace and Lordship, the Papal indulgence for the erection of the cathedral at St Peter's at
Rome. I do not so much object to the preachers of the
declaration of this indulgence, as to the erroneous idea
entertained of it by the poor, simple, and unlearned, who
are everywhere avowing openly their fond imaginations
on the subject. They fancy their souls shall be delivered
from purgatory as soon as the money clinks in the Pope's
chest. They believe the indulgence is powerful enough
to save the greatest sinner " (and here are enumerated

instances of some horrible crimes, that might well have appalled the audiences Tetzel addressed, as examples of what the Pope had pardoned). "You will incur a fearful and ever-increasing responsibility. Be pleased, noble and venerable father, to read and take into consideration the following propositions, in which is shown the vanity of the indulgences, which the preacher gives out as a certainty." Then his celebrated ninety-five propositions follow. No reply was received from the Archbishop of Maintz; so on the same day, in full anticipation of such an issue, he nailed these propositions to the door of the Schloss-kirche, a church which contains the remains of Luther and his constant friend Melancthon, Frederick the Wise, and John the Steadfast. When news of this was conveyed to Leo X., he laughed contemptuously and said, "That Luther has a fine genius," little knowing the storm there was brewing in the distance. Three of the propositions will serve as a key to the whole :—

"The Pope neither will nor can remit any penalty except that he has himself imposed, or in conformity with the canons."

"The changing of canonical punishment into the pains of purgatory is a sowing of tares. The bishops were clearly asleep when they suffered such seed to be sown.'

"Christians should be taught that if the Pope were made acquainted with the extortions of indulgence-preachers, he would prefer seeing the basilica of St Peter's reduced to ashes, to building it up with flesh, fleece, and bones of his sheep."

In addition to publishing these propositions, Luther took an opportunity to preach upon them in the vulgar tongue; and this fell like a thunderbolt in Germany, and nothing was heard on any side but disquisitions upon the new movement. The Emperor Maximilian had begged the Pope not to precipitate matters, and promised himself to look after Luther and all his heresies. But the Emperor was hardly trusted at Rome; he had made many unsuccessful campaigns upon his neighbours, which were unsuccessful in consequence of shortness of funds. His own were very large, and his private estates enormous, but they were not sufficient for a war with such a king as Louis XII.; and at times he almost forgot his proper place, as, for example, when he served under our own Henry VIII. at the siege of Terouenne for a hundred crowns a-day. Maximilian himself, in order to retrieve his broken opportunities, resolved to endeavour to make himself the Pope; but Leo X. did not appear to entertain the same views of the Pontifical crown. Some speeches, also, of Maximilian's, were reported at Rome, and these did not tend to improve his position with the Pope. He was known to have said to Pfeffinger, the minister of the Elector of Saxony, "What your monk is doing must not be looked on with contempt; the game with the priests will soon begin, so make much of him —you may want him yet." Then, again, he was well known to have indulged in bitter complaints against the priests and the hierarchy. He said, when alluding to Leo X., "The Pope has behaved to me like a knave; but I never met with good faith in any Pope, and with the blessing of God I hope this will be the last." This was not such language as would be commended at Rome, and it was the less welcome when Leo remembered that

Maximilian himself had entertained the idea of becoming Pope. Thus it happened that Maximilian was not much trusted, and Luther felt far more secure under the protection of the much more consistent and able man, the Elector of Saxony. This prince had always admired and trusted Luther. He paid the expenses which were necessary for his taking his doctor's degree at Wittenberg, and in many ways he showed himself to be his true friend. There can be no doubt that Luther had assurances of protection from the Elector, for he writes to the Bishop of Salzburg,—"Our prince has taken me and Aulstadt under his protection, and this without being entreated. He will not allow of my being dragged to Rome; this they know, and it is a thorn in their side." Still Luther, with a very natural desire to save his friend, writes soon after to Spalatin in a confidential letter,—"I do not see how I can avoid the censure with which I am threatened unless the Prince comes to my aid, and yet I would rather endure all the censure in the world than see his Highness blamed on my account. The best step I can take, in the opinion of my friends, is to ask the Prince for a safe-conduct. I am sure he will refuse me, so that they say I shall have a good excuse for not appearing at Rome. Have the kindness, therefore, to procure me from our most illustrious Prince a rescript that he refuses me a safe-conduct, and leaves me, if I will, to undertake the journey to Rome on my own risk and peril. You will be doing me a great service, but let it be done quickly, for time presses, and the day appointed is at hand." Luther might, however, have spared himself the trouble of writing this letter, because the prince had already made abundant preparations for Luther's safety. He had so managed affairs that Augsburg, and not Rome, was the town where Luther was to be examined, and that this examination was to be conducted by a legate, where he himself happened to be at the time. Luther, on being apprised of this, went straight forward, without knowing what was before him or what would be done in his favour. The Italian legate was not a man to be much feared by Luther, as his own writings were broad and liberal, and indeed he was supposed to hold heretical opinions, such as the freedom of the laity to read Scripture. But he set about his work in a business-like way, and only attacked Luther upon the subject of his attempting to shake the political power of Rome—the kingdom the Popes most prized, even though, indeed, it was of this world. The disputations do not seem to have been conducted very rancorously; and Luther left Augsburg for his own home, greatly fearing to be sent to trial to Rome. These fears were well enough founded, for Luther had left Augsburg, and the legate entreated Frederick to bring him back, or else to consider his own good name and have him sent to Rome, and even went so far as to say that it would sully the fair fame of his ancestry if he hesitated. Many were the temptations offered to the Elector to deliver Luther up, and the Pope even offered him the order of the " Golden Rose," the highest distinction it was possible to confer, which was only given to kings as some reward of their affection to the interests of the Church. Luther at once offered to quit the dominions of the Elector of Saxony, writing to him, " I will go whithersoever God in His mercy may direct me, trusting whatever may befall in His divine will. I therefore respectfully bid farewell to your Highness, and among whatever people I take my abode I shall remember your kindness with never-ceasing gratitude." It is exceedingly difficult at this time to appreciate the loftiness of the principles which guided the Elector of Saxony. He was himself a true Catholic, and quite submissive to the Pope, Leo X., who, it may be remarked in passing, was one of the most brilliant Popes that ever lived. But at any rate, through Germany, and also through Italy, it was clear that the matters in question were now beginning to assume proportions which the Pope, and most probably even Luther himself, never for a moment had contemplated.

The history of the controversy is extremely interesting, but in the end Luther himself assumed the offensive at Wittenberg, and even offered to meet the champions of indulgences and of the other errors of Rome that he wished to controvert. This seems to have been too much for his Catholic biographer Cochlæus. "He had the effrontery," he says, "with the authority of the Prince his protector, to issue a summons to the ablest of the inquisitors—men that you would think could split iron and swallow rock —to a disputation; and the Prince not only offered them a safe-conduct, but agreed to pay the expenses of their lodging." Luther's addresses to the Pope are very pathetic and very loyal. He tells him again and again that it is not with Leo his quarrel is, but with the whole system of the Papacy; and we know now that he spoke the truth when he told him that if he tried to reform the abuses he saw around him, he would hardly live a day. "Yes, dear Leo, I think of thee as Daniel in the pit or Ezekiel among the scorpions. What canst thou among these monsters, thou and some three or four learned cardinals? You would all be certainly poisoned. The doom has gone forth against the Court of Rome. The measure of God's wrath has been filled up, for that Court hates councils, dreads the name of reform, and fulfils the words uttered of its mother, of whom it is said, 'We would have healed Babylon, but she would not be healed.' Forsake Babylon, O hapless Leo, to sit on that accursed throne! I speak the truth to thee, for I desire thy good!" Perhaps this extract may throw a little lustre round the Pope, with whom Luther has so long been associated as an implacable foe. We know more of the life of this brilliant potentate from Roscoe, a Liverpool gentleman and a thorough scholar, than we know of the life of any other Pope that lived.

A new learning had, it is true, begun in Luther's time, and we have such names as Erasmus, Melancthon, and the numberless enlightened doctors of Oxford and Cambridge, as well as the multitudes of learned professors on the Continent, besides More and Wolsey; and it requires a very fair mind indeed to properly adjust the place Luther should take as a Reformer. We have seen the gentle letter of Erasmus,—himself, it need not be said, a friend of Leo X., the Pope with whom Luther's difference unfortunately happened to be, for we all could have wished it had been with some of his predecessors, instead of a prelate that Roscoe delighted to honour,—and a recent history has said, "The young king" (Henry VIII., England), "proud of a theological knowledge, in which he stood alone among the sovereigns of Europe, entered the lists against Luther with an 'Assertion of the Seven Sacraments,' for which he was rewarded by Leo with the title of 'Defender of the Faith.'   The insolent abuse of the Reformer's answer called More and Fisher to the field.   As yet the new learning, though scared by Luther's intemperate language, had steadily backed him in the struggle.   Erasmus pleaded for him with the Emperor.   Hutten attacked the friars in satires and invectives as intemperate as his own.   But the temper of the 'revival' was even more antagonistic to the temper of Luther than that of Rome itself.   From the golden dream of that new age, wrought peaceably and purely by the slow progress of intelligence, the growth of letters, the development of human virtue, the Reformer of Wittenberg turned away with horror.   He had little or no sympathy with the new culture.   He despised reason as heartily as any Papist dogmatist could despise it.   He hated the very name of toleration or comprehension.   He had been driven by a moral and intellectual compulsion to declare the system of Rome a false one, but it was only to replace it by another system, a doctrine just as elaborate, and claiming precisely the same infallibility. To degrade human nature was to attack the very basis of the new learning; but Erasmus no sooner advanced to its defence than Luther declared man to be utterly enslaved by original sin, and incapable, through any efforts of his own, of discovering truth or of arriving at goodness. Such a doctrine not only annihilated the piety and wisdom of the classic past from which the new learning had drawn its larger view of life and of the world—it trampled

in the dust reason itself, the very instrument by which
More and Erasmus hoped to regenerate both knowledge
and religion. To More especially, with his keener per-
ception of its future effects, the sudden revival of a purely
theological and dogmatic spirit, severing Christendom into
warring camps, and annihilating all hopes of union and
tolerance, was especially hateful. The temper which
hitherto had seemed so 'endearing, gentle, and happy,'
suddenly gave way. His reply to Luther's attack upon
the king sank to the level of the work it answered.
That of Fisher was calmer and more argumentative,
but the divorce of the new learning from the Reformation was complete."

This is the language of one of the greatest historians
of modern days, and one whose views command respect,
and that deservedly, from readers of every class, and
every tendency of thought. But with the highest admiration for his great work, I cannot help thinking that
the evils of the Papacy were almost too deeply rooted
for such mild and holy remedies as Erasmus in his
letter suggested. The quiet and learned Melancthon
was a close friend of Luther's. He indeed thought
that Luther was too impulsive, and too uncompromising.
Perhaps his friendly counsels may have moderated some
of Luther's impetuous courses, but the clear facts must
remain. In spite of the learned and courtly Leo, the
Papacy had become a scandal; and the Spanish representatives at Worms treated the Reformer with contumely,
as they shouldered him on leaving the town-hall. These
gentry were, from whatever reason, the most servile of all
the subjects of the Pope; and the institution called the

"Spanish Inquisition" was already in force, though not in quite the same shocking proportions which it acquired in after-days—for it soon began to spread its tremendous arms to Antwerp and India, and even sent an Armada to England with its racks and screws, some of which are yet preserved, to stifle free thought. Now Luther, in his antagonism to the Papacy, must have remembered that it was not intended for temporal profit. The money-changers in the Temple probably were not more peccant than ordinary money-lenders of the present day,—there is nothing to imply it in the Gospels,—but even their tables were overthrown. The traffic in licences, on the contrary, attacked every inducement to right doing, and even placed temptations in the way of any man who felt that when he wished to do good evil was present with him. "I see the good, and I approve it too; the evil which I would not that I do," was quite inverted, and that in the fewest and most shameless words, by the Papal indulgences. When Luther first came to the front and saw all this; and when he knew, as he did know, that the Spanish Inquisition would develop into the wickedest of all tribunals of which any record is left in history, he might have said with Macbeth—

> " We have scotched the snake, not killed it :
> She'll close, and be herself; while our poor malice
> Remains in danger of her former tooth."

It would be unjust to Leo X. not to record a letter which Erasmus wrote to his friend Luther. Many of us have pleasant recollections of this great scholar, if only from the court at Queen's College, Cambridge, where he took up his abode, at the invitation of his friend Bishop

Fisher, a college which, for picturesque beauty, has no competitor, either in Cambridge or Oxford. Erasmus wrote the following admirable letter to his friend: "I reserve all my powers to contribute to the revival of elegant literature, and it strikes me that greater progress is to be made by politic moderation than by passion. It is thus that Christ has brought the world to be subject, and thus that Paul abolished the Judaic law, by applying himself to the interpretation of the letter. It is better to exclaim against such as abuse the power given to priests than the priests themselves, and so likewise with regard to kings. Instead of bringing the schools into contempt, it would be well to bring them back to healthier studies. Whenever the question is of things too deeply rooted in the mind to be eradicated by one pull, discussion and close and cogent reasoning are to be preferred to affirmations, and it is essential to be on one's guard saying or doing anything with an arrogant or rebellious air: such, in my opinion, is the course of proceeding consonant to the spirit of Christ. But I do not say this by way of teaching you what you ought to do, only to encourage you to go on as you are now doing."

Luther's summons to the Diet of Worms, under the safe-conduct of the Emperor, is too well known to need repetition here. Some of his foes endeavoured to prevent his proceeding as far as that town, assuring him of the danger that awaited him if he went; but he never hesitated. He perhaps, however, hardly realised their actual design; for if he could only have been delayed three days longer on the road, the date of his safe pass would have expired, and his escort would have dispersed. There are some curious details of the conference written immediately after, and M. Michelet even suggests that Luther may himself have been the author, though they are in the third person. The day after his arival, the Master of the Ceremonies came to Luther's hotel, and took him by secret passages to the assembly, that he might avoid the crowd which pressed in all directions to see him; but numbers hastened to the town-hall and tried to gain an entrance with Luther, and were only with difficulty hindered by the guards. When he entered, many nobles came up to him and shook hands with him, speaking words of encouragement. "Be bold," one said; "speak the truth like a man, and fear not those that can kill the body only, but have no power over the soul." "Monk," said the famous Captain Frundsberg, laying his hand on his shoulder, "you are about to hazard a more perilous march than we have ever done, but be of good courage; if you are on the right road, God will not forsake you." Luther admitted that the books on the table were his writing, and entered upon a very strong defence of them, urging that even by the Papacy, the errors he spoke against had already been condemned; and he ends his powerful discourse in the following remarkable way: "Were I to revoke, I should only fortify the Papists in their tyranny and oppression, and open doors and windows to their horrible impieties. It would be said I recanted my charges against them at the order of his Imperial Majesty and the Empire. God! what disgraceful cloak I should become for their perversity and tyranny! The third and last part of my writings is of a polemical character, and herein I confess that I have often been more rough and violent than religion and my gown warrant. I do not give myself out for a saint. It is not my life and conduct that I am discussing before you, but the doctrines of our Lord and Saviour Jesus Christ. I can defend my doctrines only after my divine Saviour's example, who, when smote by the servant of the high priest, said, 'If I have spoken evil, bear witness of the evil.' Therefore I, with all humility, beseech your Imperial Majesty, and your Electoral and Seignoral Highnesses, not to allow yourselves to be indisposed towards my doctrine, save my adversaries produce just and cogent reasons." In vain the Emperor's orator started to his feet and said Luther had spoken beside the question, and that which once had been decided by councils could not be again handled as doubtful; and that all Luther had to say was whether he retracted or not. Of course Luther saw from such a reply that his adversary was delivered into his hands, for there were enough friends at the board to insure for Luther at least some sort of a hearing; and at the last conference the Bishop of Trèves seems to have moderated his tone, and to have asked Luther himself what he would recommend to bring the matter to a happy conclusion; and Luther said he could not do other than quote the advice of Gamaliel, in the Acts of the Apostles—" If this counsel or work be of men, it will come to nothing; but if it be of God, ye cannot overthrow it." The Emperor was true to his promise for a safe pass, and he sent to Luther a safe-conduct from Worms to his home at Wittenberg. I do not know the route which, in those days, would be considered the shortest; but as he seems to have gone through Friedburg, it is probable that his journey would be about 300 miles.

The safe pass lasted for twenty days; and if we consider the road and the difficulties, this would appear to be about a reasonable time for such a distance. Luther was enjoined by the Emperor not to preach on his way—an injunction that he was induced to disregard when passing through Friedburg.

We come now to the most dramatic of incidents in the life of Luther—and that is where he was befriended by the Elector of Saxony—and the one which connects his career so closely with the line from which Prince Albert springs. The episode on Luther may be a little lengthy, but it is so closely interwoven with our subject, and his romantic sojourn in the residence of Prince Albert's forefathers, that this part of the early homes of the Prince would hardly be complete with any less; and Wartburg was a great delight of Prince Albert, as I am credibly informed by those who remember him in his youth. It is only by recollecting the appalling straits to which Luther was driven, that we can appreciate the heroic efforts of the Elector of Saxony in his defence; and the anecdote is a very stirring one. Luther was passing by Eisenach on his road to Wittenberg, still under the safe-conduct of the Emperor, when his escort was attacked by superior numbers and dispersed. Perhaps all Luther had cause to fear was some kind of ambush, or else assassination in a covert form—a way but too common in those days for disposing of an inconvenient antagonist. The Elector of Saxony, as he well knew, incurred risks from the Holy See, and might be laid under an interdict and excommunicated, but he certainly rescued Luther from foes that were quite prepared for him;

and but for the growing power of the issues Luther had raised, it is very possible that the Elector's intervention might have brought evil on the house of Saxony. When Luther left Worms under the escort of the Emperor, he was, as we have mentioned, enjoined not to preach on his way; but he says that the Abbot of Hirsfeld almost compelled him to preach there. He sent his chancellor and a troop of horse to meet him, and treated him sumptuously every day. It was on the fifth day they begged him to preach. Luther pointed out that they might lose their *régales*, and they ran great danger—but all to no effect; they insisted—and he said that he had never consented to tie up the Gospel. "So," he writes to a friend at Worms, "you may hear it said that I have broken my word, but I have not." At Eisenach he also preached before a terrified clergyman and congregation; but a notary, before witnesses, entered a protest in order to save themselves from the consequences. Shortly after this the seizure above spoken of was made. How far the guard were themselves aware of the nature of the arrest is uncertain, but it seems not improbable that something like an explanation was arrived at during the *mélée*. Luther himself had no idea of where he was going, or could he think of an explanation. But he was hurried up the steep hill from Eisenach, which, at the end of an hour's climb, leads to the grand old castle of Wartburg. This has in part been restored, but very much of the old portion remains, and it is a most conspicuous object over the surrounding country. It is difficult to decide whether the situation of Coburg Castle or Wartburg is the grander; but either of them towers loftily above the plain, and seems well able to defy any kind of attack that it was possible, with the weapons at their disposal in those days, for enemies to make.   It needs no telling that the views from Wartburg are simply grand.   As we ascend the beautiful hill, great reaches of country open out; and when we arrive at the summit, we can see vast ranges of plain as far as the eye can stretch in every direction.   I saw it in August, when a very prosperous harvest and a second crop of hay was being gathered in; and certainly the dark black Thuringian forest, cut up with patches of broad farming lands, which, under the summer sun, looked like frosted gold, was a sight not to be forgotten.

The Elector of Saxony had really done all that lay in his power to preserve Luther.   The decree, both of the Pope and the Emperor, had gone out against him. The latter respected his guarantee of safety, which only lasted for twenty days; and after that, as all thought in Germany, it behoved Luther to look to it, for evil days were before him.   Nothing could have excelled the prudence of the Saxon Elector in the steps he took.   He was not then quite powerful enough to afford him protection, for he had the Emperor and the Pope to reckon with, and Luther's followers, though indeed numerous, were only growing.   To conceal him for a time was sure to strengthen them; for a rumour ran that he was made away with by the supreme ruling powers, either temporal or spiritual. A cry of anguish ran through Germany that their champion should have perished, and both the Emperor and the Pope were openly charged with being guilty of his undoing.   In fact, the very best way to advance the Reformation was to let this be commonly believed.   The actual history of Luther's friendly captivity is most engrossing. We can see at once into what a frenzied state he had wrought himself. Two youths were intrusted to bring him his meals, and among other delicacies they brought

Wartburg Castle.

him a bag of nuts, which he put in a chest—but these he heard rattle and tumble against each other. This he did not trouble himself, as it would appear, very much about; but he was awakened after by a great noise in the staircase, which sounded as if a hundred barrels were being rolled up, which certainly is a larger supply of Rhenish wine than he would require. He knew, however, that the solid staircase was secured against all comers by chains and bars, and a strong iron door barred the way. Luther got up and repeated the eighth Psalm, " Omnia subjecisti pedibus ejus." He went to other parts of the castle, but the spiritual remembrances seem to have haunted him ; and his throwing the ink-stand at the author of evil, and leaving the ink-stain on the wall, is a well known story. There seems to be some romance, with which we can sympathise very strongly, in Luther's abode at Wartburg. The engraving of Wartburg will show its great natural strength ; and then it was under the protection of a powerful prince, but one who could hardly have measured swords with the Pope and the Emperor combined. In the present day, with telegraphs, and daily papers, and special correspondents engaged at fancy prices in every part of the world, it seems difficult to realise so singular a state of things ; but in reality Luther was hidden in the high fortress away from the world, and was generally believed to be dead. He writes to his friend Spalatin, " The priests and monks, who played off their pranks while I was at large, have become so alarmed since I have been a prisoner, that they begin to soften the preposterous tales they have given out against me. They can no longer bear up against the pressure of the increasing crowd, and yet they set no means to escape. See you not the aim of the Almighty of Jacob in all that He works, while we are silent, and rest in patience and in prayer ?   One of those of Rome writes to a peewit [1] of Maintz,—‘ Luther is lost just as we could wish ; but such is the excitement of the people, that I fear we shall hardly be able to escape with life, except we search for him with lighted candle and bring him back.’ ”

We can see easily from Luther’s letters how secure and happy he felt in his eyrie.   The room shown is high

Luther’s Room.

up in a tower, and the view from it is very grand.   The oak furniture is that which Luther used, and the chamber is very much as he left it.   The ink-spot, which is so notable in history, has been cut out long ago by enterprising pilgrims.   Luther dates his letters “ From the region of the clouds,” or “ From the region of the birds ; ”

[1] Lapwing.

or else he takes a wider range, and says, "From amidst the birds singing sweetly on the branches, and lauding God day and night with all their strength." Again he says, "From the mountain," or "From Patmos." It was here that he wrote many of his best hymns and most beautiful letters. The libraries at Wartburg were not on an extensive scale; indeed the books there were few, but he made the best use of the little stock, and devoted himself ardently to the study of Greek and Hebrew. He says, "When I revolve these terrible times of wrath, my sole desire is to find in my eyes floods of tears to bewail the desolation of souls brought on by this kingdom of sin and of perdition. The monster sits at Rome in the midst of the Church, and gives himself out for God. Prelates flatter, sophists offer him incense, and there is nothing that the hypocrites will not do for him. Meanwhile Hell makes merry, and opens its immense jowl. Satan revels in the perdition of souls. For me, I sit the day long drinking and doing nothing. I read the Bible in Greek and Hebrew. I shall write something in German on auricular confession. I shall also continue the Psalter and the Commentaries as soon as the materials I require are sent me from Wittenberg." All the while that Luther's active mind and pen were at work, his foes wondered at his whereabouts. It slowly came to them that he must be above-ground, for the writings which were issued with his name attached to them were no forgeries. Matters, however, came to a head so quickly, that Luther found he could no longer remain in his luxurious prison, but he must at once go to Wittenberg without the permission even of his friend the Elector of Saxony; indeed he may be said to have stolen away from the friendly fortress. There is a singular incident recorded of the journey which shows how deeply his discourses and his writings had taken root in the public mind. John Kessler, who was a young theologian of St Gall, was going with a friend to Wittenberg to finish his studies at Luther's college. He happened to meet Luther at Jena, near the gates of the town. Luther wore a riding-dress, and his companion did not know him. The horseman had a little book before him, which, as it turned out, was the Psalter in Hebrew. He saluted them very courteously, and requested them to be seated at his table. During their conversation he asked what was thought of Luther in Switzerland, and Kessler said that there were many who hardly knew how to praise him enough, and thanked Heaven for having sent him on earth to exalt the truth; but others, especially the priests, denounced him as a heretic who should not be spared. From something which the landlord of the inn said, they supposed erroneously enough that Luther was Von Hutten. Two traders came in, and one of them took a newly published work of Luther's from his mantle, and put it on the table, and asked the company if they had seen it. Luther made some general remarks, and said he hoped the Gospel would not be perverted by Papal errors. One of the traders said, " I am unskilled in these questions, but to my mind Luther must be either an angel from heaven or a devil from hell; at all events, I will spend the last ten florins that I have saved up in going to confess to him." This conversation took place during supper. Luther had settled beforehand with the

T

landlord that he would pay the reckoning of the whole company. The two Swiss, after the traders departed, were left with Luther, and as they were going to Wittenberg, Luther said, " Convey my services to Dr Jerome Schurff" (their countryman), "as soon as you have arrived." They inquired very naturally whose message it was they were intrusted with. He replied, " Simply tell him that he who is to come salutes him ; he will be sure to understand from whom the message comes." When the traders returned and found it was Luther, great was their confusion to find that it was the Reformer who had been speaking to them, and they regretted that they had not shown him more respect, and the following morning they were up early to tender him their humble respects ; but Luther still declined to say if he was the veritable Luther or not.

There are few names more familiar to Englishmen, and none that are held in more affectionate regard, than Martin Luther. His name is as much a household word as that of John Bunyan or William Shakespeare. We are familiar from early childhood with the history of his foes and his dangers, and with the courageous way in which he overcame all. We admire his courage, and his modesty, and his quaint simplicity, and especially the crowning fact that he directed and guided the reformation which was beginning to dawn in the dark parts of Europe.

In a recent history of England it is well said that one of the great holds which Prince Albert had on the affections of Englishmen, was the circumstance that he was an ardent admirer of the great Reformer, and in his sketch-book were many careful drawings of the localities which he frequented,—the castle of Wartburg, and the room which he occupied; the pulpit where he used to preach, and the cell which he occupied at Wittenberg and Eisenach, which has so many reminiscences of him. Two drawings of Eisenach are given: one is a fine example of picturesque combination of water and buildings; and the other, which shows the square, is a beautiful group of German architecture.

It singularly happened that when Prince Albert first came to England, there was a sort of revival of the old Lutheran controversy, and one which promised for a time to bear considerable fruit; and by a curious coincidence, the cause nearly resembled the one which led to the first protest of Luther against the pretensions of the Pope, and which laid Christendom under a debt to the Prince's ancestors for the protection they gave to the great Reformer. There are few persons who have seen the grand old cathedral at Trèves that will be likely to forget it. Trèves is delightfully situated on the Moselle, and lies, so to say, between Luxemburg and St Goar. The cathedral is of vast proportions, hardly inferior to one of the largest in England. It has been built at many different periods, and is really an epitome of nearly all we can learn on architecture. It was founded by Helena, the mother of Constantine, and it was almost the pride of her life. She had taken great pains, it would seem, to discover the coat that was without seam, and it was said that she had found it. This was deposited in the church of Trèves, and all recollection of it was lost; but some centuries after, by a most unaccountable accident, it was rediscovered, and turned to useful account. The coat forms one of an interesting collection of about twenty that could be enumerated, in various cathedrals of Europe, and which all claim to be the vesture without seam. It is said that about the same amount of probability attaches to the genuineness of each relic. The Bishop of Trèves may speak for himself about his own treasure. Hommer, who once occupied the see, says: "The preceding is all I have been able to collect respecting the holy coat. Till future sources of information shall either confirm or refute what I have adduced, we must content ourselves with what has been brought forward. The decision of any ancient matter which cannot be *fully proved*, must be referred to a constituent principle in the mind of man. If, from whatever cause, he is prejudiced against anything, he will always be opposed to that which contradicts his views; but if he is predisposed in its favour, he readily accepts partial proofs as valid ones,—that which he wishes is really true. An unbiassed mind will, without reference to the question, always reverence whatever is venerable for the sake of its antiquity." This is Bishop Hommer's very candid statement of the plea for the holy coat, and, for one, I respect him. It is not often that a Catholic dignitary descends from his high position, and gives his reasons for any belief which should be accepted. In this instance he has done so, and with what result let his audience judge. It is not a little singular that in the last sermon of Martin Luther's,—the last, at any rate, of which a record is kept,—he directs much of his eloquence against the holy coat of Trèves, and he says that it was the means of falsehood and delusion. He winds up with some energetic language about it, which is in his own style. Now, when Luther first came forward as the champion of freedom, he was only the exponent of the thoughts of many who had gone before, but who began to waver; and it would almost seem as if the departure of Prince Albert, and the transfer of the Duchy to an English line, signalled an attempt to revive the old delusions which his forefathers had done so much to disperse. And the excuse was the same when Leo X. sent Tetzel with his indulgences to Germany. Leo wished to raise funds for the reopening and finishing of St Peter's at Rome; and when the pilgrimage to Trèves was announced, it was said openly that the object was to raise funds for the restoration of Trèves cathedral. "During the course of the present year the said holy relic will be exhibited in the cathedral church, on the 18th of August next, for a period of six weeks, to gratify the pious desires of those who have formed a desire to undertake the pilgrimage to Trèves to honour the holy coat of our divine Redeemer by direct inspection, and thus obtain the entire absolution promised by Pope Leo X. on the 26th of January 1514." According to that celebrated bull, the said Pope, "desiring that the cathedral of Trèves, which enjoys the honour of being the repository of the seamless coat and of many other holy relics, may be distinguished in a corresponding manner by magnificent ceremonials and splendid ornaments, grants full and perfect absolution, *through all succeeding ages*, to those of the faithful who shall have made a pilgrimage to Trèves on the exposition of the holy coat, sincerely repenting of their sins, and doing penance for them, or who have formed the steadfast resolution to do so, and, moreover, contribute *liberally* towards the suitable endowment of the cathedral at Trèves." The experiment was a bold, not to say an audacious one, but the marvel is that it was quite successful. The circular of Bishop Arnoldi, in which such excellent things were promised for the faithful and the liberal, was issued in July, and the exhibition of the coat commenced on the 18th August, and in less than two months it is estimated that a million and a half of pilgrims had congregated to see this relic ! Steamers ran up the Moselle gaily decorated,—they carried enthusiasts from nearly every part of Germany, and from France, Belgium, and Holland; and on their landing, by way of keeping alive the enthusiasm, they were greeted with salvos of artillery and the ringing of bells. It was well managed, and it produced a plentiful harvest; but we can only judge of the greatness of the work that Luther had to contend with when we remember that the pilgrimage to Trèves took place when the nineteenth century was well advanced, and when monachism had become almost a thing of the past; while, in Luther's time, even a hint that the Pope was not infallible would have been dangerous in nearly every part of Germany.

CHAPTER XIX.

THERE can be no doubt that the influence of Baron
Stockmar greatly assisted to develop Prince Albert's
character, and fitted him more particularly to adapt himself to English ways and habits. Max Müller, in his
preface to Stockmar's life, says: "History cannot begin
too soon, and there cannot be a better lesson to living
sovereigns and statesmen than to have a presentiment of
the difference between the voice of history and the voice
of flatterers and political partisans. Like everything else,
history travels faster now than formerly, when two or even
three centuries had to elapse before it was considered safe
to publish State papers, and when statesmen and diplom-
atists required at least two generations to have passed
away before their papers could see the light. With
us, the events of 1830 and 1848 belong completely to
the past; the controversies roused by the *coup d'état*
of 1857 are settled; and the Crimean war has found an
historian such as few other wars have met with." Men-

tion has been made at some length of the cruel tyranny of France over Germany in Napoleon's days, and the general despair and gloom that overshadowed the country, when indeed right and wrong almost seemed to have changed places, and what was wrong prevailed. Stockmar's university career was during the terrible French domination, and he was one of the heroic spirits that never lost heart. Nothing can more closely commend him to Englishmen than his absolute certainty that above the black sky an eternal sun was shining, and that, in the words of Shakespeare—

> " Right is right,
> And wrong is no man's right."

At one time the youth of Germany meditated in their not well-directed patriotism the murder of Napoleon, and these ideas were broached when Stockmar was present. To say nothing of the wickedness of the suggestion, it would have been very bad policy; for Napoleonic ideas were then rife in France, and Ney, Massena, Soult, and other generals, who almost rivalled Napoleon himself in genius, would have been left behind, and soon Germany would have been the centre of more wars and outrage. The memory of their idol would have made the soldiers furious; and " Cæsar's spirit, ranging for revenge, would in these confines, with a monarch's voice, cry 'Havoc,' and let slip the dogs of war." Of course, evil as the suggestion was, it would not compare with the detestable wickedness of those who have killed their own rulers for some unpopularity; because Napoleon was a conqueror and a cruel invader, and had broken up for the time all the Germans held dear in their country, and they saw in him a tyrant who did not even speak their language. But when this conversation was ended, an old officer, who felt for his country quite as much as any of them, said that what he heard was the talk of very young people; that the French domination could not last. He had seen, he said, much more of the world than any of them, and they must trust to the everlasting justice of things, for the end of the tyranny was drawing near. This quiet confidence of the old German officer made a profound impression on Stockmar, and he was led, he says, to think of a moral power that worked among nations, and which was beyond the strength of armies.

It gives great pleasure to reproduce a letter here which has appeared before, but which quite expounds the liberal ideas of the distinguished man who was through life brought into such intimate association with Prince Albert.

Baron Stockmar to the Prince.

"Your Royal Highness in your political argument uses the phrase 'Conservative' several times. Conservative, in a strict sense, is nature, and nature only, which maintains, uninterruptedly and in continuous action, a portion of the old, rejects a portion of what has grown too old, and in its stead creates and establishes a portion that is new. If our statesmen would in their own department imitate this process of nature as closely as possible, then I would not dispute their right to call themselves Conservative. These gentlemen must, however, at the same time, not overlook the fact that the art of preserving a productive faculty is essential, wanting which there can be but the semblance of preservation. As, however, the so-called Conservative policy of our day has either no productive faculty at all, or, if it has, practises and applies it either not at all or only to the very smallest extent, I am inclined to feel very great distrust both of the phrase and its professions.

"The standing-point taken by Combe in his pamphlet seems to me the only right one. To subvert the power of dogma, as it now exists in England, and to adapt it to the wants and spirit of the age, will require great courage and perseverance, combined with great gifts. And yet England will have to take her share, along with the rest of Europe, in solving this problem of the age.

"Be so kind as to furnish me with some authentic intelligence as to the present state of affairs in Sicily and Naples. One must own the way things have been going on of late in the world threatens to make old Metternich's last days anxious and unpleasant. It is a lesson that the happiest of men—for such Metternich has hitherto been in a singular degree—should hold himself ready to be put to the test of reverses, so long as the final limit of his days has not been reached."

The influence of Baron Stockmar on Prince Albert lasted through his life, and indeed Stockmar only survived him for some two years. He was born about four miles from the natal place of Prince Albert;

and though he belonged to what in England, and perhaps in Germany, would be called the middle class,
and was certainly free from what may be termed personal
ambition, he seems, owing to circumstances, to have
become the guide, philosopher, and friend of princes and
kings, and to have spent his life among them. He only
became well acquainted with Prince Albert when the
Prince was nearly twenty years of age. He had some
slight knowledge of him before, from occasionally seeing
him and his family when he visited Coburg; but no real
friendship sprang up between them until he went with
the Prince to Italy in the years 1838 and 1839.

It was hardly possible for the Prince to have found a
more worthy and honest counsellor in his travels through
this classic land. As a scholar he was perhaps at least
on a level with his more experienced companion, but in
knowledge of the world the latter had few equals. A
very brief review of his life will show at once what
opportunities he must have had for acquiring it.

Stockmar was the son of a Coburg lawyer who seems to
have been a man of energy and great precision. He passed
the latter part of his life at Rodach, a quiet, quaint county
German town almost unvisited by Englishmen. It lies on
the Callenburg road, and is a pleasant walk of some three
hours from Coburg. The Thuringian forest stretches in-
definitely in patches in nearly all directions, as we travel
along the highway. He held the post of *Justizamtmann*,
which literally means a bailiff of justice, perhaps not
quite unlike our own "recorder" in some of the county
towns; and his end was singular. It occurred at the age
of 65, when in the full vigour of his life. A fire broke

out in his dwelling, and his first care was to secure the public papers of which he had the charge, and also the strong-box with the public funds, which happened to be in his keeping. Then he returned to his house to secure his own books, which were in the back part of the premises, but he found these in flames, and the sight so shocked him that he fell down in a fit of apoplexy and expired immediately.

Stockmar was originally brought up to the practice of medicine, and right well he understood his profession. He practised largely and conscientiously, and had an extensive *clientèle*. He studied medicine at Jena, when the memories of the terrible battle that laid Prussia low were still fresh in men's memories; and some of his contemporaries quaintly enough seem to say that his knowledge of medical diagnosis enabled him more easily to see the causes of political ills, and to apply a proper remedy for their removal. After he had finished his course of study here he returned to Coburg to practise his profession, and at that time he was some twenty-three years of age. He was an assistant to his uncle Dr Sommer, and even at that age he showed great ability and address. This was in 1810, and two years later he became in his own words town and country physician, and then he organised the Coburg military hospital, which was conducted with consummate ability and success. It was filled first with the French and their allies, and later on with Russians. His own account of what happened to him at this benevolent institution is curious and interesting, and conveys a very favourable impression of the man. With all the sick and wounded in the wards, that terrible scourge hospital typhus made its appearance, and one by one the doctors left in fear. Stockmar alone, with one old surgeon, had the courage to remain, but finally he was compelled to succumb to a severe attack of the dreaded foe. He was carefully attended by the old physician who remained with him at his post; and though for nearly three weeks his life was wavering in the balance, his recovery at the end of this time was as rapid as his attack, and in a comparatively short space of time he was able to resume his duties, and joined the Saxon contingent on the Rhine which was furnished by the Grand Duke. He received the appointment of physician-in-chief, a post which he filled, as might fairly be expected, with consummate judgment and skill. After the battle of Waterloo, Stockmar again returned to his native town of Coburg, and resumed the comparatively obscure position of a town and country doctor. But other and more important spheres were opening out for him. Prince Leopold of Coburg had made his acquaintance during the campaigns, and had become attached to him for his sterling honesty and his devotion to duty; and an event now occurred which changed the whole tenor of his life, and, with all sincerity be it said, was of advantage to England itself. When Prince Leopold's marriage with the Princess Charlotte was settled, he was invited to act as Physician in Ordinary to the household, and he accepted the appointment.

There is a very curious picture of England which we gather from his memoirs. The party landed at Dover on the 29th of March, when surely the days were fairly long, but it was decided not to travel too late at night "for fear of highwaymen." The long conflict with Napoleon, it is true, was recently over, and perhaps the "road" was recruited by many venturous spirits that found a quiet life wearisome after so many years of campaigning; but it is to be feared that even without this contingent, travelling in England was less secure in the year 1816 than we could now easily suppose. Stockmar was still quite a young man, and as he was so intimately connected in after-life with the Prince, a slight sketch of him, which is drawn by his son, may be of interest.

"Stockmar's character was a curious compound. To a straightforward understanding that simplified all questions presented to it, a sober habit of observation and great objectivity of apprehension, he united deep feeling, good nature, and love of mankind. For the conduct of business he was endowed with fearless activity and courage, with acuteness, insight, and contrivance; but general principles, and the tracing back of isolated facts to prime causes, were with him a matter of necessity. At one time he astonished the observer by his sanguine, bubbling, provoking, unreserved, quick, fiery, or humorous, cheerful, even unrestrainedly gay manner, warming him by his hearty open advances where he felt himself attracted or encouraged to confidence. At other times he was all seriousness, placidity, self-possession, and scepticism. These contrasts, already sufficiently startling, were still further increased by a weak physical organisation, which first seriously asserted its influence during his university career, frequently checking his aspirations and the activity of his mind, and developing by bodily sufferings the deepest hypochondria, which at times, and even in his early years, weighed down his spirits."

In addition to other excellent qualities, Stockmar had a great aptitude for seeing events far ahead, and he always believed in the wisdom of fostering feelings of nationalities. He earnestly desired to see a united Germany, with Prussia for its head, and predicted that such an arrangement, which seemed to be in the natural course of events, must finally prevail. North Germany, he used to say, might be united in his time, but it would not be for him to see the union of the north with the south; and when it did come, as come it must, he feared it would not be without bloodshed. Stockmar seems to have taken court life very easily: he was relieved from many formalities of court etiquette, all of which were distasteful to him; and he used to leave the royal dining-room, and retire to his own apartment, with very little ceremony indeed. His son relates that when spring came he used suddenly to disappear, and betake himself to his own beloved Fatherland. He disliked anything so formal as leave-taking, and some fine morning his room would be empty. Letters would follow him from the palace, and generally before summer was over he would be urged to return to England. But when he went to revisit his native land, his thoughts and his energy were bent upon his favourite theme, the foundation of a new Germany. He had indeed to witness relapses, but he never ceased to have courage and hope in the future. " The Germans," he used to say, " are a good people, easy to govern; and the German princes who do not understand this, do not deserve to rule over such a people. Do not be frightened; you younger ones are quite unable to estimate how great is the progress which the Germans have made towards political unity.   I have lived through it, and I know this people. You are marching towards a great future.   You will live to see it,—not I; but think then of the old man."

Stockmar's influence with Prince Albert began at a time when impressions are the deepest and the most lasting, and it is hardly possible to overestimate the importance and the value of his wise counsels.   He maintained the difficult position he held at the English Court throughout his long and useful life,—trusted by men of various shades of opinion, by Melbourne and Palmerston, as well as by Peel and Lord Aberdeen.   His total unselfishness prevented misunderstandings, and gained the respect and confidence of all who knew him.   To those who were not informed of his character, his position used to appear somewhat anomalous; and some of the rancorous papers used to go so far as to attack him very severely, and he was called the "intriguer Stockmar, the agent of the Jesuit Leopold."   But though it might have been supposed that, to one of his sensitive nature, such attacks would have been very bitter, he was utterly indifferent to them, having so thorough a consciousness that they were wholly unfounded in fact.   How his constant care over the Prince's early years met with their reward, the position which Prince Albert occupied at last in the hearts not only of Englishmen, but even of colonists, is the best proof.

The high station of Prince Albert in England, as has been shown, was not an easy one to fill.   There was a general disposition on the part of the press to advise and lecture, and perhaps a general mistrust of the Prince, from his youthfulness and his foreign origin.   English people are jealous, and somewhat peculiar.   If he had possessed, for example, the genius of Pitt and Canning combined, we know that he could never have taken any active part in English politics, simply because the English people are so very sensitive. Yet he was the very reverse of a mute, or a cipher, in public affairs. His praise must be that, notwithstanding the difficulties of his position, he passed away, after twenty years, without leaving an enemy or even a detractor behind him. He may indeed have done, as Wolsey advised Thomas Cromwell, and in his right hand carried gentle peace to silence envious tongues; but even that is not always enough. It is hardly possible to steer any course that shall "cope malicious censurers;" and the great triumph of the Prince must be that, after so many years passed among us, he had none. There is, unhappily, always a wish to find flaws and faults with our neighbours, and it hardly needs that these should be true to insure their circulation. If the subjects of calumny are raised above their fellows in worldly circumstances, can any one say that the tales are the less welcome? Then, in such cases, there is perfect safety and immunity. It is much more secure to spread any untrue anecdote of those who are high in power than of those less highly placed.

But I only speak the truth when I say that even calumny never touched him; and a few extracts from his speeches on three occasions—and these extracts are short ones—will be sufficient to show how thoroughly Prince Albert had learned to appreciate the sympathies of the people with whom he lived, and how thoroughly he was able to add life and to give direction to their interests. At the dinner of the Royal Academy, 1851, he said:—

"Gentlemen,—The production of all works in art or poetry requires, in their conception and execution, not only an exercise of the intellect, skill, and patience, but particularly a concurrent warmth of feeling and a free flow of the imagination. This renders them most tender plants, that will thrive only in an atmosphere calculated to maintain that warmth; and that atmosphere is one of kindness towards the artist personally as well as towards his productions. An unkind word of criticism passes like a cold blast over their tender shoots, and shrivels them up, checking the flow of the sap which was rising perhaps to produce multitudes of flowers and fruit. But still criticism is absolutely necessary to the development of art, and the injudicious praise of inferior work becomes an insult to superior genius. In this respect our times are peculiarly unfavourable as compared with those when Madonnas were painted in the seclusion of convents; for we have now, on the one hand, the eager competition of a vast array of artists of every degree of talent and skill— and on the other, as judge, a great public, for the greater part wholly uneducated in art, and thus led by professional writers, who often strive to impress the public with a great idea of their own artistic knowledge by the merciless manner in which they treat works that have cost those who produced them the highest efforts of mind and feeling.

"The works of art, by being publicly offered for sale, are becoming articles of trade, following as such the unreasoning law of marches of fashion; and public and even private patronage is swayed by their tyrannical influence."

The next extract will more concern the practical part of life; and it not only appeals to all kinds of academic institutions, but broaches views that were then almost new, but have since made great progress.

At a banquet in Birmingham, on the occasion of laying the first stone of the Birmingham and Midland Institute in 1853, the Prince said: "The study of the laws by which the Almighty governs the universe is therefore our bounden duty. Of those laws our great academies and seats of education have rather arbitrarily selected only two spheres or groups (as I may call them), as essential parts of a national education. The laws which regulate quantities and proportions, and form the subject of mathematics; and the laws regulating the expression of our thoughts through the medium of language, that is to say, grammar, which finds its purest expression in the classical languages,—these laws are most important branches of knowledge. Their study trains and elevates the mind. But they are not the only ones. There are others that we cannot disregard—that we cannot do without. There are, for instance, the laws governing the human mind and its relation to the Divine Spirit (the subject of logic and metaphysics); there are those which govern our bodily nature and its connection with the soul (the subject of physiology and psychology); and those which govern human society and the relations between man and man (the subject of politics, jurisprudence, and political economy, and many others); whilst of the laws above mentioned, some have been recognised as essentials of education in different institutions, and some will, by the course of time, more fully assert their right to recognition. The laws which regulate matter and form, are those which will constitute the chief objects of *your* pursuits; and as the subject of the subdivision of labour is the one most congenial to our age, I would advise you to keep to this specialty, and to follow with undivided attention, chiefly the science of mechanics, physics, and chemistry, and then the fine arts in painting, sculpture, and architecture."

The Prince is equally happy in the next quotation, which is from a speech at a meeting of the Society for the Propagation of the Gospel in Foreign Parts, in 1851. It refers to the spread of the Gospel,—and here he might fairly claim to be, as it were, on his own ground; and when he spoke of what "our" ancestors had gained at the Reformation, he might have said "my ancestors." "We cannot help deploring that the Church whose exertions for the progress of Christianity and civilisation we are to-day acknowledging, should be afflicted by internal dissensions and attacks from without. I have no fear, however, for her safety, so long as she holds fast to what our ancestors gained for us at the Reformation, — the Gospel, and the unfettered right to use it."

But the best way to appreciate the Prince's influence in England is to contrast his reception in that country (with indeed its cordiality—such, at least, as politeness would require) with the heartfelt genuine grief when he was removed from our midst. Nothing can be more instructive or curious than to compare, as we often may, the events of the past with the same events as they have developed in later years. Often if they are those connected with our own life, they slide into each other so gently and so imperceptibly that no change is noticed. The boy is the father of the man; and when in after-years he takes his place in the battle of life, he can hardly believe that the widest possible difference separates him from the youth of early days. But often this is brought vividly forward by some slight local event or accident. He may remember, possibly, some seaside resort where he was taken to, and where everything wore an air of novelty. There was the spacious residence; the fleet of white - sailed vessels ploughing through the waves, and the gigantic fishermen jumping, regardless of their safety, into the waves, and carrying enormous loads of fish on their shoulders, which have been captured from the vast mysterious ocean beyond. But when the place is revisited, the spacious residence is a yellow-washed house of the most moderate dimensions, let by the month or the week. The fleet is only a lot of trawlers, and the venturesome fishermen that brave the deep with their load, only jump over the side of grounded yawls in their waterproof boots, and carry on their backs such plaice or ray as they have had the good fortune to capture. Or if he may remember to have gone to some neighbouring church on a Sunday, and he has all the recollections of a vast edifice of quite cathedral dimensions, he will find on revisiting it after many years, that it is only a grey stone parish church of no extravagant proportions. Though perhaps, in this instance, it may have been wrecked by restoration, and at least some of the antiquity he had looked for has been swept away, still, the building itself is far from what he had expected. Changes in everything are a part of our system, and it is often interesting when we can compare writings of anticipation with the results of after-years, and see how strange everything appears. In the present instance the articles of perhaps our most prominent journal are given, and we cannot but be struck with the contrast. The views of this journal in 1840 probably represented the average opinions of the best-informed men in England. The writer of this article, which appeared on the day of the Royal wedding, begins by saying how much we sympathise with any wedding-day, whatever the condition of the people ; and after adding that he will then, and naturally for the last time, state his views, he proceeds as follows :—

" Were Prince Albert eight or ten years older, we should augur more confidently the moral and political points to be drawn from this alliance. As it is, the position of his Royal Highness appears difficult ; and the responsibility which rests upon him as confidential and bosom counsellor of the Queen of England—to whose judgment, high principle, and steadiness of conduct, the country must look for a counteraction of many evil influences, and for the separation of some very grievous errors—is one of which it would be too sanguine to anticipate that he will be able for a long time to acquit himself with credit. But the youth and inexperience of the Prince, and the consequent snares that may be laid for him, and the unenviable disqualifications under which he must labour for his own release, and that of his Royal consort, from the embarrassments which have already accumulated round them, are our only grounds of regret or alarm in connection with the great forthcoming event of this important day." The same journal proceeds to say

that a pamphlet had recently been issued addressed to
" The People of Great Britain ; " and he says that, even
taking a moderate view of the circumstances, the title is
a little ambitious. " Why exclude Ireland ? " he asks,—
though indeed this question is less pertinent than another
one that follows. The tract or pamphlet would seem
to have been issued by some one who was at the time in
a prominent position, and this journal, which has always
held the leading position in England, asks why it was
written. It would seem to have been designed, as it
said, to shield Prince Albert from many aspersions that
would appear to linger round himself and his family and
race, and in it his pedigree is traced back to remote ages.
It may, of course, easily date back a thousand years or
more, but what do average Englishmen care for that ?
Doubtless during this long period there were many extravagances and vices and errors, but surely Prince Albert
is not to be brought to his trial for these : and finally, it
adds that " no Englishman would desire to connect any
man, whatever his position or rank in life, with any act
that was not his own ; " and that, so far as was known, " the
antecedents of the Prince were in his favour." It concludes : " Prince Albert has now become one of us. He
is actually now an English subject. He is tied to us by
law and self-interest. Let us bind him to us by gratitude
and affection. The happiness of our youthful Queen is
in his hands. He has the means of so directing and so
assisting her future footsteps, as to retrieve for her
Majesty much of what (we speak with frankness, but
with all respect) she has forfeited in the hearts of the
most loyal and virtuous of her subjects, through her

unhappy bias towards factions and principles which are hourly undermining the deep foundations of the throne. . . . We put it to the same great 'People of Great Britain,' to whom the letter in defence of Prince Albert is addressed. Is it right that the Court of England should be so composed that the well-educated German Prince, who is to live in the centre of it, should not be able to discover within reach of him a single companion capable of carrying on a conversation with him on any subject more elevated than a fox-hunt, a field-day, or a battue ? "

In the 'Memoirs of the Prince Consort' there is a note already alluded to, it will be remembered, where he said—" I don't understand people making a business of shooting, and going out the whole day. People here [in England] are given to make a business of it." And, in a similar strain, many other papers at that time discussed the situation. There was every desire to be at any rate *safe* prophets of the future; and who could possibly predict what the future of a man, who had hardly reached man's estate, would be ? He came from a duchy that would rank in area among the small English counties, and where all the surroundings to which he had been used would not, it was supposed, be considered extravagant in an English squire's house, and he became at once the head of the wealthiest and most splendid Court in the world. In addition to this, the times were very far from being favourable for a foreign Prince to cast his lot in England. For long there had been a growing feeling of what was called Chartism, or some kind of attempt to do as the Communists have at a later period done in

France. There were riotous demands for a "people's charter," as they termed it; and this included universal suffrage, vote by ballot, equal electoral divisions, annual Parliaments, the abolition of all property qualifications for members of Parliament, and payment for the services of the representatives; and it is not a little singular to reflect that two of the points have since become incorporated in the law of the land. But of course some of the claims were not only out of the question, but opposed to the oldest traditions of England, yet they stirred the country from end to end. Again, it was supposed to be through the policy of those high in station that the disastrous war of Cabul had been commenced; and all these things were culminating at the period of Prince Albert's arrival in England. Many an old head shook ominously at the prospect of the "young German Prince" coming to England, and making things no better, but much worse. The writer is just old enough to recollect some of these prognostications, and the sage innuendoes that we knew what to expect from a German dukedom:

> " For now a time is come to mock at form,—
> Henry the Fifth is crowned : up vanity !
> Down royal state ! all you sage councillors hence ;
> And to the English court assemble now
> From every region, apes of idleness."

All was uncertainty, and, as it happened, the English people were in a state of discontent at the disordered condition of their internal affairs, and almost in despair of ruling Ireland, which was in one of its periodical commotions. How Prince Albert answered any expectations will be best learned by reproducing the eloquent remarks of the 'Times,' and comparing them with the article written twenty-one years before, which has been already quoted from :—

"The nation has just sustained the heaviest loss that could possibly have fallen upon it. Prince Albert, who a week ago gave every promise that his valuable life would be lengthened to a period long enough to enable him to enjoy, even in this world, the fruits of a virtuous youth and a well-spent manhood, the affection of a devoted wife, and of a family of which any father might be proud,—this man, the very centre of our social system, the pillar of our State, is snatched suddenly away from us, without even warning sufficient to prepare us for a blow so abrupt and so terrible. We shall need time to fully appreciate the magnitude of the loss we have sustained. Every day will make us more conscious of it. It is not merely a prominent figure that will be missed on all public occasions—not merely a death that will cast a permanent gloom over a reign hitherto so joyous and prosperous; it is the loss of a public man whose services to this country, though rendered neither on the field of battle nor in the arena of crowded assemblies, have yet been of inestimable value to the nation,—a man to whom more than any one else we owe the happy state of our internal polity, and a degree of general contentment to which neither we nor any other nation we know of have ever attained before.

"Twenty-one years have just elapsed since Queen Victoria gave her hand in marriage to Prince Albert of Saxe-Gotha. It was an auspicious event, and has more than surpassed all prognostics, however favourable.

The Royal marriage has been blessed with a numerous offspring. So far as it is permitted to the public to know the domestic lives of sovereigns, the people of these islands could set up no better model for the performance of the duties of a wife and mother than their Queen; no more complete pattern of a devoted husband and father than her consort. These are not mere words of course. We write in an age and in a country when the highest position would not have availed to screen the most elevated delinquent. They are simply the records of a truth perfectly understood and recognised by the English people. It has been the misfortune of most Royal personages that their education has been below the dignity of their position. Cut off by their rank from intimate association with young persons of the same age, they have often had occasion bitterly to lament that the same fortune which had raised them above the nobility in rank had sunk them below them in knowledge and acquirements. Thanks to the elevated mind and the sterling good sense of the Prince Consort, no such charge will be brought against the present generation of the Royal family of England. Possessing talents of the first order, cultivated and refined by diligent and successful study, the Prince has watched over the education of his children with an assiduity commensurate with the greatness of the trust, and destined, we doubt not, to bear fruit in the future stability of our reigning family, and its firm hold in the affections of the people. Had Prince Albert done no more than this,—had he limited his ambition to securing the happiness of his wife and children,—this country, considering who his wife and children are, would have owed him a debt which the rank he occupied among us, and the material and social advantages attached to it, would have been quite inadequate to repay.   But there is much more which the Prince has done for us.   It was a singular piece of fortune that the Queen should find in a young man of twenty years one whom a sudden and unlooked-for elevation could not elate, nor all the temptations of a splendid Court and luxurious capital seduce ; who kept the faith he had pledged with simple and unswerving fidelity, and in the heyday of youth ruled his passions and left no duty unperformed.   But it is still more singular that in this untried youth the Queen should have found an adviser of the utmost sagacity, a statesman of the rarest ability and honesty of purpose.   Perhaps all history cannot afford an instance of the performance of high and irresponsible but strictly limited duties, with a dignity and singleness of intention comparable to that which has made illustrious the reign of Queen Victoria.   .   .   .

" Now and for a long time to come the heart of her Majesty can find room but for a single thought ; but when the first agony has spent itself, we trust that it may suggest some slight consolation to her to reflect that she as implicitly commands the sympathy and sorrow as she had always commanded the loyalty and affection of the subjects who have had the happiness to live under her rule, and to be instructed by her example."

APPENDIX.

I WOULD be wanting to the subject in hand if a few words were not added regarding Thuringian legends. Thuringia is indeed rich in legendary lore, and many tales that have enlivened an English fireside are derived from its hills and valleys. From the Carpathian hills to the Thuringer-wald it is commonly said that many legends are to be found in their primitive form; and as these tales were circulated in different parts, they acquired a local fame. It is recorded of Prince Albert that one of his great delights was to recount some of these to his family at open-air breakfasts, and it is natural to suppose that his store of them was boundless. We see the origin of the " White Doe of Rylstone" in a fine old legend which is given. The "Death of Gellert," which Southey has sung and a tomb at Llanberis commemorates, is a verbatim copy of a Thuringian legend. The "Carp of the Sea" has been told by Grimm, but only partially, and it is generally domiciled at one of the large lakes in Bohemia.

LEGENDARY LORE OF THURINGIA.

Prince Albert's early life was spent in a land rich in legendary lore, and some of the tales that especially belong to German literature have their centre in Thuringian mountains and valleys. For him, as for all single-minded people, these had always a charm, and he was greatly impressed with the tale of his ancestors being carried away by Kunz von Kaufingen from Altenburg Castle, and taken into Bohemia. The Duchess of Coburg in 1823 writes: "Ernest's boys have got a picture-book. One of the pictures represents the carrying off of the Saxon princes. This interests them greatly, and Albert makes wonderful eyes in telling that one was called Albert like himself." The native German fairy-lore stands quite by itself, though much that we read in Grimm and Hans Andersen is derived from foreign sources. In the Roman army were many German soldiers. Julius Cæsar formed so high an opinion of their valour, that he induced many warriors to enter his legions; and after his time it became quite common for Germans to enlist, until at length they formed by far the greater part of the Roman army; and when they returned to their native country, it is easy to see that they must have had many opportunities of bringing Roman legends and tales with them.

But we find at a later period a further element in German mythology. Germany, as we know, took little part in the First Crusade—she had troubles enough at home; but Conrad, whose name so often appears in romance, joined the second one with 70,000 men, and many a tale was brought to the Hartz and Thuringian mountains by the "faithful" warriors who accompanied him back to Germany. The next Crusade has furnished a legend that brings us back to modern days, and is redolent of German lore. Frederick I. spent much of his life in the famous struggle with the Papacy and the cities of Lombardy, and those who have a taste for the romantic might indeed find much in his career to gratify them. The struggle between Frederick and the Pope was always popular in Germany; and the Pope found, as he found in other lands, that the people of any monarch who himself opposed him were insensible to his anathemas. It was at the end of the twelfth century that Frederick, then an old man, decided to devote some of the few years that remained to him, to an expedition against the infidel — just the time when so many cross-legged knights are left to us in church chancels in England; but he was not destined on this occasion to reach the battle-field. In June 1190 he was stopped at a bridge over the Calycadnus in Asia Minor, and, not able to brook further delay, he dashed into the stream and was drowned. Here a curious legend, which belongs to a class indigenous to the country, appears. He was in reality buried at Antioch, but tradition says that he returned in the spirit, at least, to Germany.

There is in Thuringia, in the midst of the early homes of Prince Albert, a high hill on the range called Kyffhauser Berg, which is bluff and steep, and has in it some caverns of considerable magnitude. Into this it was the popular belief of the Germans that the soul of Frederick retired with his knights, and here they held high revel. They used also to say that when ravens had ceased to fly round the cliffs and peaks of the hill where he was, Germany would arise and assert her greatness among the kingdoms of Europe, led by a Prince Frederick. They fly there probably still, unless the railway has scared them; but, as it happens, a Prince Frederick, who was immediately connected with the descendants of the lords of Thuringia, was the first to lead a German army across the Vosges Mountains, after the battle of Wörth, and was soon joined by those who, in recent times, have placed Germany at the head of European nations. This would, of course, have been an excellent theme in old days for a genuine German legend. The soldiers who returned from the Crusades brought home many a romance, and we can find nearly every incident of the 'Arabian Nights' in the pages of Grimm or Hans Andersen. These charming writers have each of them their own stories, but they have tales in common in a few instances. It was a great delight to me often, in wandering through the ancient towns in Thuringia, to go into an old inn. One has been shown before, which is the perfect picture of a German hostelry of bygone days. It would well serve for a model of the inn at Rochester, in the graphic scene in "Henry IV.," where the two saturnine carriers had come down at four o'clock in the morning to harness up.

Very commonly the legend or fairy tale has a moral,—less cynical than Æsop's fables, indeed, but often as apt and true. Here is one that seems to preach the desirability of tender-heartedness, even in a huntsman. A fine young soldier had been brought up on the Saxon dominions of Henry the Lion. Henry the Lion was a cousin to the great Frederick Barbarossa, and he accompanied him in his celebrated Italian campaign, in his struggle with the Papacy. It is an old tale how the cousins disagreed, and Frederick, to whom he owed so much, took away his duchies; but the disinherited cousin ultimately came to England and married the king's daughter, and became the ancestor of the present Royal family of England. A young Saxon soldier, who had been a follower of Henry, returned to his native land, and used to devote much of his time to his old favourite amusement of the chase. He had formed the acquaintance of a Lombard damsel during the wars, who would seem to have nursed him on one occasion when he was wounded. She accompanied him home as his wife, and they went to live on the borders of Thuringer - wald, and were greatly beloved by every one about. The Lombard wife was as beautiful as she was kind; but she only lived to enjoy her married life for a short time, and she died shortly after having given birth to a daughter. True it is that his wife was the daughter of an enemy,—one was a " Welf," and the other was a " Waibling,"—but the affection he felt for her was none the less, and he laid her, almost broken-hearted, in the grave. But time heals all sorrow, and is often the only sweet oblivious antidote. As his daughter grew, he saw more and more the likeness of her Italian mother, and doted more upon her every day. At last the crossbow and the hunting-spear were refurbished, and once again the widower solaced himself with the chase. When he came down the hill, on his road home, his young daughter was always looking out for his return, and darted away like a roebuck when her keen eyes detected him far away in an opening in the pine-woods; and often she would wander for half a mile in the direction she fancied he might be coming, and dart off when she saw him emerge into a forest-clearing. Her delight was to search his leather game-bag, and to endeavour to demonstrate her pleasure at what she found. When she was about nine years old, he had gone into the Thuringian hills, and after toiling for some time, he was about to give up the chase and return home, which he rarely did empty-handed, when he heard the baying of his two hounds in pursuit of something. The noise seemed to approach him, and he got his bow and hunting-spear in readiness, and sheltered behind a tree. The noises approached, and soon a cream-coloured doe bounded through the woods to where he was standing, and by an impulse he could not avoid, his weapon became powerless in his hand. The doe had passed him, but there was such a sweetly plaintive look in its eyes that he almost saw in it the vision of his lost wife; and when the dogs came up directly after, he sternly called them in, and the cream-coloured deer was soon lost in the woods. When he came home he told his little daughter what he had seen; and she said she thought she had seen it several times, and it looked so tame that she tried to catch it, but it went into a small thicket and was lost. She never told her father, she said, for fear of him laughing at her, and thinking her a fanciful child. Not long after this the hunter was in the forest, and was on his road home with a roebuck. He was crossing a narrow valley, and laid his load down while he rested and had a long draught from the stream that sparkled through the gorge. He thought he heard the howl of a wolf, and listened more closely, when the baying of two wolves was quite audible, and these were approaching the spot where he was. To snatch up his hunting-spear and bow was the work of a moment, and he hid himself

x

behind a large stone. Directly after, he saw the cream-coloured fawn, and it passed close by him. This time he heard its hoofs gently disturb the gravel which lay in the gorge where he was concealed. The wolves came close by the stone, and as he was thoroughly prepared for them, he stepped out, and drove his hunting-spear through the heart of the first one, which gave one piercing howl and rolled over never to stir again. The other one, after a cry of rage and fear, turned round and slunk away. And now the huntsman wondered where his daughter could be. At the end of the valley she used to come to meet him, though it was nearly two miles from home, and as the day was pleasant and bright, he expected to see her. Some apprehension about the wolves he found it hard to shake off, and he went rather nervously forward, hoping to hear her call him. After passing through a thicket that concealed his house, which was not more than a mile off, he became more alarmed, and then he remembered that she had told him she would hang out a white cloth from the gable-window of her bedroom whenever she had left the cottage to find him. The sun was shining full in the front of the house, and the white cloth was there. His alarm grew greater and greater, and he called her name aloud, but all in vain. Just as he was leaving the opening in the woods to make a shorter track home which he well knew, he saw his daughter's little basket, half full of blackberries, and not far from that was her cap in a bramble! He searched about wildly, and even started to try and find the other wolf, and rip it in two; but he decided that it would be wiser to go back to the cottage and see if there were any trace of the missing damsel. He hurried along, and his heart fell within him when he saw the door closed, for he knew she must have gone. He knocked loudly, but no answer came, and then in terror he went round to the garden-door and called her name. This was also fastened; but what was his joy when he saw the fastenings give way, and the young girl was alive before him! She wept with joy when she found she was really safe in her father's arms, and as soon as she was able she narrated her own adventure. She said that early in the afternoon she had gone up to the woods through which he was to come back home, to gather blackberries and wild-flowers. Some of the bushes were almost black over, and the blackest were those inside the trees. She had not gone very far when she thought she saw a curious light in the deep part of a jungle, opposite to where she was. At first it was like two green lamps, but as she looked again to see what it was, there were three or four. She turned to get out of the wood into the open place between it and home, and as she looked back she saw two gaunt wolves emerging. One of them, as they slunk along, put up its head and gave such a terrible howl that it nearly took her senses away; and just as she expected to be eaten up, the cream-coloured doe skipped lightly between her and the wolves. They then howled dreadfully, and she saw it go along the valley, where it afterwards passed her father. The doe went slowly at first, and she thought the wolves would have caught it, but it skipped lightly away after she seemed to feel safe, and then for the first time she thought of running home. She locked and bolted the door, and hardly remembered what happened till she heard her father's voice at the garden-door. The white doe was never seen again till a year afterwards, when the young soldier was going to the fair at Erfurt, to make some purchases. He was tramping along a very uneven road, when it suddenly appeared and cantered before him into a path in the woods. This time he had no hesitation at all in following it, and it gently preceded him, so as not to overtax his strength; but the moment the towers of Erfurt were in sight it disappeared into the forest, and was never seen again. He slept at an old hostelry in Erfurt, and in the morning he went into the market-square to make his purchases and meet old friends. He saw three men of ferocious appearance brought in, shortly after his arrival in the square, and they were soon surrounded by a crowd. They were heavily manacled, and seemed to be very notorious. He followed them into the court-house, and heard the charge against them. They were notorious robbers and highwaymen, and only the night before they had waylaid and murdered a traveller who was on his road to Erfurt fair to make some purchases. His leather bag, with his money in it, was found on one of them; and the axe which had murdered him was found on another, with part of the same cloth that his cap was made of adhering to it. The huntsman went to the court-house, and followed the proceedings with intense interest and surprise; for before the charge against them was concluded, he found that they were stationed on the road that led to Erfurt, over which he was about to pass when the white doe led him off into the woods, and so saved his life. Whether she was real or not he never could make out. He had heard the small pebble-stones rattle under her feet as she fled from the wolves, and even heard her rapid breathing as she flitted past, and that, in his mind, settled the matter; but he never could account for the almost uncanny way in which she had appeared three times over, and he resolved in future to stay his hand against everything of the deer kind, and to direct his spear and his bow against bears and wolves. In this legend we see something of the Pythagorean system, that supposes the body of an animal is made the receptacle for the life of a man, sometimes for good and sometimes for evil. Shakespeare, who was imbued with all fairy-lore and mythology of his day, makes Gratiano say to Shylock,—

> " Thou almost makes me waver in my faith
> To hold opinion with Pythagoras,
> That souls of animals infuse themselves
> Into the trunks of men : thy currish spirit
> Governed a wolf."

The reverse of a wolf, of course, is the case with the legend before us, but the mythical lore is the same. Good fairies, doing all kinds of services for those who deserve them, are not always comely—often quite the reverse; and their form is often assumed to test the amiability of the mortal they address.

There is one legend which is common both in France and Germany, and is told in many forms—one of the best of which is as follows: A Thuringian tradesman had gone to Frankfurt to try his fortune, and there by dint of energy and thrift he acquired a competency. The large city was not, however, to his taste, and he never ceased to long for the glories of his native hills and valleys. At last he returned, and easily bought a small estate. His family increased, and he told two of his sons that they must go into the world and seek their fortune. "But you shall not go," he said, "as I went; you shall have money in your purse, enough to help you till you can find something to earn. Be industrious and frugal, and never spend more than half you make. And be kind and civil to all ; make as many friends as you can,—in the day of need these may be too few: but never make an enemy, for in the day of need he will be one too many." The elder son took this to heart, and thought over it all as he left his father's gate : the younger one, who had always been a torment to his brothers and sisters, did not think much more about it. But he was his father's favourite, and had twice as much money given to him as his brother. He made his brother spend his sum while it lasted; and then, when they slept in a cottage that they had made their resting-place for the night, the younger one got up to leave his brother, but he found that he did not know the road they were to travel along. They were bound for Dresden, and it was only the elder brother that knew the way. The younger soon returned, and said he had gone for a short walk and lost his way, and his brother believed his tale. They came to a large ant-hill, and the younger brother kicked it over, saying he wished to see the ants scamper away with their eggs ; but the elder brother, though the weaker one, persuaded him to let them live. Then they came to a lake, on which there was a flock of teal-ducks floating. The younger brother at once put up his crossbow to kill one; but his elder brother arrested his arm, and said—"Nay, the wind is from the shore, and you could not get it when you killed it." And then they came to an enchanted castle, where everything was stone: the horses and serving-men were all statues, and one old crusty warder alone was human. "Find the key," he said; "it's in the lake there. But if you try, and cannot, you will be stone too; if you can—the castle and all its lands are yours." Then the brothers went to the lake, and the younger one outran the elder, who heard soon after an arrow from a crossbow; and he said—"Can my brother wish to kill me?" and went back to the castle gates. But when he saw him return, he went towards the lake himself and saw a flight of teal-ducks—the very ones he had noticed before. They lit upon the lake, and dived down, and soon one came flapping and swimming along the water with a small golden key. This was the key to the castle. Then all the stone horses began to move, and the serving-men appeared in livery; but the old warder came forward again, and said that there were fifty pearls hidden in the wood near an ant's nest, and whoever found them when the castle gates were open, should be the owner over all other comers. So the younger man, who thought to forestall his brother, went to the wood; but he was so badly stung that he sat down to ease his pains, and the elder brother went forward to the nest. The ants had burrowed round their dwelling and found all the pearls, and when the elder brother came back to the castle with them he found his selfish relative transformed into a stone statue in a niche in the castle gateway.

Sometimes the legend contains reflections on human nature, and one of the best of these appears in Grimm's tales, though he would seem to differ in his reading from the commoner version. The tale is called the "Fisherman and his Wife," but I think it should more properly be the "Rustic and his Wife." Grimm speaks of a carp as being caught in the sea; but nothing of the carp kind lives in the sea, excepting an allied species, which is never called by the name of carp. The story in Germany would seem to refer to a rustic that used to go to a pool and cast in a line for fish, and a golden carp took his bait—some carps are of a very golden colour. But when he hooked it, it ran out his line to the bottom of the lake, which was very deep, and finally gave itself up when it could not get the hook from its mouth. When the fisherman unhooked it, it said: "Now listen for one moment to me: there is no value in me, for my flesh is not good, and if you kill me it will do you no good, but it will do me a very great deal of harm. I am an enchanted prince, and I can do nearly anything you wish; so if you desire a boon, you may say what it is." The peasant replied, "I'm sure I don't want to kill a fish that speaks; so now that I have got the hook out of your mouth, off you go." When he reached home he told his wife all that had happened, and said that he didn't like such fishes about his hooks, and he never would fish there again. "You fool!" his wife replied, "just go again and catch him once more, and don't be in such a hurry to let him go again." "But he won't come to the hook again—a burnt child avoids the fire." "Well, then," his wife said, "just send the same bait into the pool again, where you caught the carp before, and it will come to it; but tie it with a string to show there is no hook at all. We want a nice new cottage, with vines and roses." The rustic followed this astute advice, and shortly after he threw in his line. A strong pull told him that the carp was at the bait. He pulled up his line, which was followed by the golden carp, and as he trailed it along the surface the carp followed. He lifted the fish out of the water, and it seemed wonderfully pleased to meet its captor again. "There is to be no killing, mind you, though you would have no trouble at all if you desired it; but I can do nearly anything for you. If you kill me, I cannot; but till you ask me something I cannot do, my enchantment is not broken—though when you do, I return to my proper form. Ask me anything you like, and especially ask your wife to tell you what she wants, and I shall swim away into the lake very happily." He then told it about his wife's request, and the carp said, "Go home at once; your wife has all she wants." As he left the road leading up from the lake, he thought, as he turned back, that in the light of the setting sun he saw the carp leap out of the lake, as their custom sometimes is, and it was accompanied in its frolics by some others that evidently shared its joy. When the peasant returned home he went to the hovel where they had been accustomed to live, and found it was empty; but hard by he discovered a beautiful cottage, with every accompaniment of roses and vines. Great was his joy; but he was very much disturbed when his wife finally began to tire of her cottage, and to say that he should go to the golden carp again and try to mend their condition. The husband rather complained, but went away with his tackle, and very soon he enticed the carp from its cells under the rocks of the lake. The carp, as before, came after the bait smilingly; and so great was its pleasure to see him, that it said, even before the rustic spoke, "Well, how is your wife, and how does she like her new cottage?" "Fairly well, but I am afraid she wants something more,—she is not quite satisfied yet;" and the carp replied, "Go back and ask her what it is, and I will grant it to her. I can do nearly anything; and when I am asked to do something I cannot do, then my spell is broken, and I go back to my kingdom again." The rustic, however, did not hear the last part of the speech, and told his wife only what he had heard. She sent him back to the lake, and he found it calm, but of a deep indigo colour, and the sky was heavy and lowering; but he saw by a wake in the water that a large fish was coming to him, and that was the carp, as he had expected, and in its anxiety it floundered out on a bed of rushes. "Well, what does she want?" said the carp.

"Oh," said the man, more than half afraid, "she wants to go and live in a stone castle."

"Go home," said the carp; "she is standing before the door already."

So the man went away thinking to go home, but when he

saw a great stone castle his heart failed within him; but his wife took him by the hand and showed him the vestibule inlaid with marble, and the tables were all laid out with viands of the most costly description. The park was filled with deer and roebucks, and there was everything a man could desire. And his wife said, "Is not this fine?"

"A great deal too fine for me," he said. "I would almost rather be back at the cottage."

"Nonsense," she replied; "you'll tire of this before long. I shall."

In the morning, when they woke, his wife got up and looked over the grand valleys and the flat plains beyond, with all the woods, and the silvery stream that showed itself in lengths, and was lost again in foliage, as it sparkled in the morning sun on its unceasing journey to the main. She woke her husband up to see the glorious sight, for he was snoring soundly after his journeys to the lake of the previous day.

The husband was quite as much delighted as his wife, and said, "This is very grand, and in time I shall like it better than the cottage."

"Better, indeed!" his wife replied. "There is no doing anything with some people."

One fine morning in August his wife called from the casement, "Get up, you lazy dog!" and the rustic at once obeyed, though he was tired out with a reception they had given the previous night, at which, indeed, neither of them appeared to great advantage. "Now, look here," she said; "would it not be grand to be king and queen here?"

"Oh, wife," he said, "we are far too high up already; do be content. Besides that, there is no king and queen; it is a grand duchy we are looking over."

"Well, that is better than as we are; let us be grand duchess and duke."

"I won't go to the carp any more; you may go yourself,— I won't."

"Very well—we will see about that later on in the day. I
rather think you will."

And she was quite correct, for early in the afternoon he was
seen plodding away to the lake. He spent some time over his
tackle, and to be very sure he climbed to the top of the rock
under which the carp lay, and threw out his line, so that it
would be sure to reach it; but this was not necessary, as the
carp had been basking in a shallow, and made for the shore
when he came. It called from the rock, and went quickly
away to the bed of rushes. He went there, and when he could
not see it he called out—

> " Oh carp of the lake, it was all a mistake,
>   So do come and hear me for pity's sake ; "

and soon he floundered up into the bed of reeds.

"Well, what does your wife want now ?" the carp said—for
he knew very well she would not be content, and his hopes
were centred on this belief.

"She wants to rule over all the vast lands we see, and she
shall be the princess and I the prince ; and she has threatened
me with awful things if I do not get your consent."

"Well, now," said the carp, "there is a palace you can see
from your castle ; all the servants are there, and it only wants
some one to live in it."

"And can I go now to it with my wife, for she will scold me
dreadfully ? "

"Most certainly you can. The palace is mine, and I can
give that, if nothing more."

The rustic returned to his wife, and she was highly pleased
with the news, and before long she had moved into the palace ;
and when he came into the palace everything was of pure
marble and gold, and velvet covers to the chairs and tables,
with great gold tassels. Then the doors of the hall flew open,
and showed the whole splendour of the court ; and his wife
was sitting on a lofty throne, and had a crown on her head,

and in her hand a sceptre of gold. The husband was very much astonished, and when they retired he said, "Surely now you are content."

"We will see about that," she replied. "I want to be a little higher up yet: we are not quite at the top of the tree, for all we have the carp's palace. So just go back and tell him I want to be Pope, and control the sun, and the moon, and the stars."

"But, wife, I cannot do that; the Pope himself cannot control the sun."

"Oh, he can't, can't he? I know better than that."

"But, wife, you are a lady—now how can you be Pope? popes are men." And here the wife became so violent that he ran to the lake once more and called out—

> "Oh carp of the pool, my wife is a fool;
> She wants all the stars to be under her rule."

The carp was at the bed of reeds, and said, "What a time I have been waiting for you! I knew you would come again, but my spell is broken, for you have asked me what I cannot grant: however, go home, and I shall see you there." The rustic in amazement went to the palace and saw a prince sitting where his wife had been; and he saw his wife, as he thought, in the courtyard. The transformed carp said, "You broke my spell by asking for something I could not grant, and you may join your wife again." But the wife had entered the throne-room, and taken her husband by the arm, leading him to the door with many invectives. The transformed carp heard her say, "I always told you so,—it's just your way; you never do know when you are well off. You are a lout; and now I suppose we must go back to the hovel again,"—which they did, and the legend says that they are there yet. Another version of the legend lays the scene further north, and Grimm's Fables speak of the fish as some kind of sea-fish: these are never golden in colour; but the rustic says on each occasion—

> "Oh fish of the sea, come listen to me,
> For my wife won't let be as I'd have it be."

The moral of the tale is not so clearly drawn out in Grimm. It really is intended to show that a striving man may be overcome by his wife's extravagances; and though it seems natural and proper to her, she never thinks of the straits she often puts her husband to, and his repeated expostulations lose their weight by repetition.

There can be no doubt that the legendary lore of the Germans has done much to form the excellences of their character. Often we see in the legend a repetition of some Eastern tale, such as we meet with in the 'Arabian Nights,' and even in classic lore. There is no difficulty in seeing how such anecdotes may have found their way into Germany, but one would hardly expect to find the same thread of humour running through a Cheshire history. Yet nearly the same appears in some of the English traditions,—one especially in Cheshire, in the history of the notable Nixon, the Cheshire prophet. He had a wonderful career, and was sent for by Henry VII. after Bosworth field, to be "clemmed" (or starved), as he said. His fame as a prophet was established during the battle: when he was driving his cart along the highway, suddenly he stopped, and the yokels about him declared that he called out, "Now Henry, now Richard," until he said, "Cross the ditch, Henry, and you win." This was reported to Henry VII., and he sent for the Cheshire prophet. The tale is an old one how the king asked the Cheshire seer where a ring was that he had lost, and the half-witted rustic only repeated a saying, "Those that hide can find." But this was sufficient for the king, who had hidden the ring himself, to test the skill of the wise man.

The tale of "Dr Knowall" is very popular yet in the Thuringian mountains. He was a poor peasant named Crabb, and he carried a load of pine-timber for winter firing to a doctor. He was so very much astonished at the luxury, as it appeared to him, in which the doctor lived, that he asked him how he could be a doctor. The doctor was sitting down with his wife to a roasted loin of venison and a bottle of red wine. Crabb said, "I should like to be a doctor—how can I?" and the doctor, after paying him for his wood, said, "It's the simplest thing in the world; just go and sell your oxen and your cart, and advertise yourself as Dr Knowall. You do not need to know anything about medicine, but look grave when any one comes, and let them talk: if they have any ailments they will do that long enough for you to ask a fee; and if they have none, they will talk all the longer, and these are always the best customers." "Well, but what about medicine?" the rustic said. "You cannot go wrong," the doctor replied, "if you confine yourself to very simple remedies. I never use anything but water, salt, and pepper, and a few colouring ingredients to suit the case and please the eye of the patient. Colour does a very great deal, but put 'Doctor Knowall' above your door,—don't forget that." The peasant literally followed the doctor's advice, and when any client came he looked as grave as he could, and said so little, that his fame as a sage was soon established. The king of the country had heard of the fame of the great Saxony soothsayer, and sent for him in a very troublesome matter. He had lost a large sum, and he wanted to discover the thieves. He asked the peasant to bring his wife and sit down to dinner with them. When a footman came in with some fish, he knew he was a guilty party, and the peasant doctor, in allusion to the dish, said to his wife, "That is one of them,"—for she, poor creature, had no idea of any dinner that consisted of more than a single course. The servant slunk away, and was succeeded by another who brought in roasted fowls. "There is another, which makes two," the adventurer said; and the third and the fourth were greeted with similar observations. They, when they got together and compared notes, decided that the best thing they could do was to bribe the doctor when they had a chance, for they said he looked little more than a fool; but when the fourth dish came in, the nobleman stayed the servant from raising the cover, and said that he wished to see some of the cleverness he had heard so much of, and he asked him what lay under the covering. The so-called doctor was quite confounded, and thinking of the trouble that he had brought on himself, he said, reflectively, "Goose,"—and the dish was actually one of goose-livers and truffles. This confirmed him as a presager. But the last part of the history was even more remarkable; for one servant who should have brought in a dish persuaded another to take his place, being in terror for his life, and went to hide in a closet; and the rustic took a seat hard by the closet door, very glad to get away from the worshipful company. A tankard of beer was brought to him, and he said to a moth that had fallen upon the foam, "Come, get out of this; I see you." The speech was clearly heard by the servant, and he came from the closet and confessed everything, and said where the money could be found. The pseudo-doctor had just wit enough to see his advantage, and the servant, at his request, summoned the other delinquents. They brought the treasure to him, and gave him a large sum to say nothing about the matter. Their master owed his revenue to very doubtful sources, and they were apt imitators of his thrift. He went away from the castle almost a rich man, and returned to the town, where his fame was soon noised about; but he made a point of never giving advice again, except when he was asked for medicine. He became at last so skilful in the preparation of bread-pills and toast-and-water, that he always had his doors crowded with patients.

There is another class of tales that always contain a moral, and the following one is not unlike the story of Franklin and the whistle. A peasant lived near Gotha who had a very industrious son, and he sent him to Hanover to be apprenticed to a cloth-maker; and here he worked so well that he improved his master's business, and the cloth he used to weave was the best in Hanover. He worked away for seven years, and gave so much satisfaction to his master, that he gave him a bag full of silver. With this he went homewards quite overjoyed. But it was soon clear that he had not been brought up in the counting-house,—only in the workrooms. He found the silver bag getting heavier and heavier, and at last he sat down and put it by his side while he rested. A man soon passed him on horseback, who led another horse besides his own. Indeed he had been following him, and he thought he looked as if he wished to be relieved of his burden. "You have been carrying a heavy weight there, neighbour," the horseman said; "will you get up and have a ride? Get upon the horse with a saddle, and put your weight in the saddle-bag. The young weaver was overjoyed at his good fortune, and went for a mile or two merrily along; and then the trader said, "Would you not like the horse yourself? You shall have it for that heavy bag that is tiring you." The bargain was concluded on the spot, and the mechanic went on his way rejoicing. He was not, however, a skilled horseman, and, as is often the case with beginners, he was thrown into the roadside, and the horse would certainly have run away but that it was stopped by a peasant who happened to be working in a field hard by. He caught it up. Jack, which was the name of the weaver, was in very ill humour as he gathered himself up, and declared he would never mount the horse again; and he said to the peasant, "I would give my horse, and the saddle and bridle, for such a cow as that in the field."

"It is yours," said the peasant; "I will drive it into the road for you."

Jack said to himself, "Now I am in luck; a cow to milk, and to take home to my mother;"—and the legend says that he went home full of visions of cheese, and butter, and milk, all of which he supposed he could never want any more. He halted at an old gabled inn on the way, and refreshed himself powerfully, tying up his cow to a stanchion in the porch, and then he resumed his journey to the small Gotha village where his mother lived. He had been some few days in all on the road, but he came at last to a heath that he remembered as a boy, and he knew his mother's cottage was only half a day's journey off, so he tied up his cow to a rail, and began to try to milk her. But his skill in this was not greater than his skill as a horseman, and the cow kicked him over very soon indeed. Fortunately a butcher was passing in a cart, and he had a young pig in it. "What sort of tricks are you up to there?" he said, as he helped him to his feet again; and Jack told him the whole business. The butcher looked critically over the cow, and said, "Why, you have only a miserable old animal, fit for nothing but the shambles or else for a waggon; who can have sold you such a beast as that? Now I have a nice little pig here that you can exchange for it, and I will do what I can to fatten it, and make it fit for the shambles, though it will never pay me; so think yourself well off."

"Thank you very kindly indeed," Jack replied; "I have been in luck ever since I left Hanover, and every bargain leaves me better off." And then he went away, driving his porker before him, till he reached a village-green only a mile from his mother's house, and there he saw a small crowd of children round a knife-grinder, who was plying his wheel, and singing—

> "Grind knives, grind scissors, my wheel doth go!
> I never care how the wind may blow."

Jack watched him working, and at last he said, "You seem very merry and well at grinding."

"Yes, yes," replied the knife-grinder; "a good knife-grinder always has his pockets full of money. He never wants for anything. But where did you buy that fine young pig?"

"I didn't buy it at all; I got it in exchange for a cow."

"And the cow?"

"The cow was given me for a horse."

" And where did you get the horse from, I wonder ?"

"The horse was given me in exchange for a leathern bag full of silver."

" You have managed very well indeed," the knife-grinder said, " so listen to me, and if you take my advice you will have money in your pocket every time you put your hand there. I will give you a whetstone in exchange for your pig, and something more too. See here, this is a grand new flintstone to hammer out your nails upon ; take it home, and don't break it." And as he said this, he picked up a stone that happened to lie near him in the street.

Jack was greatly delighted, and soon cleared the space that lay between the knife-grinder and his mother's house. His mother's joy was very great, when she saw him after his seven years ; and as she saw him put down his burden, she said, " Is that your wages, Jack ? for I have heard how you pleased your master."

" No, mother, it is better than wages,—it will keep us rich for ever ;" and the good lady in amazement looked at his last attempt at trading.

" You don't call this wages, surely ; where can you have got such rubbish from ?"

" Mother, mother, don't call it that ! I got it from a knife-grinder for a young pig."

" And where did you get your pig from ?"

" I got the pig in exchange for a cow that was very vicious, and wanted to kick me over."

" Well, I must say ! But never make your own bargains any more. Let some one always trade for you. However, go on. Where did you get your cow from ?"

" Mother, I got it for a large horse and a saddle and bridle."

" And where did you get the large horse with the saddle and bridle from, I wonder ?"

" Mother, I got it for a bag of silver dollars, which I earned for seven years' work."

Y

"Why, Jack, you are a simple! and I heard you were so clever at your work."

"So master said, mother; but don't you think I spent my wages well?"

"Well, indeed! why, you have thrown them away; so go back to-morrow to your master and begin to work again; and when you have made any money, don't spend it on horses or paving-stones; and remember what I tell you,—'Fools *make* money, but wise men keep it.'"

The same proverbial philosophy is heard even now all over Europe.

There is another Thuringian legend which is only a paraphrase on the very old saying, that misfortunes never come alone. A peasant who lived in a Thuringian valley was so poor that he could not afford a fagot to burn in his stove, and he went out quietly at daybreak to cut a few sticks from the Crown woods. He wandered through them for some time, but he could not find a tree to his mind—that is to say, such a one as he could fell and cut into lengths, and bring home on his sledge, which he drew with a cord behind him. At length, however, he met with a beech-tree to his mind, and at once began to hew it down. Right merrily he began to hack it through, though he was not very sure if he was not trespassing; but soon he heard a well-known howl, and he knew that a pack of wolves was watching him, and they came in full cry out of the thicket, making straight for the tree he was cutting down. "Well," he said, "they would not find me very delicate eating, I am sure: there may be bones and skin, of course, but they would not find very much beyond, I fancy." Still he resolved not to give them a chance of trying for themselves, and ran away with all his might to the river, hotly pursued by the pack of wolves the moment he began to fly. He ran towards some smoke he saw, but the river intercepted his course. At length he saw an old wooden bridge, which was not far from the thin curl of blue smoke, and he rushed towards it. The wolves were almost at his heels, when the bridge he was crossing broke down, and he was precipitated into the river. The wolves, of course, beat a retreat. He was not able to swim, and two fishermen, or rustics, pulled him out of the water, and brought him to land : one of them, indeed, went into the water to fetch him out, as he was on the point of drowning. Then they laid him in the sunshine to recover him, and lit a fine fire for him by the wall of a deserted convent. He slept for a little, but soon came to himself, and asked who his friends were. He was told about his misfortune, for he had almost forgotten it in his amazement. And just as he was about to narrate his own misadventures, the wall of the old convent gave way and killed him.

Sometimes, of course, the legend has nothing of the supernatural about it, and is only a fireside story. There is little more in the following anecdote than we find in 'Gil Blas,' and it is nothing like so extravagant as Homer's Odyssey.

Strong Hans was born somewhere on the Thuringian mountains, and his father was a steward to a rich nobleman. He was much away at times looking after a castle and estate his master possessed near the Rhine ; and on one occasion when he had left his house, and his wife and young son had gone for a walk into the valley, they came across a band of five brigands, who made them go to the cave where they lived, and there they made the lady cook for them, and told the son that when he grew strong they would make him a robber too. He and his mother used to pass their days talking over their hard fate, and he said, "But never mind, mother ; I shall soon be able to go out with them, and then I will deliver them up to the officers of justice, and you shall soon be free. I'll chop the firewood to make me strong, and able to use an axe ;" and when the robbers were away after their wicked trade, he used to chop so much wood, that they were quite pleased when they came. Besides the gold the robbers brought into the cave, they used to bring in venison and game, which showed clearly enough that they were adept poachers as well as robbers.   There was a clear spring of water at the farthest end of the long cavern, and this found its way to the deep valley below by a small opening that let in a little light; but the hillside was so steep that no one could climb up it, and this opening was quite invisible from below, and so the brigands lived in security.   They stood in need of nothing to eat and drink, and to wear; everything the country could supply was theirs, and on more than one occasion kids and poultry were recognised as their own by their unwilling guests.   So great was the skill of Hans at the axe, that they let him come out with them at daybreak, to begin cutting when no one would hear their axes.   This opened again a further chance for liberty, but Hans resolved not to say a word till the time came, when he would be sure to succeed.   One day—for their days and nights often changed order—Hans said he would split a large block of wood sooner than any one in the hut.   They laughed at him, as he was only about fifteen years old.   He tried with a strong brigand who could split a block first, each block being of equal size, and the brigand won; but the struggle that Strong Hans made, excited the admiration of the robbers, and they said that very soon he should join their company.   This both he and his mother heard with secret delight.   But things happened differently from anything they had planned or contemplated.   The robbers were joined by some more freebooters from the Hartz Mountains, and these were much more ferocious than the captors of Hans.   It was one evening that Hans was lying down after cutting wood, and his mother was thinking of their terrible fate, that her ear was struck by a word of Burgundy French.   She was a Burgundian by birth, and the note was more familiar even than German.   In a short time she heard her husband's name, and she felt speechless: he was still alive, but what could they be talking of him there?

" He comes home the day after to-morrow from the Rhine, and always has plenty of money with him.   You see his master has another castle there, and he brings the rents."

"But has he not got an escort ? Surely he must have."

"Only a couple of mounted servants, and we will dispose of them fast enough."

"Well, yes, there are ten of us now." And then the conversation stopped for a little. The last robbers had been at the wars in Burgundy, and had learned the language of the country perfectly, and used it more frequently than their own. After a little pause—

"You know the way he comes, and you are sure it is the day after to-morrow ?"

"If nothing stops him."

"When will our fellows come back to-day ? It is a business I don't much like."

"Stay at home, if you don't. You'll be glad enough to finger the dollars."

"I don't mean I'm afraid, but somehow I fancy we shall come to grief."

"Nonsense, man : I've seen you this way before. There's no coming to grief except for cowards."

"We've got talking rather loud ; I wonder if the woman heard," the first one whispered.

"Heard ! no—how could she ? Besides that, what can she know of our lingo ?"

"I forgot that," said the companion, reflectively.

Every single word, however, had reached the lady's ears, and she had made up her mind how to act when the morning came, but she was resolved not to speak to her son about it that day. All her anxiety was for the morrow, and to see how the cave would be left, for latterly they always let two of their number remain behind. The morning dawned on the sleepless woman, and her terror was great when she saw the band all stay at home, and not offer to go out for their plunder. "We shall have work enough to-morrow," one of them said, "and good pay too." She then saw nothing but the cruel robbing and murder of her husband, and could not think of any device to move them.   At last she said to one of them, "What day is this?" and when the brigands told her the day of the year, she said, "I thought so; the deer are all driven into the wood for a great hunt, and nobody can go—not even the keepers—for three days, till the company comes;" and then she left them, and went to the further end of the cave, where she always used to stop with her son.   It was just as she had hoped.   She soon heard a stirring among the men, and they got their crossbows and hunting-spears, and all went but two of the very worst from the band that had come in last.   One of them said with an oath, "Get us some wine, can't you? you found it last night," —and she was overjoyed at the request.   She said there was plenty in the cave, and got a jar of the strongest.   When they sat down to it they soon began to get noisy, and she took some things to the spring to pretend to wash, and told her son to follow.   Then she narrated what she heard, and that his father was doomed by the murderers to die the next day.   "We shall see that very soon," Hans said; and taking his axe, he went as if to cut a log that had been rolled into the mouth of the cavern.   One of the murderers he felled, and the other he disabled as he rushed at him, and then they got out of the cavern. He had found the entrance by long practice, for it was very winding and difficult.   But their escape was not a moment too soon.   They were puzzled and dazed with the light, and did not know where the roads lay; and shortly after they had left the cavern, they heard voices, and supposed the gang had met the gamekeepers and slunk away.   But whether that was so or not, they never knew; at any rate, they crept into the wood quietly, and waited till the voices were gone.   Then she told Hans to look round for a castle with three towers, and when he had looked for a short time, he saw it about three miles off; and in this his father was the head-steward, and he was expected home, as we have seen, the next day.   They made the best of their way there, but it was so long since they had left that nobody knew them, till an old butler came and remembered them.   Then she told the perils that awaited her lord and master; and the under-steward, who was an old warrior, and had fought in Germany and France, organised an expedition and collected twenty men who were well armed, and pushed on overnight along the road the steward must come. They met him a long way off, and not only saved his life and the treasure, but captured all the thieves. Then the lord of the steward pressed gifts of great value on his son and his wife, and asked the son what he would like to do; and when the son said he would like to travel, he gave him a splendid palfrey, and a purse half full of gold. He was going on his quest of adventures when he saw a man pulling down a fairly large fir-tree, and he noticed that he twisted it up very easily, as though he would make a rope out of it; and he was amazed at his strength, and said, "Will you leave Thuringia and follow me for adventures, and you shall be called Tree-twister?" and he offered him a piece of gold. "Most willingly will I come," he said, and followed his horse. Then he saw another man also of gigantic strength, and he was amusing him-self by knocking a large rock to pieces with his clenched hand. "Will you leave Thuringia," he said, "and follow me for adven-tures, and you shall be called Rock-splitter, and here is a piece of gold?" "Most willingly will I come," he said, and fol-lowed his horse. They travelled some time in company, and Strong Hans's stock of money, which he spent frugally, gave them all they required, till they came to a deserted castle, and Hans said, "Now Rock-splitter and Tree-twister, clear out the hall and the great kitchen, and make things comfortable, and I will go to the village for provisions." This was done; and Hans returned in due time, and they all slept comfortably round a vast kitchen-fire. "You laid in wood, I hope," he said to Tree-twister; "you ought to be rather good at that." In the morning it was agreed that they should hunt game in the woods that surrounded the castle, and two of them should go out at a time, leaving one behind. Rock-splitter was left, and in the course of the day a very ugly dwarf came to the door, and said,

"I want some meat." But Rock-splitter said, "There is none in the castle," though there was a large joint of wild boar and some loaves; and then he used the dwarf roughly, and said he would throw him over the castle wall and break his bones, unless he took himself right off. But the dwarf said, "It takes two to make a bargain;" and he bounded into the hall, threw Rock-splitter down, and beat him very sorely till he cried for mercy, and then left him. When the two returned to the castle they brought a stag from the woods, and some wild fruit, and ground-nuts, and truffles, and had a great feast. But when the fire burned up brightly they saw many bruises on Rock-splitter, and asked him how they came. He made some excuse —that he had slipped down a great flight of stone steps into the courtyard, because there were some rotten leaves that had become very slippery. Every one thought it a little strange, but had no cause to disbelieve him; for why should he invent? And then, what could it be? The damages did not, indeed, look like a fall down a flight of steps, but no one dreamt of doubting the truth of the statement. The next day it was Tree-twister's turn to stay at home, and the very ugly dwarf came and said, "I want some meat." But Tree-twister said there was none in the castle, though now there was plenty in the larder; and then he spoke to the dwarf roughly, and said he would throw him over the castle walls and break his bones, unless he took himself right off. But the dwarf said, "It takes two to make a bargain;" and he bounded into the hall, threw Tree-twister down, and beat him very sorely till he cried for mercy, and then left him. When the two returned from the woods they brought a fine buck, and wild fruit, and ground-nuts, and truffles, and had a merry feast. But when the fire burned up brightly they saw the bruises on Tree-twister, and asked him how they came. He said something about tripping over a branch on the stairs leading to the great wine-vaults, and the bruises he had were caused by the fall. This time Strong Hans was the only one that believed the story, and the other two exchanged significant looks at each other. The next day it was the turn for Hans to stay in, and the other two to hunt. "We shall do poorly to-day, thought Hans; "these men are nothing in the shape of huntsmen, and they cannot kill a deer or a boar in twenty shots." So he went to the larder to count up what provisions there were, and found a large piece of wild boar and half a deer. This seemed well, for it was Saturday, and a storm was brewing; besides, the next day was Sunday, and they wanted to rest. He was going to cut some wood when the dwarf thundered at the castle door, and said as usual, "I want some meat." And Hans cut him two pounds of venison, and told him to take home what he could not eat. But the dwarf sat down on the floor, and soon ate it all up; and Hans gave him another piece. When this was done the dwarf demanded more; but Hans told him their supply of provisions was limited, and he thought he had had enough for one day. In an instant the dwarf jumped up, and refreshed with his meal and a draught of wine that Hans had kindly given him from a cask they had found in an inner cellar, he flew at him. Hans was thunderstruck; but this time the dwarf met with his match, and got roughly used. He ran away from the castle, and Hans pursued him to learn something of so extraordinary a being. There was a hole like a large rabbit-burrow just outside the castle gates, and he saw him disappear like lightning into this. The two huntsmen came home early with no more success than Hans had anticipated, and he related all his experience with the wonderful dwarf. The two men gave knowing looks at each other, and Hans said quickly, "What! you know him? That accounts for the falls down the cellar and the castle steps," and he laughed heartily. They decided that next day they would investigate the matter further, and make an expedition to the hole, and they took the bucket and rope from the draw-well in the castle yard. Rocksplitter easily carried the winch; and then they let Hans down. There was soon a terrific noise, and they were aware that a battle was going on below. In the course of time Hans called out, "Hoist up there, and take care of your burden," for he had found a beautiful young lady bound up in the cave, and the dwarf in charge of her. He soon waged battle with the dwarf, and the lady was released, while he bound the dwarf to a rock; and he could not tell when he looked at his eyes, which gleamed like a wolf's at night, if he were human or a fiend. The men called out, "All right; look out for the bucket," and they threw it down. He did not like this proceeding exactly, for if he had been under it, it would have fallen on his head, and he began to suspect the men. So he put three large stones in the bucket, and told them to hoist up. Up the bucket went, and then Tree-twister cut the rope, and all fell down again. "Now," he heard them say, "we can carry the lady off." And then the dwarf said, "I thank you, good friend—the spell is broken, and to-morrow you will see me again in the shape of a man. And now let us get out of the cave another way," which he showed him. When they got upon the road, Hans hardly knew which way to take: at first he thought it must be to the left, and then he thought it must be the other way. But the dwarf, who, as it turned out, had been an under-gamekeeper at the vacant castle Hans had left, had a very ready wit, and saw some foot-marks of a deer and a hare, and said, "I know the way they have gone; these marks are not many minutes old, and the roebuck and the hare have passed along it, you may be sure, in the same way—they run from people, not to them." So Hans went in the way the dwarf showed him, and they soon came up with the two men and the lady. The men ran away when they saw them, and Hans took the lady back to the castle he had been at, which he found was her own. She had it left her by her father, whose sole heiress she was.

There is a fine old legend of Albert, Landgrave of Thuringia, which belongs rather to history than romance. Whatever foundation there may be for the story, it has even yet plenty of believers in the mountains of Germany. A short way from the

eastern limit of Saxony, and on the Silesian frontier, is the small
commercial town of Hirschberg. This is frequented partly on
account of its extreme salubrity, and partly, also, to bathe in its
sulphurous baths. A high mountain-range shelters it, and it
is worthy of note that this range contains springs which find
an outlet in three different parts of Europe. One reaches the
Baltic through the Oder, another the German Ocean through
the Elbe, and the waters of a third are carried into the Black
Sea by the Danube. The stream which runs along the beautiful valley in which Hirschberg is situated, is celebrated for
the size and quality of its trout, which form a great feature at
the *table d'hôte,* and are well known in all that part of Germany. Near where this stream rises is the grand old castle of
Kynast, which for picturesqueness and rugged beauty has no
equal, or at any rate no superior, in all Fatherland. Kynast
Castle was originally founded by a Roman patrician named
Bolco. It is perched on the cliff of an inaccessible rock, and is
surrounded on all sides by dells which are nearly precipitous.
It defied all the forces of the Swedes and their allies during the
Thirty Years' War, though they made havoc of the principal
fortresses in Germany. And they were obliged at last to
abandon the siege. The watch-tower is still in good preservation, and from its summit the view is very grand. On one
side we have the beautiful vale of Hirschberg, with its silvery
trout-stream and smiling villages, and white farmhouses set in
beech-trees and firs ; and on the other a stupendous cliff of the
Carpathian Mountains shuts out the view. This forms a dark,
gloomy chasm of frightful depth, which is called the Hölle, and
into this chasm the bluff rock on which the castle stands pro-
jects. A walk along this precipice, even on the top of the
castle boundary-wall, which is supposed to be a place where
pedestrians of the Blondin kind may adventure, is not without
considerable danger, and not worth the risk. In the days of
Albert the Thuringian Landgrave, this castle was in its pride
and power, as it remained long after. Indeed, its end was

worthy of its appearance and traditions. After having stood for a thousand years and defied its foes, it was struck by lightning, and a fearful storm attacked it for some time. Flash after flash crumbled its towers, and the elements effected a destruction that no human foes could compass. This was about a quarter of a century after the peace of Westphalia, which concluded the Thirty Years' War. The legend, which dates back 900 years, states how the castle and the rich domains round it fell to the lot of Kunigunde, the sole heiress of the powerful baron who owned it. She was very beautiful, but a cruel heart beat under her comely form. As might be expected, suitors were not wanting, of all degrees, for her estates were very large; but she was exceedingly hard to please. In the course of a short time she had taken, she said, such an aversion to all men she ever had seen, that she went into the oratory of the castle, and made a solemn vow that she would accept no one who could not ride round the outer castle walls on a high-spirited steed; and she knew that when they passed the long black chasm which is yet called the bottomless pit, their nerves must give way. One after another of her suitors, when they heard what the conditions were, became less ardent, and left her in possession of her castle and broad lands quite undisturbed, and they were jeered as they left the ancient halls as cravens and cowards. This at last had the effect of bringing some of the more reckless connections of the robber-knights, who had nothing but their lives to call their own,—not their arms, certainly, for they were generally come by without much reference to any legal distinctions between *meum* and *tuum.* They supposed that they and their horses were proof against giddiness or any danger a shapely lady would dare them to; and as the attempt was always preceded by a costly banquet in the lady's company, they were sure of one good day. They might be, as Richard said of Henry's troops—

> " A scum of Bretagnes,
> Whom their o'er-cloyed country vomits forth
> To desperate ventures and assured destruction."

But they had nothing to lose and all to gain. The gentle lady sat in a turret and saw them on each occasion mount the walls, and topple over the terrible abyss when they came to it, and said, doubtless, with Portia, "May all of his complexion choose the same." Remorse she had none, nor pity either, and would rather have liked new suitors to come and share the same fate. But one suitor came for whom she was not quite prepared, and he was singularly handsome and nobly attended. He wore a grave look over his handsome features, and, unlike any of his predecessors, he was sparing in his diet and in the wine-cup. His followers would not reveal his name, but they treated him with the profoundest respect. Kunigunde was taken captive at once, and ordered the most splendid banquet to be served that the castle would afford, with the most precious wines in the cellars. She was surprised to see how slightly he regarded the preparations, and it was quite clear that no entertainment she could have provided in the castle would astonish him as it had surprised the adventurous host that she had numbered among her admirers. She felt that her happiness depended on him; and at the end of the second day, when he said he would attempt the great feat, she threw herself before him and begged of him not to attempt it, as no one could do it; and she ended by begging him to take her and her castle and lands without trying. "But, gentle lady," the knight said, very courteously, "I will never let a lady break her oath for any danger to me;" and then he mounted his palfrey and cantered round the court-yard twice before mounting the wall by the slope. Kunigunde fled in speechless anguish to the chapel, and prayed aloud to all the saints; but her prayers were needless. She heard a great shout, and concluded at once that it must be for the gentle knight who had fallen over the precipice, and ran out to know the worst. The first object that met her eyes was the rider, who had accomplished the circuit with perfect ease. The Carpathian mountain was ringing with acclamations when she rushed out to throw herself in his arms. But he received her with perfect coldness, and said, "Proud woman, I am Albert,

Landgrave of Thuringia, and I spurn any one that has blood on her hands."   She could neither believe her eyes nor her ears.   " But," he added, " I was resolved to humble your murderous pride; and as for the castle, I could ride round it again ! " and then he signalled his escort together to leave Kynast Castle for ever.   " I have a wife in Thuringia," he said, " who is infinitely your superior in beauty, and she is not a murderess !   And as for Kynast, I have two larger of my own, and my lands are many times as broad."   When Albert and his train swept away, Kunigunde had received such a shock that it was long before she was able to leave her bed ; and when she did, she was a maniac.   Often she used to peer over the " bottomless pit," as it is yet called, and break out into a hoarse laugh, and run back to the castle ; and sometimes she would be all day wandering through her woods, and only return to her broken slumbers at night.   The legend says that her spirit will for ever haunt these woods.

These are only a few out of thousands, and they have been chosen as being representative, rather than as exceeding others in ingenuity.

THE END.

PRINTED BY WILLIAM BLACKWOOD AND SONS,

II.

SECOND EDITION.

A LADY'S CRUISE IN A FRENCH MAN-ÒF-WAR.

By C. F. GORDON CUMMING.

New and Cheaper Edition, in One Volume, post 8vo.
With numerous Illustrations, 12s. 6d.

"Another delightful book.......Another charming account of several among the too idyllic Pacific archipelagoes."—*Athenæum.*

"We are transported by a series of vivid pictures of easy lives and glorious scenery, to the clustering islands of the Southern Pacific.......The volume is extremely entertaining, and it contains much valuable information."—*Saturday Review.*

"Her readers owe her nothing but thanks for having given them yet another glimpse of perhaps the most attractive region in the whole world."—*Pall Mall Gazette.*

"It is a record of all that is quaint, curious, beautiful, and majestic in the regions of the distant south, from Fiji all round to Tahiti."—*Newcastle Chronicle.*

"She lets nothing slip her notice by sea or by land. Her power of delineation is most graphic and picturesque.......'A Lady's Cruise' is one of those books that is not only readable, but highly instructive. It is historic, romantic, artistic, picturesque, and fascinating."—*Christian Union.*

III.

This Day is Published.

FIRE FOUNTAINS.

THE KINGDOM OF HAWAII:
ITS VOLCANOES, AND THE HISTORY OF ITS MISSIONS.

By C. F. GORDON CUMMING.

With Map and numerous Illustrations.

Two Volumes, 8vo, 25s.

WILLIAM BLACKWOOD & SONS, EDINBURGH AND LONDON.